CRIMINAL LAW CASE STUDIES

Fourth Edition

■ ■ ■

By

Paul H. Robinson

Colin S. Diver Professor of Law
University of Pennsylvania

AMERICAN CASEBOOK SERIES®

A Thomson Reuters business

Mat #40892849

    610 Opperman Drive
    St. Paul, MN 55123
    1–800–313–9378

Printed in the United States of America

ISBN: 978–0–314–90862–9

ACKNOWLEDGEMENTS

───────────

This work is the product of many people. Special thanks to Matthew Majarian, of University of Pennsylvania Law School, for his exceptional work on the Fourth Edition, which introduces the cases of *Landis, Bailey, Daschner,* and *Yates.* Mark Plichta, Kevin Metz, Alex Paul, Hallie Mitchell, Stephen Haedicke, Michelle Guardino, Benjamin Ellenbogen, and Roshna Bala, of Northwestern University Law School, and Cat–Uyen Vo of University of Pennsylvania Law School, worked on earlier editions as research assistants and contributed enormously to it. Marcia Lehr, librarian at Northwestern University Law Library, unstintingly helped with the often challenging and sometimes bizarre research problems presented by the First Edition.

Finally, many people helped in providing facts and photographs on the individual cases. Regarding the case of DeSean McCarty, we thank Carol Kelly of the Southtown Daily News, for photographs.

Regarding the case of Bernice and Walter Williams, we thank Anthony Savage, Jr., Williams' defense attorney, for facts and insights; Gil Zimmerman, of The Sawyer Company, for field research; Chris Lane, Washington Department of Corrections, for research help.

Regarding the case of Thomas Dudley, we thank Professor Brian Simpson, of University of Michigan Law School, for photographs and insights.

Regarding the case of Canna Baker, we thank Marianne Messick, local historian in Baxter County, Arkansas, for photographs and facts.

Regarding the case of Julio Marrero, we thank Andrew Fine, Marrero's attorney with the Legal Aid Society, for court documents and insights; Mary Price, senior court clerk, Supreme Court New York County, for court records; Anna Lucena for photographs; Beth Sauer Robinson, for field research.

Regarding the case of Ray Edwin Billingslea, we thank Virginia Billingslea, granddaughter of Hazel Billingslea, for an interview; John Hagler, Billingslea's appellate attorney, for facts and help with court records; Deke Austin, Billingslea's trial attorney, for insights on the case; Ray Edwin Billingslea, for an interview; Joel Sauer for field research.

Regarding the case of Linda Ruschioni, we thank Linda Ruschioni, Ricci Ruschioni, and Dudley P. Haney, for interviews; John Ronan, Haney's attorney in the civil suit, for information and insights.

Regarding the case of Joseph B. Wood, we thank Professor Randy Roth, of Ohio State University in Columbus, Ohio, for facts and newspaper citations; Paul Carnahan, reference librarian at the Vermont State Historical Society in Montpelier, Vermont, for photographs and research leads; Paul Donovan, reference librarian at the Vermont State Historical Society, for photographs and facts; Jeffrey D. Marshall, archivist and curator of Manuscripts at University of Vermont, for photographs and facts.

Regarding the case of Larry Eugene Phillips, we thank Sgt. Ian Grimes of the Glendale, California police department, for his interview; Tom Reisinger, Editor of Soldier of Fortune magazine, for facts and photographs; Gene Blevins, freelance photographer for photographs.

Regarding the case of Roger Thomas, we thank James Rockwell, of Northwestern University, for help in obtaining documents; Anita Coley, United States Navy, Judge Advocate General Office, for documents; and Ralph Coon, prosecutor on appeal, for his interview.

Regarding the case of Joseph A. Bailey, we thank David Damico, Bailey's defense attorney, for newspaper clippings and insights; Joshua Nowocin, for photographs.

Regarding the case of Jordan Weaver, we thank Joyce Perry, Office of County Clerk of Court, Marion County Superior Court, for documents and photographs; Marcel Pratt, trial defense counsel for his interview; Dawn Mitchell, of the Indianapolis Star, for research; and Jordan Weaver, for an interview.

Regarding the case of John Charles Green, we thank Beverly Holder, reference librarian at Little Dixie Regional Library in Moberly, Missouri, for facts and newspaper photographs; Joan Krauskopf, Green's defense counsel, for facts and insights; C.M. Hulen, another Green defense attorney (retired), for research leads; Tim Kneist, director of public relations, Missouri Department of Corrections, for photographs.

Regarding the case of Johann Schlicht, we thank Judge Michael Bohlander, for help finding German court documents; Delf Buchwald, for court documents, other information, and field research in Germany; Sarah Schaeffer, for translations.

Regarding the case of Wolfgang Daschner, we thank LL.M. candidate Dominik Brodowski of University of Pennsylvania Law School for research and translations.

Regarding the case of Motti Ashkenazi, we thank Jonathan von Samek, for interviews of Israelis; Dr. Ron Shapira of Tel Aviv University Law Faculty, for Israeli statutes and newspaper articles; Ronen Avraham for translations and field research in Tel Aviv.

Regarding the case of Janice Leidholm, we thank Irvin B. Nodland, Leidholm's defense attorney, for documents and insights; and Professor Tom Lockney at the University of North Dakota School of Law, for research leads.

Regarding the case of Barry Kingston, we thank Charles Taylor, Kingston's barrister, for documents, an interview, and for assistance in arranging an interview; Colin Wibley, Kingston's solicitor, for documents; Professor Keith Topping, at University of Dundee, for help in locating Mr. Kingston; Barry Kingston, for an interview and photographs.

Regarding the case of David Kenny Hawkins, we thank Mike Spechio, Washoe County (Nevada) public defender, for facts; John Petty, also of the public defender's office, for an interview and court documents; Tim Randolph, the Reno prosecutor of Hawkins, for an interview; Edwin Basl, also of the prosecutor's office, for an interview; Officer Roger Linscott, Reno Police Department, for an interview and field research in Reno; Carol McHenry, of Gladding and Michel, Inc., for field research.

Regarding the case of Richard R. Tenneson, we thank Frederick Hess, Director, Office of Enforcement Operations, Criminal Division, U.S. Department of Justice, for help obtaining Department records; John Andrews, Intelligence Specialist, U.S. Army Materiel Command, for research help.

Regarding the case of Alex Cabarga, we thank Lt. Richard Gordy, of Concord (California) Police Department, for an interview.

Regarding the case of Robert Sandifer, we thank Professor Tom Geraghty at the Northwestern University School of Law, for documents and research leads.

As always, my greatest thanks go to my family for their patience and support.

PAUL H. ROBINSON

Philadelphia
August 2009

N.B.—The facts recounted in these stories are true, as best as we can determine from our research of court documents, newspaper articles, and personal interviews. In places, I have added what I think is reasonable speculation about a person's motivation or state of mind as it appears from the person's conduct and circumstances.

TABLE OF CONTENTS

Acknowledgements v

Chapter 1.   The Basic Requirements of Criminal Liability 1
   1.   The Case of DeSean McCarty (Illinois, 1997) 1
       A.   The Facts 1
       B.   Then Existing Law 5
             Illinois Compiled Statutes (1997) 5
       C.   Current Law That Would Be Applied Were the Case Prosecuted Today 7
   2.   The Case of John Landis (California, 1982) 8
       A.   The Facts 8
       B.   Then Existing Law 10
             California Penal Code (1982). 10
             California Education Code (1982) 12
             California Labor Code (1982) 12
             People v. Matta 12
             People v. Penny 12
       C.   Current Law That Would Be Applied Were the Case Prosecuted Today 13
             California Labor Code (2009) 13
   3.   The Case of Bernice J. and Walter L. Williams (Washington, 1968) 14
       A.   The Facts 14
       B.   Then Existing Law 16
             Revised Code of Washington (1968). 16
             State v. Hedges 17
             State v. Stentz 17
       C.   Current Law That Would Be Applied Were the Case Prosecuted Today 18
             Revised Code of Washington (2006). 18

Chapter 2.   Principles for the Distribution of Criminal Liability and Punishment 21
   4.   The Case of Thomas Dudley (England, 1884) 21
       A.   The Facts 21
       B.   Then Existing Law 25
             Hale's History of the Pleas of the Crown 25
             Blackstone's Commentaries on the Laws of England: Of Public Wrongs . 25
             The Works of Francis Bacon 26
             United States v. Holmes 26
       C.   Current Law That Would Be Applied Were the Case Prosecuted Today 26
             Draft Criminal Code for England and Wales (1989) 26

5. The Case of William James Rummel (Texas, 1973)............................ 28
    A. The Facts 28
    B. Then Existing Law 29
        Texas Penal Code (1973)... 29
    C. Current Law That Would Be Applied Were the Case Prosecuted Today 30
        Texas Penal Code (2006)... 30

Chapter 3. Do We Know What the Criminal Law Commands of Us, and Does the Law
        Care If We Don't? Legality, Mistake, and Omissions..................... 35
  6. The Case of Canna Baker (Arkansas, 1948) 35
    A. The Facts 35
    B. Then Existing Law 38
        Arkansas Statutes (1948) 38
        Corpus Juris 39
        Wharton's Criminal Law 39
        Kanavan's Case 39
        State v. Bradbury 39
        Thompson v. State 39
    C. Current Law That Would Be Applied Were the Case Prosecuted Today 39
        Arkansas Statutes (2006) 39
  7. The Case of Julio Marrero (New York, 1977)............................... 41
    A. The Facts 41
    B. Then Existing Law 42
        Consolidated Laws of New York—Penal Law (1977) 42
        Consolidated Laws of New York Annotated—Criminal Procedure Law
          (1977) 47
    C. Current Law That Would Be Applied Were the Case Prosecuted Today 52
        Consolidated Laws of New York—Criminal Procedure Law (2006) 52
  8. The Case of Ray Edwin Billingslea (Texas, 1984) 62
    A. The Facts 62
    B. Then Existing Law 64
        Texas Penal Code (1984)... 64
        Texas Family Code—Annotated (1984) 66
    C. Current Law That Would Be Applied Were the Case Prosecuted Today 67
        Texas Penal Code (2006)... 67
  9. The Case of Linda Ruschioni (Massachusetts, 1993)........................ 69
    A. The Facts 69
    B. Then Existing Law 70
        Laws of Massachusetts, Chapter 266—Crimes Against Property (1993).. 70
        Laws of Massachusetts, Chapter 134—Lost Goods and Stray Beasts
          (1993) 71
        Commonwealth v. Titus 71
        Commonwealth v. Everson 71

C.   Current Law That Would Be Applied Were the Case Prosecuted Today 71

Chapter 4.   The Significance of Resulting Harm: Causation, Attempt, and Impossibility . . 73
   10. The Case of Joseph B. Wood (Vermont, 1879) 73
      A.   The Facts 73
      B.   Then Existing Law 74
            Vermont Statutes, Chapter 189 (1879) 74
            Acts and Resolves of Vermont (1878). 75
            State v. Tatro 75
            State v. Scates 75
            Commonwealth v. Webster 76
      C.   Current Law That Would Be Applied Were the Case Prosecuted Today 76
            Vermont Statutes, Title 13—Crimes & Criminal Procedure (2006) 76
   11. The Case of Larry Eugene Phillips (California, 1993) 78
      A.   The Facts 78
      B.   Then Existing Law 82
            California Penal Code (1993). 82
            People v. Dillon 85
            People v. Lopez 85
      C.   Current Law That Would Be Applied Were the Case Prosecuted Today 85
   12. The Case of Roger Thomas (U.S. Military, 1961). 86
      A.   The Facts 86
      B.   Then Existing Law 89
            Uniform Code of Military Justice (1961) 89
      C.   Current Law That Would Be Applied Were the Case Prosecuted Today 89
            Uniform Code of Military Justice (2006) 90
   13. The Case of Joseph A. Bailey (Virginia, 1983). 94
      A.   The Facts 94
      B.   Then Existing Law 97
            Code of Virginia (1983) 97
            Harris v. Commonwealth 97
            Pugh v. Commonwealth 97
            Albert v. Commonwealth 98
            Collins v. Commonwealth 98
      C.   Current Law That Would Be Applied Were the Case Prosecuted Today 98

Chapter 5.   Can There Be Criminal Liability Without Proving That the Defendant Satis-
         fies the Elements of an Offense? Doctrines of Imputation. 99
   14. The Case of Keith Mondello (New York, 1989) 99
      A.   The Facts 99
      B.   Then Existing Law 103
            Consolidated Laws of New York (1989) 103
      C.   Current Law That Would Be Applied Were the Case Prosecuted Today 106

15. The Case of Jordan Weaver (Indiana, 1991) 107
    A.   The Facts 107
    B.   Then Existing Law 110
        Indiana Code (1991) 110
        Zickefoose v. Indiana 112
        Rhode v. State 112
        Terry v. State 113
    C.   Current Law That Would Be Applied Were the Case Prosecuted Today 113
        Indiana Code (2006) 113
        Sanchez v. State of Indiana 113

Chapter 6.   Can Committing a Crime Be Doing the Right Thing? Justification Defenses .. 115
    16. The Case of John Charles Green (Missouri, 1967) 115
    A.   The Facts 115
    B.   Then Existing Law 118
        Missouri Statutes (1967) 118
        State v. King 118
        State v. St. Clair 118
        People v. Richards 118
    C.   Current Law That Would Be Applied Were the Case Prosecuted Today 118
        Missouri Statutes (2006) 118
        City of St. Louis v. Klocker 120
    17. The Case of Johann Schlicht (Germany, 1919) 121
    A.   The Facts 121
    B.   Then Existing Law 122
    C.   Current Law That Would Be Applied Were the Case Prosecuted Today 123
        Federal Republic of Germany—Penal Code (2002) 123
    18. The Case of Wolfgang Daschner (Germany, 2002) 126
    A.   The Facts 126
    B.   Then Existing Law 129
        Federal Republic of Germany—Penal Code (2002) 129
        Federal Republic of Germany—Criminal Procedure Code (2002) 131
        Hessian Law on Security and Public Order (2002) 131
    C.   Current Law That Would Be Applied Were the Case Prosecuted Today 132
    19. The Case of Motti Ashkenazi (Israel, 1997) 133
    A.   The Facts 133
    B.   Then Existing Law 134
        Israeli Penal Law (1997) 134
    C.   Current Law That Would Be Applied Were the Case Prosecuted Today 136

Chapter 7.   Is Wrongdoing Ever Blameless? Excuse Defenses 137
    20. The Case of Janice Leidholm (North Dakota, 1981) 137
    A.   The Facts 137

B.   Then Existing Law 139
        North Dakota Century Code (1981). 139
C.   Current Law That Would Be Applied Were the Case Prosecuted Today 142
        North Dakota Century Code (2006). 142
21. The Case of Barry Kingston (England, 1991) 144
A.   The Facts 144
B.   Then Existing Law 146
        Sexual Offences Act, 1956, 4 & 5 Eliz.2, ch. 69 146
        Cardle v. Mulrainey 146
        Regina v. Court 146
        Regina v. Court 146
C.   Current Law That Would Be Applied Were the Case Prosecuted Today 146
22. The Case of Andrea Yates (Texas, 2001) 147
A.   The Facts 147
B.   Then Existing Law 150
        Texas Penal Code (2001) 150
        Bigby v. State 152
C.   Current Law That Would Be Applied Were the Case Prosecuted Today 152
23. The Case of David Kenney Hawkins (Nevada, 1986) 153
A.   The Facts 153
B.   Then Existing Law 155
        Nevada Revised Statutes (1986) 155
        Shrader v. State 155
C.   Current Law That Would Be Applied Were the Case Prosecuted Today 155
        Nevada Revised Statutes (2006) 155

Chapter 8.   Are We Responsible for Who We Are? 157
24. The Case of Richard R. Tenneson (Federal, 1954). 157
A.   The Facts 157
B.   Then Existing Law 160
        Uniform Code of Military Justice, 50 U.S.C.A. (1954) 160
C.   Current Law That Would Be Applied Were the Case Prosecuted Today 161
25. The Case of Alex Cabarga (California, 1982). 162
A.   The Facts 162
B.   Then Existing Law 165
        California Penal Code (1982). 165
C.   Current Law That Would Be Applied Were the Case Prosecuted Today 166
26. The Case of Robert "Yummy" Sandifer (Illinois, 1994) 169
A.   The Facts 169
B.   Then Existing Law 171
        Illinois Compiled Statutes (1994) 171
C.   Current Law That Would Be Applied Were the Case Prosecuted Today 173
        Illinois Consolidated Statutes (2006). 173

Appendix A: Selected Provisions of the Model Penal Code 175

Appendix B: Criminal Law Case Studies 213

CRIMINAL LAW CASE STUDIES

Fourth Edition

CHAPTER 1.   THE BASIC REQUIREMENTS OF CRIMINAL LIABILITY

1.   THE CASE OF DESEAN MCCARTY (ILLINOIS, 1997)

A.   THE FACTS

It is September, 1997. DeSean McCarty is a 17–year old African American who was born on the south side of Chicago on July 24, 1980. His particular part of Chicago is known for its high crime rate. The Fourth District, which includes the towns of Markham and Harvey, where DeSean grew up, is predominately African American. DeSean grew up with his mother and five siblings at 180 E. 152nd Street. DeSean's mother and father had a common-law marriage, but DeSean had little contact with his father, who did not provide financial or emotional support to the family. Rather, DeSean's mother had a live-in boyfriend, with whom DeSean interacted frequently. The boyfriend was an abusive drunk and often beat DeSean, his mother, and his siblings with belts, sticks, and extension cords. DeSean would frequently run away from home. He began using drugs at the age of 11 and later joined the "Four Corner Hustlers," a local street gang. He was smoking approximately 4 blunts (a combination of marijuana and PCP) and $100 of marijuana a day. At the age of 13, DeSean was arrested for possession of cocaine and was transferred to juvenile division custody. The charges were subsequently dropped. DeSean was also arrested twice for possession of controlled substances.

Figure 1. DeSean McCarty.
(Illinois Department of Corrections)

The Markham police department is familiar with DeSean, who is also known as DeSean Black, Ward DeSean, and Little D. One Markham officer had previously attempted to pull DeSean over on an outstanding warrant for carjacking. DeSean attempted to flee, but was caught by the officer and others. He was soon released, however, because the accusation turned out to be false. DeSean was arrested one other time for fleeing and eluding the police, but was not convicted.

Two years ago, McCarty moved away from his mother's home to live with his grandmother Deborah Black, in another part of the south side of Chicago. This move allowed him to be closer to his girlfriend, Monica Mottley, and their nine-month old son. Although DeSean has not attended school regularly, he worked at Midway airport for an extended period of time in order to provide financial support for his son. DeSean is planning to start work on his general equivalency degree in November 1997.

Andre Griffin is 28 years old, and lives in Chicago with his fiancé Renell Brown, and their daughter. In the late afternoon of Thursday, September 18, 1997, Renell asks Andre to take her 1982 Chevy Caprice to a mechanic for repairs. In addition to numerous mechanical problems, the steering column was "peeled" in a theft attempt, leaving the car broken in such a way that it can only be started with a screwdriver. Andre takes the car, but instead of getting it fixed, he takes it to 154th Street in Harvey, where he thinks he can rent it out. At the intersection of 154th and Myrtle Avenue, he pulls over to talk to a woman who calls herself CoCo. Her real name is Shilita Williams. The two have never met before, but he asks her if she wants to rent a car or knows someone who might want to rent a car in exchange for some cocaine. CoCo says that she knows of some people who might want to rent the car and tells Andre to take her to the intersection of 154th and Dixie Highway. When they get there, CoCo sees DeSean McCarty, who she knows as "Little D." CoCo asks DeSean if he knows anyone who would want to rent a car in exchange for some cocaine. DeSean says that he would, and tells them to meet him at the corner of 154th and Wood Street. At that location, DeSean gets in the car and gives Andre two "dime bags" of cocaine. The two agree that DeSean will return the car at 9:00 that evening.

Later that night, Andre arrives at the planned location, but DeSean never shows up. Andre does not report the car to the police as being stolen.

Andre sees DeSean two days later, between 10:00 and 11:00 a.m. on Saturday, September 20, at an apartment building on 154th Street. He flags DeSean down and tells him to park the car in the back of the building. DeSean drives the car around back, but when Andre walks to the back of the building, DeSean drives away. Andre still does not report the car to the police as being stolen.

Later that same morning, DeSean drives up to the house of Larry Mason, in Harvey. Larry is 19 years old and has known DeSean for close to 10 years, since they attended school together as children. When DeSean pulls up to Larry's house, Larry is playing basketball with a group of friends. DeSean asks if anyone wants to buy the Chevy Caprice that he is driving. Mason looks inside the car and notices that the steering column has been broken into. He tells DeSean that he wants no part of a stolen car. DeSean insists that the car isn't stolen—that he has the title. He puts the car in park and starts searching the vehicle for the title. Mason's friends yell at DeSean to get the car off the block, so DeSean gets back into the car and drives away.

Figure 2. Officer Sean Laura.
(Southtown Daily News)

At 7:00 p.m. on September 20, DeSean parks the car on Marshfield Street, just north of 165th Street. This location is two blocks from where his meeting with Andre Griffin and CoCo had occurred. He looks in the rearview mirror and sees a Markham Police car driven by Officer Sean Laura traveling east on 165th. A short time later, the police car passes DeSean again, this time going west. When he sees the police car, DeSean becomes nervous. He does not want to get caught in a stolen car with two ounces of marijuana and without a driver's license. DeSean starts the car and drives north on Marshfield to 163rd Street. While at a stop sign, he sees the same police car stopped at a corner on 163rd, headed east. DeSean turns left on 163rd and heads west, past the police car. He looks in his rearview mirror and sees the police car make a U-turn in the middle of the street. The police car begins following DeSean. DeSean continues and turns right on Wood Street.

At that time, Officer Laura radios in that he is following a vehicle. As he approaches the Markham–Harvey border, the end of his jurisdiction as a Markham police officer, he notifies the dispatcher that he is going to make a traffic stop for "erratic driving." By the time DeSean reaches the corner of 159th and Wood Street, Officer Laura has turned on his emergency lights. DeSean does not pull over. He turns right at a street light onto

159th Street, and continues east. He is by this point traveling at approximately 45–50 m.p.h.; the speed limit on 159th is 40 m.p.h. DeSean then turns left on Ashland Avenue and heads north, with Officer Laura close behind. He continues to drive at a speed of 45–55 m.p.h. The speed limit on Ashland is 25 m.p.h. DeSean sees the police car behind him and notices an alleyway to his right. The alley is just before the intersection of Ashland and 155th Street, and has a speed limit of 15 m.p.h. Deciding that he would be better off on foot, he turns into the alley and dumps the car in a weedy lot behind 155th Street, between Myrtle Avenue and Loomis Street. He leaves the ignition on, and proceeds to run on foot.

DeSean takes off running north through a darkened back yard and gangway on the first block of E. 155th Street. Officer Laura, after pulling up behind DeSean's abandoned car, turns off the ignition, grabs a flashlight, locks the car doors, and begins pursuing DeSean on foot. Using the radio on his shoulder, he notifies the dispatcher that he is engaged in a foot pursuit. The pursuit continues until DeSean runs between two parked cars and onto the street in front of 155th, followed by Officer Laura.

Officer Charles Brogdon, a three year veteran of the Harvey Police Department, is conducting a field interview in the area of 154th and Vine Street when he hears over the radio that an officer is pursuing a suspect coming into Harvey from Markham. He jumps in his car, turns on his emergency lights, and heads towards the direction of the vehicle pursuit. While en route, Officer Brogdon hears from dispatch that the car chase has now become a foot pursuit in the vicinity of 155th Street. Brogdon enters the area, heading south on Vine Street in his police car. He makes a sharp left onto 155th, nearly hitting a tree on the corner.

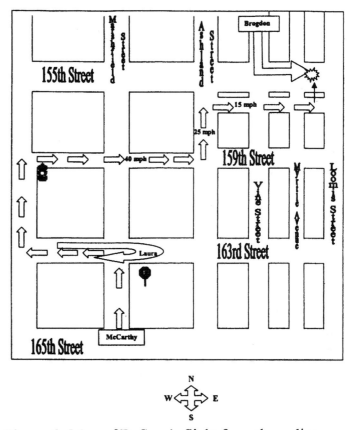

Figure 3. Map of DeSean's flight from the police.

In this area, 155th Street is a two-lane road, 40 feet wide and asphalt-paved. Residences and on-street parking spaces line both sides of the street. The posted speed limit is 25 m.p.h. in both directions. It is 7:15 p.m., and dark. The streetlights in the vicinity are obstructed by large trees lining the block. When Officer Brogdon turns onto 155th, he sees DeSean run across the street. Brogdon visually tracks DeSean and radios in, saying: "Harvey, he is running north bound going towards 154th." Brogdon applies the brake and feels a thump as the front wheel of his vehicle goes into the air.

Officer Laura, chasing after DeSean on foot, had run across 155th Street in front of the police car driven by Officer Brogdon. He slipped, causing his center of gravity to become lower than the impact point of the squad car. Rather than being thrown onto the hood of the squad car, Laura is pulled under the front tire. Officer Laura is dragged for approximately 100 feet before the police car comes to a complete stop. The lack of skid marks on the roadway indicates that there was no braking by the squad car. Officer Brogdon was traveling at approximately 40 m.p.h. when he hit Officer Laura. When the car finally comes to a full stop, Laura is pinned underneath the right rear tire.

Meanwhile, DeSean does not realize that Officer Laura has been hit. After reaching the other side of 155th Street, he continues to run, eventually hiding under a porch. After waiting there for ten minutes, he figures that the police officer is no longer following him, so he goes to a friend's house where he changes clothes.

Brogdon did not see Officer Sean Laura before hitting him. When he gets out of the car and realizes what has happened, he begins jumping up and down, crying and yelling, "That was Sean." By this time, other officers arrive at the scene and a crowd has formed. James, who is on his mother-in-law's front porch at 68 E. 155th St. at the time of the accident, says that Laura appears to be alive but is pinned underneath the back tires. The neighbors offer to jack up the car, remove Laura, and perform CPR, but police tell them to wait until the ambulance arrives. Firefighters arrive at the scene shortly thereafter. It takes them 20 minutes to pry the vehicle off of Laura. He is rushed by helicopter to Ingalls Memorial Hospital, where the emergency staff work for more than an hour to save his life. He is pronounced dead of multiple injuries at 8:58 p.m.

When Officer Sean Laura began pursuing DeSean McCarty on the day of the accident, he was in the middle of his second shift of the day. He worked his usual midnight shift ending at 8:00 a.m. that morning, and was already back at work at 4 p.m. because he agreed to fill in for another officer who had requested the night off. Brogdon has been on duty for four hours by the time he responds to the scene. He is non-medicated and complains of no ailments that would impair his performance or judgment.

At the time of the accident, Officer Sean Laura is 25 years old, 6 feet tall, and weighs approximately 222 lbs. Laura has dreamed of becoming a police officer since he was 3 years old. That dream was prodded along when he came into contact with the "nice cops" who would visit the house when, as a child, he would accidentally set off his mother's house alarm. Officer Laura's parents divorced at a young age, and Sean, the only child, remains with his mother, Patricia Laura, in Chicago. The two have a particularly close relationship, often attending basketball and football games together. In September of 1995, Sean graduated from the Chicago Police Academy and passed the eligibility tests for the police departments in Chicago, Markham, and Cook County. Markham is the first department to call and offer him a job, which he accepts. Markham Police Captain James Hunt describes Laura as one of "the newer suburban policeman, extremely well-educated, well-trained." Laura hopes to become a state police officer and eventually an FBI agent. He is taking classes at South Suburban College.

Charles Brogdon is 28 years old and three-year veteran of the Harvey Police Department. He knows Sean Laura because they were classmates at both the Chicago Police Academy and at South Suburban College. Brogdon is distraught after the accident, and quits his job as a policeman one month later. He has worked in construction ever since.

The police trace the license plates and registration of the stolen vehicle to Renell Brown. On the evening of September 21st, the police question Brown and Andre Griffin. Andre states that he left the Caprice at his father's house in Harvey a few days ago and was not aware that it had been stolen. On Monday, September 22, however, Andre Griffin is questioned again at the Markham Police Department. This time, he admits to lending the car to DeSean in exchange for drugs.

Several witnesses at the scene of the accident tell police that they saw a person who they know as "Little D" running away on the night in question. The police learn from various witnesses that DeSean McCarty goes by the name of "Little D." When questioned, McCarty admits to running away from Officer Laura on the night in question and says "I truthfully didn't mean no harm [to Laura]. When you're scared, your first instinct is to run."

DeSean McCarty is arrested on Sunday, September 21, 1997 and is charged with the death of Officer Sean Laura.

* * *

Would you convict McCarty for the death of Officer Laura? If so, what amount of punishment would you impose?

N	0	1	2	3	4	5	6	7	8	9	10	11
☐	☐	☐	☐	☐	☐	☐	☐	☐	☐	☐	☐	☐
no liability	liability but no punishment	1 day	2 wks.	2 mo.	6 mo.	1 yr.	3 yrs.	7 yrs.	15 yrs.	30 yrs.	life imprison- ment	death

B. THEN EXISTING LAW

Illinois Compiled Statutes (1997)

§ 625–5/4–103—Offenses relating to motor vehicles and other vehicles—Felonies

(a) It is a violation of this Chapter for:

(1) A person not entitled to the possession of a vehicle or essential part of a vehicle to receive, possess, conceal, sell, dispose, or transfer it, knowing it to have been stolen or converted ... It may be inferred, ... that a person exercising exclusive unexplained possession over a stolen or converted vehicle or an essential part of a stolen or converted vehicle has knowledge that such vehicle or essential part is stolen or converted, regardless of whether the date on which such vehicle or essential part was stolen is recent or remote; ...

(b) Sentence. A person convicted of a violation of this Section shall be guilty of a Class 2 felony.

§ 625–5/4–103.2—Aggravated offenses relating to motor vehicles and other vehicles—Felonies

(a) It is a violation of this Chapter for:

. . .

(7) a person:

(A) who is the driver or operator of a vehicle and is not entitled to the possession of that vehicle and who knows the vehicle is stolen or converted, ...

who has been given a signal by a peace officer directing him to bring the vehicle to a stop, to willfully fail or refuse to obey such direction, increase his speed, extinguish his lights or otherwise flee or attempt to elude the officer. The signal given by the peace officer may be by hand, voice, siren, or red or blue light. The officer giving the signal, if driving a vehicle, shall display the vehicle's illuminated, oscillating, rotating or flashing red or blue lights, which when used in conjunction with an audible horn or siren would indicate that the vehicle is an official police vehicle. Such requirement shall not preclude the use of amber or white oscillating, rotating or flashing lights in conjunction with red or blue oscillating, rotating or flashing lights as required in Section 12–215 of this Code; ...

(b) The inference contained in paragraph (1) of subsection (a) of Section 4–103 of this Code shall apply to subsection (a) of this Section.

(c) A person convicted of violating this Section shall be guilty of a Class 1 felony.

(d) The offenses set forth in subsection (a) of this Section shall not include the offenses set forth in Section 4–103 of this Code.

§ 625–5/11–204.1—Aggravated fleeing or attempt to elude a police officer

(a) The offense of aggravated fleeing or attempting to elude a police officer is committed by any driver or operator of a motor vehicle who flees or attempts to elude a police officer, after being given a visual or audible signal by a police officer ... and such flight or attempt to elude:

> (1) is at a rate of speed at least 21 miles per hour over the legal speed limit;

> (2) causes bodily injury to any individual; or

> (3) causes damage in excess of $300 to property.

(b) Any person convicted of a violation of this Section shall be guilty of a Class 4 felony....

§ 720–5/2–8—Forcible felony

Forcible felony means treason, first degree murder, second degree murder, predatory criminal sexual assault of a child, aggravated criminal sexual assault, criminal sexual assault, robbery, burglary, residential burglary, aggravated arson, arson, aggravated kidnaping, kidnaping, aggravated battery resulting in great bodily harm or permanent disability or disfigurement and any other felony which involves the use or threat of physical force or violence against any individual.

§ 720–5/4–6—Recklessness

A person is reckless or acts recklessly, when he consciously disregards a substantial and unjustifiable risk that circumstances exist or that a result will follow, described by the statute defining the offense; and such disregard constitutes a gross deviation from the standard of care which a reasonable person would exercise in the situation. An act performed recklessly is performed wantonly, within the meaning of a statute using the latter term, unless the statute clearly requires another meaning.

§ 720–5/9–1—First degree murder—Death penalties—Exceptions—Separate hearings—Proof—Findings—Appellate procedures—Reversals

(a) A person who kills an individual without lawful justification commits first degree murder if, in performing the acts which cause the death:

> (1) he either intends to kill or do great bodily harm to that individual or another, or knows that such acts will cause death to that individual or another; or

> (2) he knows that such acts create a strong probability of death or great bodily harm to that individual or another; or

> (3) he is attempting or committing a forcible felony other than second degree murder....

§ 720–5/9–2—Second degree murder

(a) A person commits the offense of second degree murder when he commits the offense of first degree murder as defined in paragraphs (1) or (2) of subsection (a) of Section 9–1 of this Code and either of the following mitigating factors are present:

> (1) At the time of the killing he is acting under a sudden and intense passion resulting from serious provocation by the individual killed or another whom the offender endeavors to kill, but he negligently or accidentally causes the death of the individual killed; or

> (2) At the time of the killing he believes the circumstances to be such that, if they existed, would justify or exonerate the killing ... but his belief is unreasonable.

. . .

Second Degree Murder is a Class 1 felony.

§ 720–5/9–3—Involuntary manslaughter and reckless homicide

(a) A person who unintentionally kills an individual without lawful justification commits involuntary manslaughter if his acts whether lawful or unlawful which cause the death are such as are likely to cause death or great bodily harm to some individual, and he performs them recklessly, except in cases in which the cause of the death consists of the driving of a motor vehicle, in which case the person commits reckless homicide.

. . .

(d) Sentence.

(1) Involuntary manslaughter is a Class 3 felony.

. . .

§ 730–5/5–8–1—Sentence of imprisonment for felony

(a) Except as otherwise provided in the statute defining the offense, a sentence of imprisonment for a felony shall be a determinate sentence set by the court under this Section, according to the following limitations:

(1) for first degree murder,

(a) a term shall be not less than 20 years and not more than 60 years, or

. . .

(c) the court shall sentence the defendant to a term of natural life imprisonment when the death penalty is not imposed if the defendant, …

(iii) is found guilty of murdering a peace officer or fireman when the peace officer or fireman was killed in the course of performing his official duties, … and the defendant knew or should have known that the murdered individual was a police officer or fireman, …

(1.5) for second degree murder, a term shall be not less than 4 years and not more than 20 years;

. . .

(3) except as otherwise provided in the statute defining the offense, for a Class X felony, the sentence shall be not less than 6 years and not more than 30 years;

(4) for a Class 1 felony, other than second degree murder, the sentence shall be not less than 4 years and not more than 15 years;

(5) for a Class 2 felony, the sentence shall be not less than 3 years and not more than 7 years;

(6) for a Class 3 felony, the sentence shall be not less than 2 years and not more than 5 years;

(7) for a Class 4 felony, the sentence shall be not less than 1 year and not more than 3 years….

C.   CURRENT LAW THAT WOULD BE APPLIED WERE THE CASE PROSECUTED TODAY

[Statutory changes are not relevant]

2. THE CASE OF JOHN LANDIS (CALIFORNIA, 1982)

A. THE FACTS

The Twilight Zone, a hugely successful American science fiction TV show, garners such recognition in the public consciousness that nineteen years after its last episode airs, Steven Spielberg decides to produce a movie adaptation. Established stars such as Dan Aykroyd, Kathleen Quinlan, John Lithgow, and Victor Morrow sign on, eager to work on what they hope will be a summer blockbuster. The film is divided into four segments, with a different director for each. The first segment is directed by John Landis, who by 1982 has already become a sought-after movie director. He is thirty-three years old, and has directed a number of highly successful films, including The Blues Brothers, Animal House, and An American Werewolf in London. As writer and director of the first segment of Twilight Zone, Landis is to be paid $150,000 by Warner Brothers.

Figure 4. John Landis.

Landis decides to make a political point with his segment of the movie, casting Vic Morrow as Bill Connor, an outspoken bigot with prejudice against Jews, Blacks, Arabs, and other racial minorities. Connor, a fifty-five year old salesman, is to open the movie at a bar, drinking away his sorrow over being passed over for promotion. When he steps outside, he is transported back to World War II-era France, where he is accused of being Jewish by Nazi officers. As Connor navigates the Twilight Zone, he is taken to various points in history and made to suffer the effects of bigotry similar to his own. Eventually, Connor is left in Vietnam as an American, desperately trying to escape Vietcong fire in a marsh.

Studio executives decide that the moral lesson of the story fails, in part because Connor is never redeemed. Landis is told to change the ending of his segment to show a changed Connor escaping from death and from his own bigotry. Landis alters the final scene, making Bill Connor realize the wrongs of his bigotry by saving two Vietnamese children in danger. The climactic scene is written such that "Bill, holding a child in each arm, makes a herculean effort and runs for the shallow river. With the village burning behind them Bill runs as best he can across the river." In making his escape from the Vietcong, he makes his escape from prejudice.

This new scene will require the construction of a village set, but more importantly will require that Landis hire two child actors to play the Vietnamese infants. California state law does not permit children of the age Landis wants to use—6 to 8 years old—to work at night, when Landis wants to film the scene. For children this young to act at all, the studio is required to apply for a permit. Furthermore, the state requires that a state-certified teacher or welfare worker must be on the set at all times, in order to stop the production if she observes anything that could be physically or morally harmful to the child.

Landis decides not to get the required permits. He reasons that the film is already behind schedule, so waiting for the state to approve his production would cost too much time. Landis also decides to film the last scene outdoors at night, for the sake of realism. Though he could film on a soundstage indoors, he decides that it would be more realistic to film the movie using real sets, real explosions, and live ammunition. July 23, 1982 is set as the filming date for the last scene.

Landis's casting department hires two Asian-American children to play the parts of the Vietnamese children. Six year old Renee Chen is the daughter of a county social worker, and seven year old My-Ca Le is the son of the director of the County Indo-Chinese Mental Health Clinic. Neither set of parents is aware of the child labor laws the govern movie productions. The parents are told that though the scene includes explosions and a helicopter, neither will be near their children. They accept the offer and are paid $500 per child for the night of filming—over five times as much as legally-hired extras are usually paid. Landis requires that the parents not tell anyone why they are on the set—if asked, they say that they are friends of Landis, there to observe the filming.

The other actor in the scene is Vic Morrow, a Hollywood veteran and noted "tough guy" actor. Morrow enjoys filming his own scenes instead of using dedicated stuntmen, and he does the same on the set of The Twilight Zone. He is nervous before filming the last scene; everyone on the set knows that it must be perfectly done the first time. Demolitions experts have loaded the woods surrounding the set with explosives designed to simulate heavy gunfire. Real shotgun shells are fired, simulating the fury of a helicopter's attack on a small village in wartime. Morrow is to wade across a bog, chased by a helicopter, while holding both children in his arms.

Landis' assistants repeatedly question the wisdom of using live ammunition and explosives in the course of filming. Western Helicopters, a contractor who owns the UH–1B Huey that is to be used in the final scene, insists that they will not sign a contract allowing the helicopter to be used in the production if there is any risk that the special effects could damage the aircraft. A production assistant working for Landis assures the company that there was no danger, simply saying "Safety first." Trusting Landis's special effects coordinator, the helicopter pilot does not come to the set to inspect the placement of explosives. The pilot does, however, repeatedly warn Landis that a hovering helicopter is extremely vulnerable to flying debris, such as that caused by demolitions explosives like those used in the film. Landis and his staff assure him that everything will be fine.

Figure 5. Vic Morrow.
(Columbia Pictures/Getty Images)

On the night of the filming, however, Landis warns his staff that the filming of the final scene could be "tricky." He arranges them so that they can run if the helicopter veers out of control, and then begins filming the scene. As Morrow runs across the marsh with a child under each arm, the helicopter gives chase, beginning a planned descent as explosions go off in the distance. "Squibs" (small explosives designed to mimic bullet impacts) detonate in the water. More explosions follow, at the rate of one per second. Landis yells "Lower, lower, lower!" into the pilot's radio, urging him to alter his rehearsed course. The pilot, wanting to comply with the director, flies lower than was planned and on a different trajectory.

Figure 6. A Huey helicopter identical to the one flown in the filming of *The Twilight Zone.*

As the pilot alters course, a pyrotechnics operator triggers a nearby explosion, thinking that the helicopter has followed its planned trajectory and is safely out of the way. The bomb detonates directly below the helicopter, engulfing its tail and causing it to spin out of control. The helicopter crashes into the water near the actors, who are still making their way across the bog. The spinning blades decapitate Morrow and My-Ca Le, and Renee Chen is crushed beneath the body of the helicopter.

Landis peers into his camera viewfinder, and asks "What the fuck is the helicopter doing in my shot?" Immediately afterwards, he rushes towards the helicopter. An assistant director sees Morrow's head lying near the shore as Renee Chen's mother kneels over her daughter's body. Seconds later, a loudspeaker crackles as a production assistant says "That's a wrap! Leave your equipment where it is. Everyone go home. Please, everyone go home!" It is 2:30 a.m.

* * *

Would you convict John Landis for the deaths of Victor Morrow, My–Ca Le, and Renee Chen? If so, what amount of punishment would you impose?

N	0	1	2	3	4	5	6	7	8	9	10	11
☐	☐	☐	☐	☐	☐	☐	☐	☐	☐	☐	☐	☐
no liability	liability but no punishment	1 day	2 wks.	2 mo.	6 mo.	1 yr.	3 yrs.	7 yrs.	15 yrs.	30 yrs.	life imprison- ment	death

B.   Then Existing Law

California Penal Code (1982)

§ 187—Murder defined

(a) Murder is the unlawful killing of a human being, or a fetus, with malice aforethought.

(b) This section shall not apply to any person who commits an act that results in the death of a fetus if any of the following apply:

(1) The act complied with the Therapeutic Abortion Act, Chapter 11 (commencing with Section 25950) of Division 20 of the Health and Safety Code.

(2) The act was committed by a holder of a physician's and surgeon's certificate, as defined in the Business and Professions Code, in a case where, to a medical certainty, the result of childbirth would be death of the mother of the fetus or where her death from childbirth, although not medically certain, would be substantially certain or more likely than not.

(3) The act was solicited, aided, abetted, or consented to by the mother of the fetus.

(c) Subdivision (b) shall not be construed to prohibit the prosecution of any person under any other provision of law.

§ 187—Malice, express malice, and implied malice defined

Such malice may be express or implied. It is express when there is manifested a deliberate intention unlawfully to take away the life of a fellow creature. It is implied, when no considerable provocation appears, or when the circumstances attending the killing show an abandoned and malignant heart.

When it is shown that the killing resulted from the intentional doing of an act with express or implied malice as defined above, no other mental state need be shown to establish the mental state of malice aforethought. Neither an awareness of the obligation to act within the general body of laws regulating society nor acting despite such awareness is included within the definition of malice.

§ 192—Manslaughter; voluntary, involuntary, and in driving a vehicle defined; construction of section

Manslaughter is the unlawful killing of a human being, without malice. It is of three kinds:

1. Voluntary—upon a sudden quarrel or heat of passion.

2. Involuntary—in the commission of an unlawful act, not amounting to felony; or in the commission of a lawful act which might produce death, in an unlawful manner, or without due caution and circumspection; provided that this subdivision shall not apply to acts committed in the driving of a vehicle.

3. In the driving of a vehicle—

   (a) In the commission of an unlawful act, not amounting to felony, with gross negligence; or in the commission of a lawful act which might produce death, in an unlawful manner, and with gross negligence.

   (b) In the commission of an unlawful act, not amounting to felony, without gross negligence; or in the commission of a lawful act which might produce death, in an unlawful manner, but without gross negligence.

   This section shall not be construed as making any homicide in the driving of a vehicle punishable which is not a proximate result of the commission of an unlawful act, not amounting to felony, or of the commission of a lawful act which might produce death, in an unlawful manner.

§ 195—Excusable homicide

Homicide is excusable in the following cases:

1. When committed by accident and misfortune, in lawfully correcting a child or servant, or in doing any other lawful act by lawful means, with usual and ordinary caution, and without any unlawful intent.

2. When committed by accident and misfortune, in the heat of passion, upon any sudden and sufficient provocation, or upon a sudden combat, when no undue advantage is taken, nor any dangerous weapon used, and when the killing is not done in a cruel or unusual manner.

§ 31—Principals defined

Who are principals. All persons concerned in the commission of a crime, whether it be felony or misdemeanor, and whether they directly commit the act constituting the offense, or aid and abet in its commission, or, not being present, have advised and encouraged its commission, and all persons counseling, advising, or encouraging children under the age of fourteen years, lunatics or idiots, to commit any crime, or who, by fraud, contrivance, or force, occasion the drunkenness of another for the purpose of causing him to commit any crime, or who, by threats, menaces, command, or coercion, compel another to commit any crime, are principals in any crime so committed.

§ 7—Words and phrases

*   *   *

The following words have in this code the signification attached to them in this section, unless otherwise apparent from the context:

*   *   *

4. The words "malice" and "maliciously" import a wish to vex, annoy, or injure another person, or an intent to do a wrongful act, established either by proof or presumption of law.

California Education Code (1982)

§ 49160—Permit to employ

No person, firm or corporation shall employ, suffer, or permit any minor under the age of 18 years to work in or in connection with any establishment or occupation except as provided in Section 49151 without a permit to employ, issued by the proper educational officers in accordance with law.

California Labor Code (1982)

§ 1391—Hours of employment of minors; violation; misdemeanor; penalty

Except as provided in Sections 1297 and 1298, no minor shall be employed more than eight hours in one day of 24 hours or more than 48 hours in one week, or before five o'clock in the morning, or after ten o'clock in the evening; but a minor may work the hours authorized by this section during any evening preceding a nonschoolday until 12:30 in the morning of such nonschoolday.

Any person or the agent or officer thereof, or any parent or guardian, who directly or indirectly violates or causes or suffers the violation of any provision of this section is guilty of a misdemeanor punishable by a fine of not less than fifty dollars ($50) nor more than two hundred dollars ($200) or imprisonment in the county jail for not more than 60 days or both.

People v. Matta, 129 Cal.Rptr. 205 (Cal. Ct. App. 1976)

"Malice aforethought is found where one acts with wanton disregard for human life by doing an act that involves a high probability that it will result in death.... Thus, malice may be implied from the doing of an act in wanton and willful disregard of an unreasonable human risk, i.e., the willful doing of an act under such circumstances that there is obviously a plain and strong likelihood that death or great bodily injury may result."

People v. Penny, 285 P.2d 926, 937 (Cal. 1955)

A lack of "due caution and circumspection," as the term is used in Penal Code § 192, is equivalent to criminal negligence. The definition of criminal negligence in California is conduct that is "such a departure from what would be the conduct of an ordinarily prudent or careful man under the same circumstances as to be incompatible with a proper regard for human life, or, in other words, a disregard of human life or an indifference to consequences." Liability for involuntary homicide can only accrue if the actor could have reasonably foreseen that his actions would have resulted in a death. The death must have been "the natural and probable result of a reckless or culpably negligent act."

C. CURRENT LAW THAT WOULD BE APPLIED WERE THE CASE PROSECUTED TODAY

California Labor Code (2009)

§ 1308.7—Hours of employment of minor in entertainment industry; penalty

(a) No minor shall be employed in the entertainment industry more than eight hours in one day of 24 hours, or more than 48 hours in one week, or before 5 a.m., or after 10 p.m. on any day preceding a schoolday. However, a minor may work the hours authorized by this section during any evening preceding a nonschoolday until 12:30 a.m. of the nonschoolday.

(b) For purposes of this section, "schoolday" means any day in which a minor is required to attend school for 240 minutes or more.

(c) Any person or the agent or officer thereof, or any parent or guardian, who directly or indirectly violates or causes or suffers the violation of this section, is guilty of a misdemeanor punishable by a fine of not less than five hundred dollars ($500) nor more than one thousand dollars ($1,000), or imprisonment in the county jail for not more than 60 days, or both.

3. THE CASE OF BERNICE J. AND WALTER L. WILLIAMS (WASHINGTON, 1968)

A. THE FACTS

Twenty-four-year-old Walter L. Williams leaves school after the sixth grade, working as an unskilled laborer and staying out of trouble, except for one arrest for public drunkenness. Bernice J. Williams, four years younger than Walter, does not finish high school. By the time she turns 20, she has two children, the youngest being a boy named William Joseph Tabafunda. Both Walter and Bernice are of significantly below-average intelligence. They live in King County, Washington.

In June 1968, Bernice marries Walter, who assumes responsibility for Bernice's two children despite not being their biological father. William has just had his first birthday. Both parents work during the day, so Walter's 85–year–old mother cares for the children while the parents are at their jobs.

On September 1, 1968, the parents realize that William is sick. He cries most of the time and eats very little. When he does eat, he usually does not keep the food down. His cheeks begin to swell. The swelling goes up and down, but never disappears. The Williamses believe that the infant is teething or has a toothache. They give him aspirin but do not take him to the doctor.

Over the next few days, William's condition visibly worsens. The couple notices that his cheek is swollen and has turned a red or purplish-red color. He runs a high fever—much higher than the mild temperature associated with teething. Moreover, they notice a peculiar odor coming from his cheek and mouth. They discuss taking the boy to a doctor, but believe that doctors and dentists would not pull a tooth when his mouth is so swollen. They decide not to seek help. Walter Williams has experienced bad toothaches and abscesses himself. He does not think that the boy is in serious danger, even without medical treatment. The parents continue to give William aspirin.

Part of their hesitation to seek medical care stems from their fear that a doctor might see the swollen and discolored cheek and think that they are abusing the child. They fear that Child Welfare might take away both their children. Both parents are Shoshoni. Government social workers actively intervened in Native American families in the 1960s. More than a quarter of all Native American children are separated from their families and placed in non-Native American foster homes. Sometimes, this results from social workers mistaking Native American culture (which emphasizes child care by members of the extended family) for neglect.

On September 12, 1968, William Tabafunda dies of pneumonia. An autopsy reveals that an abscessed tooth was allowed to develop into an infection of the mouth and cheeks, eventually becoming gangrenous. Because the child could not eat, he became malnourished, weakening his immune system. These conditions produced severe pneumonia and ultimately, his death.

Bernice and Walter are extremely saddened by the loss. Both felt a great deal of love and affection for William.

Gale Wilson, the chief pathologist for King County, determines that the infection leading to death had been present for at least two weeks. If medical care had been obtained anytime before the final week, it would have saved William's life. During the critical period when William's life could have been saved, the odor from the gangrene would have been strong—an unavoidable signal that the child suffered from more than a toothache and that medical attention was needed. The Williamses knew that the boy was sick and that a doctor was available. They were both financially and physically able to take the boy to the doctor, and were aware of his symptoms. The symptoms were such that it would have been obvious to any reasonable parent that medical attention was needed.

On October 3, 1968, Bernice and Walter Williams are charged with manslaughter for negligently failing to supply 17–month-old William with necessary medical attention, for the lack of which he died. They plead not guilty and the case is tried without a jury on January 13, 1969.

CERTIFIED COPY OF DEATH CERTIFICATE

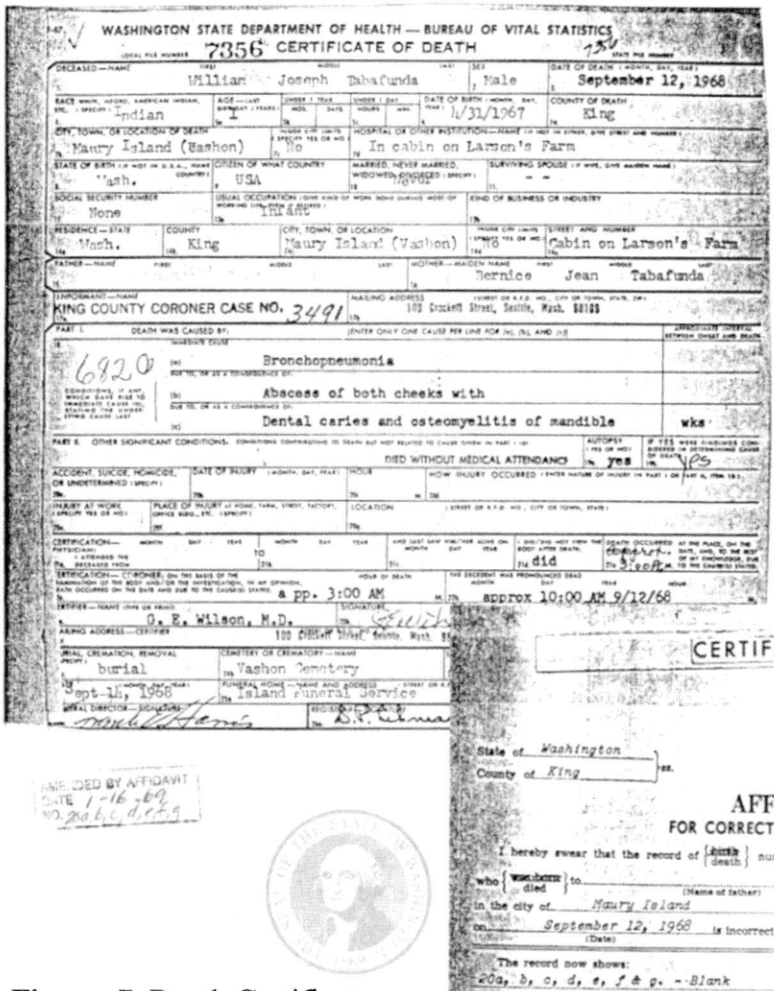
WASHINGTON STATE DEPARTMENT OF HEALTH — BUREAU OF VITAL STATISTICS

7356 CERTIFICATE OF DEATH

DECEASED—NAME: William Joseph Tabafunda
SEX: Male
DATE OF DEATH: September 12, 1968
RACE: Indian
AGE: 1
DATE OF BIRTH: 4/31/1967
COUNTY OF DEATH: King
CITY, TOWN, OR LOCATION OF DEATH: Maury Island (Vashon)
INSIDE CITY LIMITS: No
HOSPITAL OR OTHER INSTITUTION: In cabin on Larson's Farm
STATE OF BIRTH: Wash.
CITIZEN OF WHAT COUNTRY: USA
SURVIVING SPOUSE: – –
SOCIAL SECURITY NUMBER: None
USUAL OCCUPATION: Infant
RESIDENCE—STATE: Wash.
COUNTY: King
CITY, TOWN, OR LOCATION: Maury Island (Vashon)
INSIDE CITY LIMITS: No
STREET AND NUMBER: Cabin on Larson's Farm
MOTHER—MAIDEN NAME: Bernice Jean Tabafunda
KING COUNTY CORONER CASE NO. 3491
MAILING ADDRESS: 100 Crockett Street, Seattle, Wash. 98109

PART I. DEATH WAS CAUSED BY:
6820
(a) Bronchopneumonia
(b) Abscess of both cheeks with
(c) Dental caries and osteomyelitis of mandible — wks

PART II. OTHER SIGNIFICANT CONDITIONS: DIED WITHOUT MEDICAL ATTENDANCE
AUTOPSY: yes
IF YES WERE FINDINGS CONSIDERED IN DETERMINING CAUSE OF DEATH: yes
did
CERTIFICATION—CORONER: a pp. 3:00 AM
THE DECEDENT WAS PRONOUNCED DEAD: approx 10:00 AM 9/12/68
CERTIFIER: G. E. Wilson, M.D.
BURIAL, CREMATION, REMOVAL: burial
CEMETERY OR CREMATORY: Vashon Cemetery
DATE: Sept-14, 1968
FUNERAL HOME: Island Funeral Service

AMENDED BY AFFIDAVIT
DATE 1-16-69
NO. 20a,b,c,d,e,f,g

Figure. 7. Death Certificate.

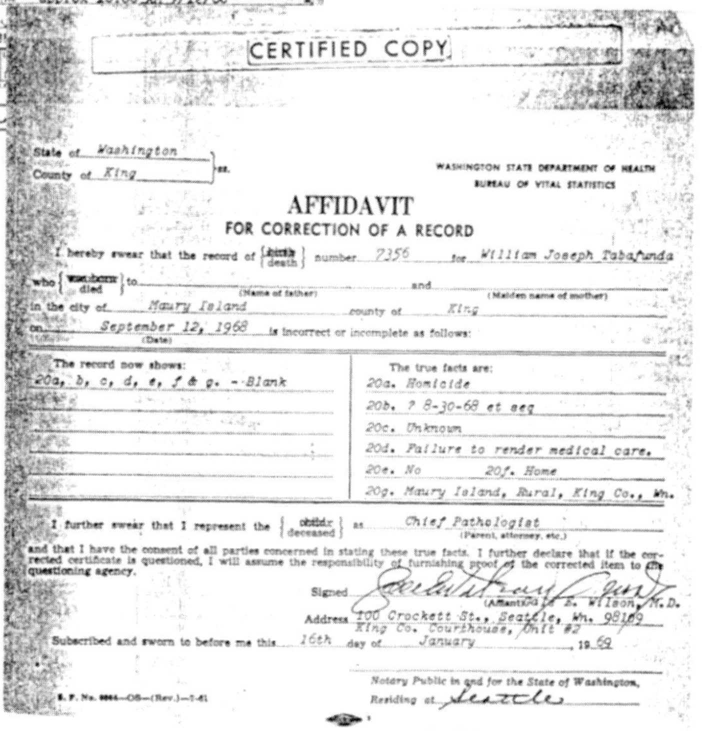
CERTIFIED COPY

State of Washington
County of King } ss.

WASHINGTON STATE DEPARTMENT OF HEALTH
BUREAU OF VITAL STATISTICS

AFFIDAVIT
FOR CORRECTION OF A RECORD

I hereby swear that the record of {birth / death} number 7356 for William Joseph Tabafunda who {was born / died} to ______ (Name of father) and ______ (Maiden name of mother) in the city of Maury Island county of King on September 12, 1968 (Date) is incorrect or incomplete as follows:

The record now shows:	The true facts are:
20a, b, c, d, e, f & g. - Blank	20a. Homicide
	20b. ? 8-30-68 et seq
	20c. Unknown
	20d. Failure to render medical care.
	20e. No 20f. Home
	20g. Maury Island, Rural, King Co., Wn.

I further swear that I represent the {child / deceased} as Chief Pathologist (Parent, attorney, etc.) and that I have the consent of all parties concerned in stating these true facts. I further declare that if the corrected certificate is questioned, I will assume the responsibility of furnishing proof of the corrected item to the questioning agency.

Signed ______ (Affiant) G. E. Wilson, M.D.
Address 100 Crockett St., Seattle, Wn. 98109
King Co. Courthouse, Unit #2

Subscribed and sworn to before me this 16th day of January, 19 69

Notary Public in and for the State of Washington,
Residing at Seattle

S. F. No. 6664—OS—(Rev.)—7-61

Figure 8. Corrected copy of William's death certificate.

* * *

Would you convict the Williamses for the death of their son? If so, what amount of punishment would you impose?

N	0	1	2	3	4	5	6	7	8	9	10	11
☐	☐	☐	☐	☐	☐	☐	☐	☐	☐	☐	☐	☐
no liability	liability but no punishment	1 day	2 wks.	2 mo.	6 mo.	1 yr.	3 yrs.	7 yrs.	15 yrs.	30 yrs.	life imprisonment	death

B. Then Existing Law

Revised Code of Washington (1968)

§ 9.48.010—Homicide; defined and classified

Homicide is the killing of a human being by the act, procurement or omission of another and is either (1) murder, (2) manslaughter, (3) excusable homicide or (4) justifiable homicide.

§ 9.48.030—Murder—First Degree—Death penalty up to jury

The killing of a human being, unless it is excusable or justifiable, it murder in the first degree when committed either—

(1) With a premeditated design to effect the death of the person killed, or of another; or,

(2) By an act immediately dangerous to others and evincing a depraved mind, regardless of human life, without a premeditated design to effect the death of any individual; or,

(3) Without design to effect death, by a person engaged in the commission of, or in an attempt to commit, or in withdrawing from the scene of, a robbery, rape, burglary, larceny or arson in the first degree; or,

(4) By maliciously interfering or tampering with or obstructing any switch, frog, rail, roadbed, sleeper, viaduct, bridge, trestle, culvert, embankment, structure or appliance pertaining to or connected with any railway, or any engine, motor or car of such railway.

Murder in the first degree shall be punishable by imprisonment in the state penitentiary for life, unless the jury shall find that the punishment shall be death; and in every trial for murder in the first degree, the jury shall, if it find the defendant guilty, also find a special verdict as to whether or not the death penalty shall be inflicted; and if such special verdict is in the affirmative, the penalty shall be death, otherwise it shall be as herein provided. All executions in accordance herewith shall take place at the state penitentiary under the direction of and pursuant to arrangements made by the superintendent thereof.

§ 9.48.040—Murder in the second degree

The killing of a human being, unless it is excusable or justifiable, is murder in the second degree when:

(1) Committed with a design to effect the death of the person killed or of another, but without premeditation; or

(2) When perpetrated by a person engaged in the commission of, or in attempt to commit, or in withdrawing from the scene of, a felony other than those enumerated in RCW 9.48.030 [robbery, rape, burglary, larceny or arson in the first degree].

Murder in the second degree shall be punished by imprisonment in the state penitentiary for not less than ten years.

§ 9.48.060—Manslaughter

In any case other than those specified in RCW 9.48.030 [murder—first degree—death penalty up to jury], 9.48.040 [murder in the second degree], 9.48.050 [killing in duel], homicide, not being excusable or justifiable, is manslaughter.

Manslaughter is punishable by imprisonment in the state penitentiary for not more than twenty years, or by imprisonment in the county jail for not more than one year, or by a fine of not more than one thousand dollars, or by both fine and imprisonment.

§ 9.48.150—Homicide, when excusable

Homicide is excusable when committed by accident or misfortune in doing any lawful act by lawful means, with ordinary caution and without any unlawful intent.

§ 26.20.030—Desertion or nonsupport—Penalty

(1) Every person who:

(a) Has a child dependent upon him or her for care, education or support and deserts such child in any manner whatever with intent to abandon it; or

(b) Wilfully omits, without lawful excuse, to furnish necessary food, clothing, shelter, or medical attendance for his or her child or children or ward or wards; or

(c) Has sufficient ability to provide for his wife's support or is able to earn the means for his wife's support and wilfully abandons and leaves her in a destitute condition or who refuses or neglects to provide his wife with necessary food, clothing, shelter, or medical attendance, unless by her misconduct he is justified in abandoning her, shall be guilty of the crime of family desertion or nonsupport.

(2) When children are involved under the age of sixteen years, such act shall be a felony and punished by imprisonment in the state penitentiary for not more than twenty years or by imprisonment in the county jail for not more than one year or by fine of not more than one thousand dollars or by both fine and imprisonment.

(3) When there is no child under sixteen years, such act shall be a gross misdemeanor and shall be punished by imprisonment in the county jail for not more than one year or by fine of not more than one thousand dollars, or by both fine and imprisonment.

§ 26.20.080—Proof of willfulness—Application of penalty provisions

Proof of the abandonment or nonsupport of a wife, or the desertion of a child or children, ward or wards, or the omission to furnish necessary food, clothing, shelter, or medical attendance for a child or children, ward or wards, is prima facie evidence that such abandonment or nonsupport, or omission to furnish food, clothing, shelter or medical attendance is willful. The provisions of RCW 26.20.030 are applicable whether the parents of such child or children are married or divorced and regardless of any decree made in said divorce action relative to alimony or to the support of the wife or child or children.

State v. Hedges, 8 Wash.2d 652, 113 P.2d 530 (1941)

"By lawful means with ordinary caution and without any unlawful intent," does not require a finding by the jury that the accused was guilty of gross negligence before conviction for manslaughter may be obtained. Only ordinary negligence is required.

State v. Stentz, 33 Wash. 444 (1903)

That defendant tried to avoid accident after it was too late is no excuse, where death was result of his negligent driving.

C.   Current Law That Would Be Applied Were the Case Prosecuted Today

Revised Code of Washington (2006)

§ 9A.32.010—Homicide defined

Homicide is the killing of a human being by the act, procurement or omission of another, death occurring at any time, and is either (1) murder, (2) homicide by abuse, (3) manslaughter, (4) excusable homicide, or (5) justifiable homicide.

§ 9A.32.030—Murder in the first degree

(1) A person is guilty of murder in the first degree when:

(a) With a premeditated intent to cause the death of another person, he or she causes the death of such person or of a third person; or

(b) Under circumstances manifesting an extreme indifference to human life, he or she engages in conduct which creates a grave risk of death to any person, and thereby causes the death of a person; or

(c) He or she commits or attempts to commit the crime of either (1) robbery in the first or second degree, (2) rape in the first or second degree, (3) burglary in the first degree, (4) arson in the first or second degree, or (5) kidnapping in the first or second degree, and in the course of or in furtherance of such crime or in immediate flight therefrom, he or she, or another participant, causes the death of a person other than one of the participants: Except that in any prosecution under this subdivision (1)(c) in which the defendant was not the only participant in the underlying crime, if established by the defendant by a preponderance of the evidence, it is a defense that the defendant:

(i) Did not commit the homicidal act or in any way solicit, request, command, importune, cause, or aid the commission thereof; and

(ii) Was not armed with a deadly weapon, or any instrument, article, or substance readily capable of causing death or serious physical injury; and

(iii) Had no reasonable grounds to believe that any other participant was armed with such a weapon, instrument, article, or substance; and

(iv) Had no reasonable grounds to believe that any other participant intended to engage in conduct likely to result in death or serious physical injury.

(2) Murder in the first degree is a class A felony.

§ 9A.32.050—Murder in the second degree

(1) A person is guilty of murder in the second degree when:

(a) With intent to cause the death of another person but without premeditation, he or she causes the death of such person or of a third person; or

(b) He or she commits or attempts to commit any felony other than those enumerated in RCW 9A.32.030(1)(c) [robbery, in the first or second degree, rape in the first or second degree, burglary in the first degree, arson in the first or second degree, or kidnaping in the first or second degree], and, in the course of and in furtherance of such crime or in immediate flight therefrom, he, or another participant, causes the death of a person other than one of the participants; except that in any prosecution under this subdivision (1)(b) in which the defendant was not the only participant in the underlying crime, if established by the defendant by preponderance of evidence, it is a defense that the defendant:

(i) Did not commit the homicidal act or in any way solicit, request, command, importune, cause, or aid the commission thereof; and

(ii) Was not armed with a deadly weapon, or any instrument, article or substance readily capable of causing death or serious physical injury; and

(iii) Had no reasonable grounds to believe that any other participant was armed with such a weapon, instrument, article or substance; and

(iv) Had no reasonable grounds to believe that any other participant intended to engage in conduct likely to result in death or serious physical injury.

(2) Murder in the second degree is a class A felony.

§ 9A.32.055—Homicide by abuse

(1) A person is guilty of homicide by abuse if, under circumstances manifesting an extreme indifference to human life, the person causes the death of a child or person under sixteen years of age, a developmentally disabled person, or a dependent adult, and the person has previously engaged in a pattern or practice of assault or torture of said child, person under sixteen years of age, developmentally disabled person, or dependent person.

. . .

(3) Homicide by abuse is a class A felony.

§ 9A.32.060—Manslaughter in the first degree

(1) A person is guilty of manslaughter in the first degree when:

(a) He recklessly causes the death of another person; or

(b) He intentionally and unlawfully kills an unborn quick child by inflicting any injury upon the mother of such child.

(2) Manslaughter in the first degree is a class A felony.

§ 9A.32.070—Manslaughter in the second degree

(1) A person is guilty of manslaughter in the second degree when, with criminal negligence, he causes the death of another person.

(2) Manslaughter in the second degree is a class B felony.

§ 9A.16.030—Homicide; when excusable

Homicide is excusable when committed by accident or misfortune in doing any lawful act by lawful means, without criminal negligence, or without any unlawful intent.

§ 9A.08.010—General requirements of culpability

(1) Kinds of Culpability Defined

(a) Intent. A person acts with intent or intentionally when he acts with the objective or purpose to accomplish a result which constitutes a crime.

(b) Knowledge. A person knows or acts knowingly or with knowledge when:

(i) he is aware of a fact, facts, or circumstances or result described by a statute defining an offense; or

(ii) he has information which would lead a reasonable man in the same situation to believe that facts exist which facts are described by a statute defining an offense.

(c) Recklessness. A person is reckless or acts recklessly when he knows of and disregards a substantial risk that a wrongful act may occur and his disregard of such substantial risk is a gross deviation from conduct that a reasonable man would exercise in the same situation.

(d) Criminal negligence. A person is criminally negligent or acts with criminal negligence when he fails to be aware of a substantial risk that a wrongful act may occur and his failure to be aware of such substantial risk constitutes a gross deviation from the standard of care that a reasonable man would exercise in the same situation.

(2) Substitutes for Criminal Negligence, Recklessness, and Knowledge. When a statutes provides that criminal negligence suffices to establish an element of an offense, such element also is established if a person acts intentionally, knowingly or recklessly. When recklessness suffices to establish an element, such element also is established if a person acts intentionally or knowingly. When acting knowingly suffices to establish an element, such element also is established if a person acts intentionally.

.　.　.

§ 26.20.030—Family abandonment; penalty; exception

(1) ... any person who has a child dependent upon him or her for care, education or support and deserts such child in any manner whatever with intent to abandon it is guilty of the crime of family abandonment.

.　.　.

(3) The crime of family abandonment is a class C felony under chapter 9A.20 RCW.

§ 26.20.035—Family nonsupport; penalty; exception

(1) ... any person who is able to provide support, or has the ability to earn the means to provide support, and who:

(a) Wilfully omits to provide necessary food, clothing, shelter, or medical attendance to a child dependent upon him or her; or

(b) Wilfully omits to provide necessary food, clothing, shelter, or medical attendance to his or her spouse, is guilty of the crime of family nonsupport.

.　.　.

(3) The crime of family nonsupport is a gross misdemeanor under chapter 9A.20 RCW [which provides a penalty of imprisonment in the county jail for a maximum term of not more than one year, or a fine of not more than five thousand dollars, or both such imprisonment and fine].

CHAPTER 2. PRINCIPLES FOR THE DISTRIBUTION OF CRIMINAL LIABILITY AND PUNISHMENT

4. THE CASE OF THOMAS DUDLEY (ENGLAND, 1884)

A. THE FACTS

In the early part of 1883, John Want, a prominent Australian lawyer and politician, arrives in England from Sydney. Want is a flamboyant yachtsman who comes to England to view and purchase a fast, 40 ton yacht to take back with him to Sydney. He eventually purchases the *Mignonette*, a 55 foot yacht built in 1867. As the yacht is too large to ship as deck cargo, Want makes arrangements to have the yacht sailed to Sydney. In November of 1883, Thomas Dudley hears of Want's purchase of the *Mignonette* and applies to sail the boat for him. Dudley is employed and arrangements are made to set sail in the spring of 1884.

Dudley, 31, grew up in the small town of Tollesbury. After his mother died when he was 9, he began his career as a seaman. He worked hard and became a sailing master, winning yachting prizes and competitions. Family friends and relatives helped him in his struggle for education and he learned to read and write. Dudley is a married man. He takes on the task of sailing the *Mignonette* to Australia because he is thinking of emigrating there to find better opportunities. When Want hires Dudley, Dudley becomes responsible for organizing and finding a crew. Dudley selects Edwin Stephens as his mate, Edmund (Ned) Brooks as the able seaman, and Richard Parker as the ordinary seaman.

Figure 9. Thomas Dudley.

Edwin Stephens, 37, is the son of a master mariner. He grew up in Southampton and is an experienced seaman. He is married with 5 children and is a respected local figure, active in the Young Men's Christian Association. Stephens, however, was responsible for a shipping accident in 1877 and has difficulty finding work. It is clear to him that his career will never flourish if he remains in Southampton, so he decides to emigrate. With the owner's consent, Dudley tempts Stephens to the journey on the *Mignonette* by offering him the captaincy of the ship once it gets to Sydney. Stephens holds a master's certificate and has considerable experience as a navigator.

Ned Brooks, 38, is the son of a mariner and went to sea early. He was a reservist in the British Navy for a time and then became a yacht hand. He married and later deserted his wife. He has known Dudley since 1879 and has been acquainted with the *Mignonette* yacht herself since the time of her building. Brooks apparently joins the *Mignonette* crew with interest in emigrating to Australia as well. Dudley offers him work on the yacht in Sydney if he wishes to stay there.

Richard Parker, the ordinary seaman, is 17. Illiterate, he comes from a traditional yachting village called Itchen Ferry. His brothers and cousins are seamen, with one serving as a ship captain. Both of his parents die by 1861, and as a 14 year-old orphan, he starts working at sea. Parker wants to join the crew because he wishes to travel abroad, having never sailed on a long ocean voyage. He also thinks that he might emigrate to Australia. He hopes "to make a man of himself" on the trip, and Dudley talks to him about the voyage as a rite of passage, promising to give Parker

Figure 10. The yacht *Mignonette* with crew of four, rigged for ocean voyage. (Barlow/Boon)

some schooling during the journey. Dudley brings books on board the *Mignonette* for this very purpose. He also promises Parker work in Sydney on the *Mignonette* if he wishes to stay on there.

As captain, Dudley is paid a large flat fee to cover his expenses and is responsible for paying for repairs and provisions out of this sum. Dick Fox, who is hired to perform repairs on the *Mignonette* prior to her departure, says he notices that her deadwood is "sick" (meaning that it has some rotten beams below the water line). Fox states that the ship needs new timbers, an expensive repair, but he is instructed to carry out repairs using the ship's existing wood, a much less expensive process. Dudley is an economical man and keeps the repair work to a minimum.

Some officials think the *Mignonette* unsuitable for the long voyage. The British Board of Trade's Marine Department feels that the ship is not fit for the voyage, but because she is not technically unseaworthy, she cannot be prevented from leaving. When Dudley is looking around for sailors to accompany him on the trip, there is a general feeling in the community that the trip is a bad idea because of the small size of the yacht. Three sailors who initially sign on think better of the trip, and Dudley eventually has to pay Stephens, Brooks, and Parker substantially more than the prevailing wage. However, yacht voyages across the ocean are not that uncommon, nor is the *Mignonette* a particularly small yacht. Dudley and the crew think that they can make it.

Dudley and his crew sail from Southampton on May 19, 1884. The voyage as planned consists of sailing somewhere between 14,000 and 16,000 miles. They intend to use the southerly route around the Cape of Good Hope, since the winds on the route to the Suez Canal are often erratic. Dudley and his navigator Stephens hope to reach Sydney within 110 to 120 days of leaving port. The boat safely arrives at Madeira on June 2, 1884, and leaves the last of the Cape Verde islands on June 8, 1884. The group then sails into the South Atlantic, where it is winter. In order to secure good winds and to reduce the chance of being run down by a larger ship, Dudley plots a course well to the west of normal shipping lanes. The crew expects and receives strong and reliable southeast tradewinds. On June 25, 1884, the wind becomes more variable. On July 3, 1884 the winds cease and the yacht is becalmed in the South Atlantic until July 5, 1884, when the *Mignonette* is caught in a storm 1600 miles from the Cape of Good Hope. During the storm, an enormous wave, half as tall as the mast, sweeps over the ship, knocking a hole in the side. The ship's side then caves in. The collapse results, in part, from a failure of the rotten beams below the water line.

Dudley realizes that the ship is sinking and orders that the dinghy be lowered. He asks Parker to go below and pass up a cask of water that is kept at the foot of the ladder leading into the hold. Parker does this and throws the cask into the sea as ordered by Dudley. Any attempt to lower the water into the dinghy would have torn a hole in the bottom of the boat. Knowing that the cask will float, Parker plans to retrieve it once in the dinghy.

Stephens, Brooks and Parker board the dinghy. Dudley retrieves six tins of provisions and the ship's compass. Dudley feels the ship start to founder and knows that he must get to the dinghy. He attempts to throw the provisions into the dinghy, but only one tin makes it.

Figure 11. As the *Mignonette* went down. (Illustrated London News)

The men are able to recover one more of the tins, along with some cotton waste. The water cask is lost, probably pushed out to sea by the strong wind.

Although maritime tradition holds that the crew need not follow the captain if their ship

Figure 12. The infamous dinghy.

founders, Dudley remains in command of the dinghy. He successfully constructs a sea anchor and positions the dinghy so that its bow is to the sea, allowing them to survive the heavy seas. There is a hole in the dinghy, so the men must constantly bail, even though they successfully plug the hole with the cotton waste recovered from the ship. A shark swims around their boat, but leaves after the men hit it on the head with an oar. The nearest land is 2,000 nautical miles to the west. The normal steamship route lays to the east.

Dudley, Stephens, Brooks, and Parker survive the first night, but they have no supply of water and no supply of food, except for the two one-pound tins of turnips they salvaged from the ship. For three days, the four eat nothing but turnips. On the fourth day, July 9, 1884, Brooks spots, and Dudley kills, a small turtle. They attempt to catch its blood, but sea water splashes over the side and contaminates it. It is believed by sailors of the time that seawater is a kind of poison causing madness and death. On that day, they consume the end of their second tin of turnips along with some of the turtle.

The main problem is not hunger, but thirst. By July 13, 1884, all four are drinking their own urine. It does little to alleviate their thirst. Their lips and tongues become parched and blackened, their feet and legs swell, and their skins develop sores from constant exposure to sea and wind and from the press of the crowded boat. They have no fresh water except the rain they from time to time are able to catch in their oilskin caps.

Stephens has been trained in survival and teaches the men to soak their clothes in seawater, but they find that this leaves them cold at night. They also try hanging naked overboard, finding that this provides some relief.

They survive by eating the turtle until July 17th, consuming both the bones and the skin. On the 12th day, the turtle has been entirely consumed. At this time, Dudley first proposes that they draw lots to determine who should be killed to save the lives of the others. Parker either does not participate in the conversation or states that he will not draw lots. Stephens and Brooks decide that discussion of the topic is premature.

At the time, cannibalism after a shipwreck is so common that discussion of the practice among surviving castaways is a routine reaction to being left adrift at sea. The traditional course of action is to draw lots, a practice viewed as legitimizing the killing and cannibalism.

For the next 8 days, the four eat nothing. On July 20, 1884, Richard Parker drinks a considerable quantity of sea water and becomes violently ill. He suffers from diarrhea which further dehydrates him. He lays on the bottom of the boat groaning and gasping for breath. He becomes delirious and then intermittently comatose. Richard has been explicitly warned that drinking sea water will kill him. Dudley again raises the issue of drawing lots. The others ignore this suggestion. They say, "We had better die together." Dudley replies, "So let it be, but it's hard for four to die, when perhaps one might save the rest."

The boat drifts on the ocean and remains more than 1000 nautical miles away from land. Although they eventually fashion a rudimentary sail out of oars and their clothing, they make only about four knots. On the 18th day, when they have been seven days without food and five days without water, Dudley and Stephens speak to Brooks about what should be done if no help arrives. Dudley and Stephens suggest to Brooks that one should be sacrificed to save the rest. Brooks disagrees and the boy, Richard Parker, to whom each understands they refer, is not consulted.

On July 24, 1884, Dudley again proposes to Stephens and Brooks that lots be cast. Brooks still refuses to consent, and it is unclear whether Parker chooses not to participate or votes no. There is no drawing of lots. On this day, Dudley and Stephens speak of their families and suggest to one another that it would be better to kill the boy so that their lives be saved. Dudley proposes that, if no vessel appears by the following morning, the boy be killed. The next day, July 25, 1884, no vessel appears. Dudley tells Brooks that the boy should be killed. Stephens agrees to this, but Brooks again does not agree. At this time, the boy lays at the bottom of the boat, helpless and extremely weakened by famine and drinking sea-water. He is unable to make any resistance. He does not consent to being killed.

Dudley offers a prayer, asking for forgiveness for them all if any of them should be tempted to commit a rash act and that their souls might be saved. Then Dudley, after ordering Stephens to hold the boy's feet if necessary, goes to the boy and says, "Dick, your time has come, poor boy." The boy then asks him, "What, me, sir?" and Dudley replies, "Yes, my boy." He stabs a two inch blade into the boy's throat, killing him. Sailors believe that it is preferable to obtain blood from a living victim. Dudley and Stephens immediately drink as much blood as they can catch, and cut out and eat the boy's heart and liver. The three men, Dudley, Stephens, and Brooks, use the oarlocks of the dinghy to cut the boy into pieces and feed upon his body and blood for four days.

If the men had not fed upon the body of the boy when they did, they would have died of famine within a few days. The boy, being in a much weaker condition, would have died before them.

At the time of the killing, there is no sail in sight, nor any reasonable prospect of relief. Under these circumstances, it appears to Stephens and Dudley that there is no other chance of saving life except by killing one of them to eat.

Four days after the boy is killed, the dinghy is picked up by a passing vessel. Dudley, Stephens and Brooks are all rescued. They are still alive, but all are near death. They eventually recover. It seems clear that none would have lived to be rescued if they had not fed upon the boy when they did.

Once on shore, none of the men make an effort to conceal what they have done and frankly confess the events surrounding Parker's death. All are sorry that the boy was killed, but none appears to think that they have done anything wrong. When a policeman asks to examine the knife used to kill Richard, Dudley asks to have it back as a keepsake.

* * *

Would you convict Dudley for the death of Parker? If so, what amount of punishment would you impose?

N	0	1	2	3	4	5	6	7	8	9	10	11
☐	☐	☐	☐	☐	☐	☐	☐	☐	☐	☐	☐	☐
no liability	liability but no punishment	1 day	2 wks.	2 mo.	6 mo.	1 yr.	3 yrs.	7 yrs.	15 yrs.	30 yrs.	life imprison-ment	death

B.   Then Existing Law

Hale's History of the Pleas of the Crown, 1st ed. vol. I, pp. 51, 54, 428

If a man be sick of some such disease, which possibly by course of nature would end his life ... and another gives him a wound or hurt ... this hastening of his death sooner than it would have been is murder or manslaughter ...

If a man be desperately assaulted and in peril of death, and cannot otherwise escape unless ... he will kill an innocent person ... the fear and actual force will not acquit him of the crime and punishment of murder ... for he ought to die himself than kill an innocent ...

Some of the casuists ... tell us that in case of extreme necessity, either of hunger or clothing, the civil distributions of property cease, and by a kind of tacit condition the first community doth return ..., and therefore in such case theft is no theft, or at least not punishable, as theft ... I do ... take it, that, where persons live under the same civil government, as here in *England*, that rule, at least by the laws of *England*, is false; and therefore if a person being under necessity for want of victuals, or clothes, shall upon that account clandestinely, and *amino furandi* steal another man's goods, it is a felony, and a crime by the laws of *England* punishable with death; altho the judge before whom the trial is, in this case (as in other cases of extremity) be by the laws of *England* intrusted with a power to reprieve the offender before or after judgement in order to the obtaining of the king's mercy.

Blackstone's Commentaries on the Laws of England: Of Public Wrongs, p. 28 (1765)

There is a ... species of necessity, which may be distinguished from actual compulsion of external force or fear; being the result of reason and reflection, which act upon and constrain a man's will, and oblige him to do an action which without such obligation would be criminal. And that is, when a man has his choice of two evils set before him, and being under the necessity of choosing one, he chooses the least pernicious of the two. Here the will cannot be said freely to exert itself, being passive rather than active; or, if active, it is rather in rejecting the greater evil than choosing the less ...

The Works of Francis Bacon, Shedding, Ellis, and Heath, eds., p. 343 (1859)

The law chargeth no man with default where the act is compulsory and not voluntary, and where there is not a consent and election: and therefore, if either there be an impossibility for a man to do otherwise, or so great a perturbation of the judgement and the reason as in presumption of law man's nature cannot overcome, such necessity carrieth a privilege in itself. [I]f a man steals viands to satisfy his present hunger, there is no felony or larceny ... So if divers be in danger of drowning by the casting away of some boat or barge, and one of them get to some plank, or on the boat's side to keep himself above water, and another to save his life thrust him from it, whereby he is drowned, this is neither se defendendo nor by misadventure, but justifiable ...

United States v. Holmes, 26 F. Cas. 360 1 Wall Jr. 1 (C.C.E.D. Pa. 1842)

In an American case brought after seaman jettisoned 18 passengers to save the lives of others on a sinking lifeboat, the judge charged the jury that generally if two persons are in a situation where only one can possibly survive, "neither is bound to save the other's life by sacrificing his own life for the only means of safety," but that this rule only applied to those on equal footing, and had no bearing in cases where there was a special duty of care, as between the sailors and the passengers jettisoned. Where there is no duty of care, the choice of whom should be cast overboard is appropriately made by drawing lots.

C. Current Law That Would Be Applied Were the Case Prosecuted Today

The opinion in *Regina v. Dudley and Stephens* remains controlling, but the Law Commission has proposed "A Criminal Code for England and Wales" (Law Com. No. 177) that contains the following provisions:

Draft Criminal Code for England and Wales (1989)

§ 54.—[Murder]

(1) A person is guilty of murder if he causes the death of another—

    (a) intending to cause death; ...

(2) A person convicted of murder shall be sentenced to life imprisonment, except that, where he appears to the court to have been under the age of eighteen years at the time the offence was committed, he shall be sentenced to detention in such place and for such period and subject to such condition as to release as the secretary of State may determine.

§ 43.—Duress of Circumstances

(1) A person is not guilty of an offence [to which this section applies] when he does an act under duress of circumstances.

(2) A person does an act under duress of circumstances if:

    (a) he does it because he knows or believes that it is immediately necessary to avoid death or serious personal harm to himself or another; and

    (b) the danger that he knows or believes to exist is such that in all the circumstances (including any of his personal characteristics that effect its gravity) he cannot reasonably be expected to act otherwise.

(3) This section:

[(a) applies to any offence other than murder or attempt to murder;]*

(b) does not apply: ...

(iii) to a person who has knowingly and without reasonable excuse exposed himself to the danger.

---

* The bracketed language was added to reflect a House of Lords decision to exclude murder and attempted murder from the scope of the defense. See Draft Criminal Code for England and Wales, Volume 2, "Commentary on Draft Criminal Code Bill," Clause 42, ¶ 12.23.

5. THE CASE OF WILLIAM JAMES RUMMEL (TEXAS, 1973)

A. THE FACTS

William J. Rummel has had trouble holding down any kind of job, although this is more from laziness than inability. He has opted instead to make his living through small-time larceny and fraud. If he were good enough, check forgery might be called his specialty. But he is not, and his arrests begin to pile up. As a con-man, the tall and thin Rummel is inept, leaving clues like his real name and signature on receipts from stolen credit cards and stolen checks. His legitimate skills are as limited as his criminal ones. His educational background consists of a few Dale Carnegie courses. At the age of 30, he has no wife, no children, and no friends. His parents are both alive, but their health is poor and Rummel rarely sees them.

Figure 13. William James Rummel. (Corbis)

William Rummel has a long criminal record. On October 20, 1959 in San Antonio, he is convicted of misdemeanor theft and unlawful possession of alcoholic beverages. On the day of those convictions at the Bexar County Courthouse, he is arrested again, this time for unlawfully carrying a Bowie knife. He is convicted of the weapons charge on January 21, 1960 and is fined $100. On May 17, 1960, he is given three years of probation on a burglary charge. On July 25, 1963, he passes a bad check for $10 at a Holiday Inn and on December 22, 1963 a $30 bad check, for which he is convicted on March 6, 1964 of two counts of swindling. He is sentenced to 30 days in jail.

On December 16, 1964, Rummel is convicted of credit-card fraud after he uses a company credit card to buy two new tires for his car. The tires are worth a total of $80, but Rummel is sentenced to three years in prison. He violates parole on July 21, 1966 and is returned to the Department of Corrections on August 25, 1966. On February 21, 1968, Rummel is convicted of aggravated assault on a female, Penny Rummel, and is sentenced to 30 days in jail. On the day of his assault conviction, he passes a bad check for $5.61 at a Gulf service station and is again convicted of swindling by check. He is sentenced to 30 days, to run consecutively with the sentence for the assault conviction. On March 11, 1969, Rummel is convicted of forging a $28.36 check and is sentenced to two to four years in prison, of which he serves 28 months.

On August 15, 1973, Rummel walks into Captain Hook's Lounge in San Antonio. It is a hot day, and the bar's air conditioning is not working. Rummel gets an idea. He approaches the bar's owner, David Shaw, and offers to fix the air conditioner. Shaw agrees and Rummel begins his inspection. After a few minutes and a little tinkering, Rummel announces the unit needs a new compressor. Cost: $129.75, labor free. Shaw quickly agrees and writes Rummel a check for the whole amount, payable to Rummel. Rummel, who has no intention of ever making the promised repair, leaves, cashes the check, and never returns. Shaw files a complaint with the police, who easily trace Rummel.

Rummel's offense, theft by false pretext, would normally render him liable under Texas Law for a maximum sentence of between two and ten years, although violators typically receive a sentence of months, not years. Rummel, however, has a criminal record.

* * *

Would you impose liability on Rummel for his $129.75 air conditioning repair fraud? If so, what amount of punishment would you impose?

N	0	1	2	3	4	5	6	7	8	9	10	11
☐	☐	☐	☐	☐	☐	☐	☐	☐	☐	☐	☐	☐
no liability	liability but no punishment	1 day	2 wks.	2 mo.	6 mo.	1 yr.	3 yrs.	7 yrs.	15 yrs.	30 yrs.	life imprisonment	death

B. THEN EXISTING LAW

Texas Penal Code (1973)

§ 1410—Theft (defined)

Theft is the fraudulent taking of corporeal personal property belonging to another from his possession, or from the possession of some person holding the same for him, without his consent, with intent to deprive the owner of the value of the same, and to appropriate it to the use or benefit of the person taking.

§ 1413—False Pretext

The taking must be wrongful, so that if the property came into the possession of the person accused of theft by lawful means, the subsequent appropriation of it is not theft, but if the taking, though originally lawful, was obtained by false pretext, or with any intent to deprive the owner of the value thereof, and appropriate the property to the use and benefit of the person taking, and the same is so appropriated, the offense of theft is complete.

§ 1421—Punishment for felony theft

Theft of property of the value of fifty dollars or over shall be punished by confinement in the penitentiary not less than two nor more than ten years.

§ 1422—Punishment for misdemeanor theft

Theft of property under the value of fifty dollars and over the value of five dollars shall be punished by imprisonment in jail not exceeding two years, and by fine not exceeding five hundred dollars, or by such imprisonment without fine; theft of property of the value of five dollars or under shall be punished by a fine not exceeding two hundred dollars.

§ 1555b—Intent to defraud; credit card fraud; punishment

Section (4)(d). For a violation of this Act, in the event the amount of the credit obtained or the value of the items or services is Fifty Dollars ($50) or more, punishment shall be confinement in the penitentiary for not less than two (2) nor more than ten (10) years.

§ 996—Forgery; punishment

If any person shall knowingly pass as true, or attempt to pass as true, any such forged instrument in writing as is mentioned and defined in the preceding articles of this chapter, he shall be confined in the penitentiary not less than two nor more than five years.

§ 1397—Punishment for burglary

One guilty of burglary shall be confined in the penitentiary not less than two nor more than twelve years.

§ 1148—Punishment [for aggravated assault or battery]

The punishment for an aggravated assault or battery shall be a fine not less than Twenty-five Dollars ($25) nor more than One Thousand Dollars ($1,000), or imprisonment in jail not less than one (1) month nor more than two (2) years, or both such fine and imprisonment.

§ 63—Third conviction for felony

Whoever shall have been three times convicted of a felony less than capital shall on such third conviction be imprisoned for life in the penitentiary.

C.   Current Law That Would Be Applied Were the Case Prosecuted Today

Texas Penal Code (2006)

[The offense definitions of Credit Card Abuse (§ 32.31), Forgery (§ 32.21), and Theft (§ 31.03) are now considerably more detailed than in 1973. Credit Card Abuse and Forgery are generally "state jail felonies." Theft is a "state jail felony" if the value of the property is $1,500 or more, but less than $20,000. If the amount is $500 or more, but less than $1500, the offense is a Class A misdemeanor. If the amount is $50 or more, or $20 or more if theft by check (§ 31.06), the offense is a Class B misdemeanor. Otherwise the offense is a Class C misdemeanor. Aggravated assault generally is a felony in the second degree. Burglary is a state jail felony if committed in a building other than a habitation, a felony of the second degree if committed in a habitation, and a felony of the first degree if committed in a habitation with intent to commit an additional felony.]

§ 12.03—Classification of Misdemeanors

(a) Misdemeanors are classified according to the relative seriousness of the offense into three categories:

> (1) Class A misdemeanors;

> (2) Class B misdemeanors;

> (3) Class C misdemeanors;

(b) An offense designated a misdemeanor in this code without specification as to punishment or category is a Class C misdemeanor.

(c) Conviction of a Class C misdemeanor does not impose any legal disability or disadvantage.

§ 12.04—Classification of Felonies

(a) Felonies are classified according to the relative seriousness of the offense into five categories:

> (1) capital felonies;

> (2) felonies of the first degree;

> (3) felonies of the second degree;

> (4) felonies of the third degree;

> (5) state jail felonies.

(b) An offense designated a felony in this code without specification as to category is a state jail felony.

§ 12.21—Class A Misdemeanor

An individual adjudged guilty of a Class A misdemeanor shall be punished by:

(1) a fine not to exceed $4,000;

(2) confinement in jail for a term not to exceed one year; or

(3) both such fine and confinement.

§ 12.22—Class B Misdemeanor

An individual adjudged guilty of a Class B misdemeanor shall be punished by:

(1) a fine not to exceed $2,000;

(2) confinement in jail for a term not to exceed 180 days; or

(3) both such fine and confinement.

§ 12.23—Class C Misdemeanor

An individual adjudged guilty of a Class C misdemeanor shall be punished by a fine not to exceed $500.

§ 12.31—Capital Felony

(a) An individual adjudged guilty of a capital felony in a case in which the state seeks the death penalty shall be punished by imprisonment in the institutional division for life without parole or by death. An individual adjudged guilty of a capital felony in a case in which the state does not seek the death penalty shall be punished by imprisonment in the institutional division for life without parole.

(b) In a capital felony trial in which the state seeks the death penalty, prospective jurors shall be informed that a sentence of life imprisonment without parole or death is mandatory on conviction of a capital felony. In a capital felony trial in which the state does not seek the death penalty, prospective jurors shall be informed that the state is not seeking the death penalty and that a sentence of life imprisonment without parole is mandatory on conviction of the capital felony.

§ 12.32—First Degree Felony Punishment

(a) An individual adjudged guilty of a felony of the first degree shall be punished by imprisonment in the institutional division for life or for any term of not more than 99 years or less than 5 years.

(b) In addition to imprisonment, an individual adjudged guilty of a felony of the first degree may be punished by a fine not to exceed $10,000.

§ 12.33—Second Degree Felony Punishment

(a) An individual adjudged guilty of a felony of the second degree shall be punished by imprisonment in the institutional division for any term of not more than 20 years or less than 2 years.

(b) In addition to imprisonment, an individual adjudged guilty of a felony of the second degree may be punished by a fine not to exceed $10,000.

§ 12.34—Third Degree Felony Punishment

(a) An individual adjudged guilty of a felony of the third degree shall be punished by imprisonment in the institutional division for any term of not more than 10 years or less than 2 years.

(b) In addition to imprisonment, an individual adjudged guilty of a felony of the third degree may be punished by a fine not to exceed $10,000.

§ 12.35—State Jail Felony Punishment

(a) Except as provided by Subsection (c), an individual adjudged guilty of a state jail felony shall be punished by confinement in a state jail for any term of not more than two years or less than 180 days.

(b) In addition to confinement, an individual adjudged guilty of a state jail felony may be punished by a fine not to exceed $10,000.

(c) An individual adjudged guilty of a state jail felony shall be punished for a third degree felony if it is shown on the trial of the offense that:

(1) a deadly weapon as defined by Section 1.07 [either a firearm or anything manifestly designed, made, or adapted for the purpose of inflicting death or serious bodily injury, or anything that in the manner of its use or intended use is capable of causing death or serious bodily injury] was used or exhibited during the commission of the offense or during immediate flight following the commission of the offense, and that the individual used or exhibited the deadly weapon or was a party to the offense and knew that a deadly weapon would be used or exhibited; or

(2) the individual has previously been finally convicted of any felony:

(A) listed in Section 3g(a)(1), Article 42.12, Code of Criminal Procedure [murder, capital murder, indecency with a child, aggravated kidnapping, aggravated sexual assault, aggravated robbery]; or

(B) for which the judgement contains an affirmative finding under Section 3g(a)(2), Article 42.12, Code of Criminal Procedure.

§ 12.41—Classification of Offenses Outside this Code

For purposes of this subchapter, any conviction not obtained from a prosecution under this code shall be classified as follows:

(1) "Felony of the third degree" if imprisonment in a penitentiary is affixed to the offense as a possible punishment;

(2) "Class B misdemeanor" if the offense is not a felony and confinement in a jail is affixed to the offense as a possible punishment;

(3) "Class C misdemeanor" if the offense is punishable by fine only.

§ 12.42—Penalties for Repeat and Habitual Felony Offenders

(a)

(1) If it is shown on the trial of a state jail felony ... that the defendant has previously been finally convicted of two state jail felonies, on conviction the defendant shall be punished for a third-degree felony.

(2) If it is shown on the trial of a state jail felony ... that the defendant has previously been finally convicted of two felonies, and the second previous felony conviction is for an offense that occurred subsequent to the first previous conviction having become final, on conviction the defendant shall be punished for a second-degree felony.

(3) If it is shown on the trial of ... a third-degree felony that the defendant has been once before convicted of a felony, on conviction he shall be punished for a second-degree felony.

(b) If it is shown on the trial of a second-degree felony that the defendant has been once before convicted of a felony, on conviction he shall be punished for a first-degree felony.

(c)

(1) If it is shown on the trial of a first-degree felony that the defendant has been once before convicted of a felony, on conviction he shall be punished by imprisonment in the institutional division of the Texas Department of Criminal Justice for life, or for any term of not more than 99 years or less than 15 years. In addition to imprisonment, an individual may be punished by a fine not to exceed $10,000.

(2) A defendant shall be punished by imprisonment in the institutional division for life if:

(A) the defendant is convicted of an offense:

(i) under Section 22.021 [Aggravated Sexual Assault], Penal Code;

(ii) under Section 20.04(a)(4) [Aggravated Kidnapping], Penal Code, if the defendant committed the offense with the intent to violate or abuse the victim sexually; or

(iii) under Section 30.02 [Burglary], Penal Code, punishable under Subsection (d) of that section, if the defendant committed the offense with the intent to commit a felony described by Subparagraph (i) or (ii) or a felony under Section 21.11 [Indecency With a Child] or 22.011 [Sexual Assault], Penal Code; and

(B) the defendant has been previously convicted of an offense:

(i) under Section 43.25 [Sexual Performance by a Child] or 43.26 [Possession or Promotion of Child Pornography], Penal Code, or an offense under section 43.23 [Obscenity] Penal Code, punishable under subsection (h) of that section;

(ii) under Section 21.11 [Indecency With a Child], 22.011 [Sexual Assault], 22.021 [Aggravated Sexual Assault], or 25.02 [Prohibited Sexual Conduct], Penal Code;

(iii) under Section 20.04(a)(4) [Aggravated Kidnapping], Penal Code, if the defendant committed the offense with the intent to violate or abuse the victim sexually;

(iv) under Section 30.02 [Burglary], Penal Code, punishable under Subsection (d) of that section, if the defendant committed the offense with the intent to commit a felony described by Subparagraph (ii) or (iii); or

(v) under the laws of another state containing elements that are substantially similar to the elements of an offense listed in Subparagraph (i), (ii), (iii), or (iv).

(d) If it is shown on the trial of a felony offense other than a state jail felony ... that the defendant has previously been finally convicted of two felony offenses, and the second previous felony conviction is for an offense that occurred subsequent to the first previous conviction having become final, on conviction he shall be punished by imprisonment in the institutional division of the Texas Department of Criminal Justice for life, or for any term of not more than 99 years or less than 25 years.

(e) A previous conviction for a state jail felony punished under Section 12.35(a) may not be used for enhancement purposes under Subsection (b), (c), or (d).

* * *

§ 12.43—Penalties for Repeat and Habitual Misdemeanor Offenders

(a) If it is shown on the trial of a Class A misdemeanor that the defendant has been before convicted of a Class A misdemeanor or any degree of felony, on conviction he shall be punished by:

(1) a fine not to exceed $4,000;

(2) confinement in jail for any term of not more than one year or less than 90 days; or

(3) both such fine and confinement.

(b) If it is shown on the trial of a Class B misdemeanor that the defendant has been before convicted of a Class A or Class B misdemeanor or any degree of felony, on conviction he shall be punished by:

    (1) a fine not to exceed $2,000;

    (2) confinement in jail for any term of not more than 180 days or less than 30 days; or

    (3) both such fine and confinement.

(d) If the punishment scheme for an offense contains a specific enhancement provision increasing punishment for a defendant who has previously been convicted of the offense, the specific enhancement provision controls over this section.

Chapter 3. Do We Know What the Criminal Law Commands of Us, and Does the Law Care If We Don't? Legality, Mistake, and Omissions

6. The Case of Canna Baker (Arkansas, 1948)

A. The Facts

It is 1947 near Mountain Home, Arkansas, a rural town 10 miles from the Missouri border. Canna Baker, born January 11, 1883, and her husband Jim, seven years her senior, live on a small piece of property with a main house, some cabins and sheds, a barn, and other out-buildings, and make their living by farming and raising milk cows. Since their marriage in 1901, they have also earned income from the state by lodging, feeding, and caring for welfare paupers. They get $1 per day for each.

Canna, or "Cannie" as she is called, is well-known in the county. The dominant force in her marriage, she can hitch up and drive a team of horses as well as can any man. On Saturday afternoons she does just that, running her team and wagon into town and around the Mountain Home County Courthouse Square. She wears a man's hat, bright red lipstick and rouge, and a cotton house dress with, maybe, a sweater for a coat. Her cotton hose is rolled below her knees. Cannie talks to everybody—long and loud.

Cannie Baker's relationship with the county welfare authorities has not been smooth. Baxter County Department of Public Welfare Director Mamie Green has held her position since 1936, and regularly objects to sending people to live with Cannie. She has heard that the boarders may not be "getting the care they should have." Busy with her duties in the office, Green rarely gets out to visit the welfare wards under her care. Instead, she must send visitors to check on them, usually about once every three or four months, sometimes less.

Figure 14. Cannie and Jim Baker in their cornfield. (Arkansas Gazette)

Margaret Bryant, the visitor who usually goes to the Baker home, regularly returns with grim reports. But Director Green has no power to move people out unless the boarders themselves request it. The few who have asked to get moved from the Baker place have quietly whispered their request when alone with the welfare worker. In all the years that she has been working in the welfare office, only three people have moved out. Two were boarders; the third was Cannie Baker's mother, an old-age pen-

35

sioner who, one day, when alone with Green, quietly asked the Welfare Director to help get her away from her daughter.

Figure 15. Cannie Baker behind the plow on her farm. (Arkansas Gazette)

The state pays its welfare recipients once a month in advance, by sending a check made out to the recipient on the first of the month. When the check arrives each month, Cannie Baker takes it to the boarder, who signs it in Cannie's presence and hands it over to her. Cannie then endorses the check herself and cashes it, keeping the whole $30 for the coming month's upkeep. The check pays for food, rent, and a few basic necessities.

On April 2, 1947, Cannie Baker reports the death of Annie Reynolds, a welfare boarder at her house. The check for Annie's April board comes on the morning of the 2nd, but Cannie does not get it signed before Annie dies. Cannie takes the check to a local shopkeeper, Fred Burrow, who regularly cashes the checks for her. Burrows and Cannie write to the state welfare department in Little Rock, informing the state of the woman's death on April 2, and asking whether Cannie can cash the check and use the money to pay for Reynolds' funeral expenses. The state refers the issue to the Baxter County welfare department, and the check is held for weeks while the case is sorted out. It is ultimately decided that the state will pay the funeral expenses directly. The check is never cashed.

Ed White has been a pauper on the Baxter County welfare rolls for as long as most residents and social workers can remember. For several years, he lived in nearby Cotter, Arkansas. He is well known in Cotter, largely because of his smell—a strong, rancid odor that hangs about him. Most think the smell comes from his dirty clothes, although others think it is caused by his ill health and kidney trouble. In 1947, White is in his late 70s and in poor health. He decides to travel from Cotter to Mountain Home in Baxter County to find a new place to live. He stops first at the courthouse, where the welfare office is located. He sleeps and putters around the courthouse as welfare workers try to figure out where to send him.

White hears from people around the courthouse that Cannie Baker takes in boarders and cares for them in exchange for their welfare checks. He asks to be sent to live at the Bakers'. Welfare workers, wary of sending boarders to the Bakers', hesitate and stall. After several days and repeated requests by White, the welfare director finally agrees. A sheriff's deputy drives White out to the Baker home that afternoon. After a short conversation, Cannie agrees to take White on as a boarder for the usual $1 a day, the $30 per month representing White's entire monthly old-age assistance check.

White arrives after the first of the month, the date when the state writes its welfare checks, so Cannie does not get paid immediately for the first few weeks of the old man's lodging. Since subsequent checks pay in advance for each following month, in Cannie's mind, the state remains several weeks behind in what they owe her.

White is already in poor physical condition when he arrives at the Bakers'. His clothes are dirty and torn so badly that he appears almost naked. His feet are black and gangrenous, and he has no feeling left in them. His odor is unbearably strong and his breath so foul that Cannie refuses to get close enough to shave him. She buys him a new suit for $3 and 65 cans of Saymon's Salve to treat the sores on his legs, neck, and back, which are open, infected, and oozing. A local doctor prescribes $2 worth of pills to fight the infections that have discolored his skin and bloated his body.

For several months, White lives in one of the small cabins on the back side of the Baker property, a short walk from the main house. Each day, Cannie fixes White breakfast, lunch, and dinner, although White usually eats little, sometimes just Jell–O, milk, and a bite or two of cake. The neighbors come to know him as a sickly old man who hangs around his cabin most of the day and hardly ever says a word to anyone. Because of his age, they give him the nickname "Daddy."

In late November 1948, White suffers a stroke. His sores continue to seep; they are infected and not responding to the medication and salves. His genitals have long since rotted and fallen off, and Cannie fashions a makeshift diaper for him.

On November 27, White dies in his cabin. Cannie discovers his body, but does not report his death to the authorities or undertaker. She knows that the state will not send White another welfare check until December 1. Cannie believes that the state still owes her for the first several weeks of White's stay at her house, before she received the first monthly check. Additionally, she recalls the difficulties in trying to cash Annie Reynolds' check after Annie died. She decides not to report White's death until after she gets his check on the first of the month, four days away.

She pulls his hat low, almost over his eyes, and sits him up in bed. During the next four days, she keeps him well-hidden by the sheets on his bed and the hat over his face. His odor, getting even worse in death, naturally keeps people from coming too close, and his non-talkative demeanor surprises no one. Occasionally, she moves White, so that no one gets suspicious. Sometimes, she props him up in a chair in his room or on the steps of the porch to his cabin.

On Tuesday, November 30, Cannie goes into town and buys another can of salve and some new clothes, making sure to tell the shopkeeper, Henry Tipton, that she is buying them for White.

On Wednesday, December 1, Johnnie McCarty, Cannie's grandson-in-law, walks over to Cannie's at about 8 or 9 in the morning to help strain the milk taken from the cows that day. He passes by the house where White lives. The old man is sitting in a chair by the front door, but he does not move a muscle or say a word. That does not strike McCarty as unusual. White almost never says anything and hardly ever moves. Although he later wonders whether the old man was alive, McCarty thinks nothing of it as he passes by. "I never saw a dead man sitting up," he thinks later.

The same day, Irene Schreiner, a neighbor, walks by White's cabin and sees him sitting on the steps to the porch. "How are you, Mr. White?" Schreiner asks. White does not answer or move, but Schreiner is not really paying attention to him and thinks nothing of it. Later, Cecil Kyter, another neighbor who lives about 100 yards from the Bakers' home, returns from work in the afternoon and goes to White's cabin between 6 and 7 in the evening to gather some hay that he stores in one of its rooms. While he is there, he looks in the door to White's room and sees the old man sitting on the bed. Kyter says a few words but does not get very close because of the "odor to him nobody couldn't hardly stand." White's body and face are swollen and discolored in spots. His legs are black, as they have been for months. Kyter says something about the weather and believes that White responds in his usual feeble voice.

The morning mail of December 2 brings White's monthly welfare check, which Cannie signs for White, endorses, then cashes.

On the afternoon of December 2, Cannie, her granddaughter, Mary Lee, and her granddaughter's husband, Johnnie McCarty, travel to Cotter to see Frank Baker about buying and slaughtering a hog. Afterwards, the group goes to a movie, returning home at 10 p.m. Cannie asks her husband if he has checked on Ed White. He tells her he has not. Cannie says, "I will go," lights a lantern, and walks out to White's cabin. As she approaches the cabin, she hollers "Daddy" but gets no response from inside. White is lying on the bed. Cannie runs back to the house and yells, "Jim, Daddy White's dead." Shortly after 10:00 p.m., Cannie sends Johnnie and Mary Lee McCarty for Denver Roller, the Mountain Home undertaker.

Later in the evening, Dr. S. W. Chambers, a practicing physician in Mountain Home and the county health officer, comes to the funeral home to examine White's body, which has been brought over from the cabin. The body is discolored, greatly swollen, and decomposed, but the limbs move easily, evidence that rigor mortis has already left the body. Because of the absence of rigor mortis and the advanced decomposition, Chambers believes that White has been dead for at least 5 or 6 days. Dr. Gerald Pearce, also a Mountain Home physician, examines the body the next day, December 3. He too concludes White has been dead for a number of days.

* * *

Cannie can be held liable for the welfare fraud, but authorities are more upset about her treatment of Ed White's dead body. Would you impose criminal liability on Cannie Baker for her handling of White's body? If so, what amount of punishment would you impose?

N	0	1	2	3	4	5	6	7	8	9	10	11
☐	☐	☐	☐	☐	☐	☐	☐	☐	☐	☐	☐	☐
no liability	liability but no punishment	1 day	2 wks.	2 mo.	6 mo.	1 yr.	3 yrs.	7 yrs.	15 yrs.	30 yrs.	life imprison- ment	death

B. THEN EXISTING LAW

Arkansas Statutes (1948)

§ 1–101—Common and statute law of England adopted

The common law of England, so far as the same is applicable and of a general nature, and all statutes of the British Parliament in aid of or to supply the defects of the common law made prior to the fourth year of James the First [1606] (that are applicable to our own form of government), of a general nature and not local to that kingdom, and not inconsistent with the Constitution and laws of the United States or the Constitution and laws of this State, shall be the rule of decision in this State unless altered or repealed by the General Assembly of this State.

§ 41–107—Common law crimes and misdemeanors—Jurisdiction—Penalty

In cases of crimes and misdemeanors committed in this State, the punishment of which has not been provided for by statute, the court having the jurisdiction thereof shall proceed to punish the offender under the provisions of the common or statute law of England put in force in this State by this act [§§ 1–101, 41–107]; but the punishment in such cases shall only be fine and imprisonment, and in such cases the fine shall not exceed one hundred dollars [$100.00] and the imprisonment shall not exceed three [3] months.

Corpus Juris, vol. 17, p. 1148

At common law it was an offense to treat a dead human body indecently, and various specific offenses were recognized. Ordinarily it is a misdemeanor for one upon whom the duty is imposed of having a dead body buried to refuse or neglect to perform such duty.

Wharton's Criminal Law, 12th ed., vol. II, p. 1704

Indecency in treatment of a dead human body is an offense at common law, as an insult to public decency. Hence it is indictable to expose such a body without proper burial.

Kanavan's Case, 1 Me. 226 (1821)

Defendant's casting of a dead body into the river, without the rites of Christian sepulture, was a common law offense against common decency, since it is "a crime to deprive [the deceased] of a decent burial, by a disgraceful exposure, or disposal of the body contrary to usages so long sanctioned, and which are so grateful to the wounded hearts of friends and mourners."

State v. Bradbury, 136 Me. 347, 9 A.2d 657 (1939)

Where defendant disposed of his recently deceased sister by burning her in their home's furnace, he was guilty of a common law offense of abuse of corpse. "[A]ny disposal of a dead body which is contrary to common decency is an offense at common law."

Thompson v. State, 105 Tenn. 177, 58 S.W. 213 (1900)

The case discusses a common law case, Reg. v. Feist, Dears. & B. Cr. Cas. 590, 27 Law J. M. Cas. 164, in which "the defendant was the master of a workhouse, and had lawful possession of the bodies of deceased paupers. He was in the habit of having the appearance of a funeral gone through, with a view of preventing the relatives requiring that the bodies should be buried without being subject to anatomical examination; and the jury found that but for that deception the relatives would have required the bodies to be so buried. The bodies, instead of being buried, as was supposed by the relatives, were delivered to a hospital for the purpose of undergoing anatomical examination, and for this service the master received from the hospital a sum of money. The prisoner was found guilty of an offense at common law, in disposing of a body for dissection."

C. Current Law That Would Be Applied Were the Case Prosecuted Today

[§ 1–101, recodified as § 1–2–119, has not been changed in substance. § 41–107 has been repealed and replaced with § 5–1–105]

Arkansas Statutes (2006)

§ 1–2–202—Liberal construction

All general provisions, terms, phrases, and expressions used in any statute shall be liberally construed in order that the true intent and meaning of the General Assembly may be fully carried out.

§ 1–2–201—Applicability of §§ 1–2–202 and 1–2–203

The rules prescribed in §§ 1–2–202 ... shall apply in all cases, both civil and criminal, unless it is otherwise specially provided or unless there is something in the context or subject matter repugnant to that construction.

§ 5–1–105—Offenses—Court authority not limited

(a) An offense is conduct for which a sentence to a term of imprisonment or fine or both is authorized by statute.

(b) Offenses are classified as follows:

    (1) Felonies;

    (2) Misdemeanors;

    (3) Violations.

(c) Nothing in this code shall be construed to limit the power of a court to punish for contempt or to employ any sanction authorized by law for the enforcement of an order, judgement, or decree.

§ 5–4–401—Sentence

(a) A defendant convicted of a felony shall receive a determinate sentence according to the following limitations:

    (1) For a Class Y felony, the sentence shall be not less than ten (10) years and not more than forty (40) years, or life;

    (2) For a Class A felony, the sentence shall be not less than six (6) years nor more than thirty (30) years;

    (3) For a Class B felony, the sentence shall be not less than five (5) years nor more than twenty (20) years;

    (4) For a Class C felony, the sentence shall be not less than three (3) years nor more than ten (10) years;

    (5) For a Class D felony, the sentence shall not exceed six (6) years;

    (6) For an unclassified felony, the sentence shall be in accordance with the limitations of the statute defining the felony.

(b) A defendant convicted of a misdemeanor may be sentenced according to the following limitations:

    (1) For a Class A misdemeanor, the sentence shall not exceed one (1) year;

    (2) For a Class B misdemeanor, the sentence shall not exceed ninety (90) days;

    (3) For a Class C misdemeanor, the sentence shall not exceed thirty (30) days;

    (4) For an unclassified misdemeanor, the sentence shall be in accordance with the limitations of the statute defining the misdemeanor.

§ 5–60–101—Abuse of a corpse

(a) A person commits abuse of a corpse if, except as authorized by law, he knowingly:

    (1) Disinters, removes, dissects, or mutilates a corpse; or

    (2) Physically mistreats a corpse in a manner offensive to a person of reasonable sensibilities.

(b) Abuse of a corpse is a Class D felony.

7. THE CASE OF JULIO MARRERO (NEW YORK, 1977)

A. THE FACTS

Julio Marrero of the Bronx, New York, is a disabled Vietnam veteran who previously worked as an undercover agent in a Puerto Rican drug enforcement operation for the Departamento de Hacienda. He now works as a prison guard at the federal prison in Danbury, Connecticut, and is the father of six: Sonya, 11; Hector Louis, 8; Ricardo, 6; Carina 4; and Joe and Vanessa, 3. His children Endira and Carlos will be born in a year and two years, respectively.

During his time as a guard at Danbury, Marrero has received death threats, as many guards have, including one from a recently released inmate. He regularly carries a pistol for protection, having received weapons training when he was in the Military Police. Marrero stores several weapons at the Military Police armory in Manhattan for use at the firing range.

Marrero purchases his pistol from a New York City gun dealer, Eugene DiMayo, who sells it to Marrero knowing that Marrero does not have a special New York gun permit, but believing and advising Marrero that, as a federal prison guard, Marrero does not need one. DiMayo knows several federal prison guards who similarly have bought weapons without a special New York gun permit. DiMayo explains to Marrero that "federal corrections officers" are considered "peace officers," under the New York firearms statute and "licenses are not required if proper identification is presented."

On December 19, 1977, while off duty, Marrero visits a social club at 207 Madison Street in New York City. As he enters the club, he is searched by police officer G. Dugan of the 7th precinct, who finds a loaded .38 caliber

Figure 16. Julio Marrero, circa 1984. (Family photo)

pistol on Marrero's person. Marrero explains that he does not have a permit but does not need one because he is a federal corrections officer. He shows his identification badge. The police call the Danbury prison and confirm that he is a guard there. Marrero is nonetheless arrested, and charges are filed. Ten days later Marrero is indicted for criminal possession of a weapon.

* * *

Would you convict Marrero? If so, what amount of punishment would you impose?

N	0	1	2	3	4	5	6	7	8	9	10	11
☐	☐	☐	☐	☐	☐	☐	☐	☐	☐	☐	☐	☐
no liability	liability but no punishment	1 day	2 wks.	2 mo.	6 mo.	1 yr.	3 yrs.	7 yrs.	15 yrs.	30 yrs.	life imprison-ment	death

B. THEN EXISTING LAW

Consolidated Laws of New York—Penal Law (1977)

§ 265.01—Criminal possession of a weapon in the fourth degree

A person is guilty of criminal possession of a weapon in the fourth degree when:

(1) He possesses any firearm, electronic dart gun, gravity knife, switchblade knife, cane sword, billy, blackjack, bludgeon, metal knuckles, chuka stick, sand bag, sandclub, or slingshot, or

(2) He possesses any dagger, dangerous knife, dirk, razor, stiletto, imitation pistol, or any other dangerous or deadly instrument or weapon with intent to use the same unlawfully against another; or

(3) He knowingly has in his possession a rifle, shotgun or firearm in or upon a building or grounds, used for educational purposes, of any school, college or university, except the forestry lands, wherever located, owned and maintained by the State University of New York college of environmental science and forestry, without the written authorization of such educational institution; or

(4) He possesses a rifle or shotgun and has been convicted of a felony or serious offense; or

(5) He possesses any dangerous or deadly weapon and is not a citizen of the United States; or

(6) He is a person who has certified not suitable to possess a rifle or shotgun, as defined in subsection sixteen of section 265.00, and refuses to yield possession of such rifle or shotgun upon the demand of a police officer. Whenever a person is certified not suitable to possess a rifle or shotgun, a member of the police department to which such certification is made, or of the state police, shall forthwith seize any rifle or shotgun possessed by such person. A rifle or shotgun seized as herein provided shall not be destroyed, but shall be delivered to the headquarters of such police department, or state police, and there retained until the aforesaid certificate has been rescinded by the director or physician in charge, or other disposition of such rifle or shotgun has been ordered or authorized by a court of competent jurisdiction.

Criminal possession of a weapon in the fourth degree is a class A misdemeanor.

§ 265.02—Criminal possession of a weapon in the third degree

A person is guilty of criminal possession of a weapon in the third degree when:

(1) He commits the crime of criminal possession of a weapon in the fourth degree as defined in subdivision one, two, three or five of section 265.01, and has been previously convicted of any crime; or

(2) He possesses any explosive or incendiary bomb, bombshell, firearm silencer, machine-gun or any other firearm or weapon simulating a machine-gun and which is adaptable for such use; or

(3) He knowingly has in his possession a machine-gun or firearm which has been defaced for the purpose of concealment or prevention of the detection of a crime or misrepresenting the identity of such machine-gun or firearm; or

(4) He possesses any loaded firearm. Such possession shall not, except as provided in subdivision one, constitute a violation of this section if such possession takes place in such person's home or place of business.

(5)(i) He possesses twenty or more firearms; or (ii) he possesses a firearm and has been previously convicted of a felony or a class A misdemeanor defined in this chapter within the five years immediately preceding the commission of the offense and such possession did not take place in the person's home or place of business.

Criminal possession of a weapon in the third degree is a class D felony.

§ 265.20—Exemptions

a.   Sections 265.01, 265.02, 265.03, 265.04, 265.05, 265.10, 265.15 and 270.05 shall not apply to:

(1) Possession of any of the weapons, instruments, appliances or substances specified in sections 265.01, 265.02, 265.03, 265.04, 265.05 and 270.05 by the following:

(a) Persons in the military service of the state of New York when duly authorized by regulations issued by the chief of staff to the governor to possess the same, members of the division of state police, and peace officers as defined in subdivision thirty-three of section 1.20 of the criminal procedure law and persons appointed as railroad policemen pursuant to section eighty-eight of the railroad law.

(b) Persons in the military or other service of the United States, in pursuit of official duty or when duly authorized by federal law, regulation or order to possess the same.

(c) Persons employed in fulfilling defense contracts with the government of the United States or agencies thereof when possession of the same is necessary for manufacture, transport, installation and testing under the requirements of such contract.

(d) A person voluntarily surrendering such weapon, instrument, appliance or substance, provided that such surrender shall be made to the sheriff of the county in which such person resides and in the county of Nassau to the commissioner of police or a member of the police department thereof designated by him, or if such person resides in a city having a population of seventy-five thousand or more to the police commissioner or head of the police force or department, or to a member of the force or department designated by such commissioner or head; and provided, further, that the same shall be surrendered by such person only after he gives notice in writing to the appropriate authority, stating his name, address, the nature of the weapon to be surrendered, and the approximate time of day and the place where such surrender shall take place. Such notice shall be acknowledged immediately upon receipt thereof by such authority. Nothing in this paragraph shall be construed as granting immunity from prosecution for any crime or offense except that of unlawful possession of such weapons, instruments, appliances or substances surrendered as herein provided. A person who possesses any such weapon, instrument, appliance or substance as an executor or administrator or any other lawful possessor of such property of a decedent may continue to possess such property for a period not over fifteen days. If such property is not lawfully disposed of within such period the possessor shall deliver it to an appropriate official described in this paragraph or such property may be delivered to the superintendent of state police. Such officer shall hold it and shall thereafter deliver it on the written request of such executor, administrator or other lawful possessor of such property to a named person, provided such named person is licensed to or is otherwise lawfully permitted to possess the same. If no request to deliver the property is received within two years of the delivery of such property to such official he shall dispose of it in accordance with the provisions of section 400.05 of the penal law.

(2) Possession of a machine-gun, firearm, switchblade knife, gravity knife, billy or blackjack by a warden, superintendent, headkeeper or deputy of a state prison, penitentiary, workhouse, county jail or other institution for the detention of persons convicted or accused of crime or detained as witnesses in criminal cases, in pursuit of official duty or when duly authorized by regulation or order to possess the same.

(3) Possession of a pistol or revolver by a person to whom a license therefore has been issued as provided under section 400.00; provided, that such a license shall not preclude a conviction for the offense defined in subdivision three of section 265.01.

(4) Possession of a rifle, shotgun or longbow for use while hunting, trapping or fishing, by a person, not a citizen of the United States, carrying a valid license issued pursuant to section 11–0713 of the environmental conservation law.

(5) Possession of a rifle or shotgun by a person who has been convicted as specified in subdivision four of section 265.01 to whom a certificate of good conduct has been issued pursuant to section two hundred forty-two, subdivision three of the executive law.

(6) Possession of a switchblade or gravity knife for use while hunting, trapping or fishing by a person carrying a valid license issued to him pursuant to section 11–0713 of the environmental conservation law.

(7) Possession, at an indoor or outdoor rifle range for the purpose of loading and firing the same, of a rifle of not more than twenty-two caliber rim fire, the propelling force of which may be either gunpowder, air or springs, by a person under sixteen years of age but not under twelve, who is a duly enrolled member of any club, team or society organized for educational purposes and maintaining as a part of its facilities, or having written permission to use, such rifle range under the supervision, guidance and instruction of (a) a duly commissioned officer of the United States army, navy, marine corps or coast guard, or of the national guard of the state of New York; or (b) a duly qualified adult citizen of the United States who has been granted a certificate as an instructor in small arms practice issued by the United States army, navy or marine corps, or by the adjutant general of this state, or by the National Rifle Association of America, a not-for-profit corporation duly organized under the laws of this state.

(8) The manufacturer of machine-guns, pilum ballistic knives, switchblade or gravity knives, billies or blackjacks as merchandise and the disposal and shipment thereof direct to a regularly constituted or appointed state or municipal police department, sheriff, policeman or other peace officer, or to a state prison, penitentiary, workhouse, county jail or other institution for the detention of persons convicted or accused of crime or held as witnesses in criminal cases, or to the military service of this state or of the United States.

(9)

(a) The regular and ordinary transport of firearms as merchandise, provided that the person transporting such firearms, where he knows or has reasonable means of ascertaining what he is transporting, notifies in writing the police commissioner, police chief or other law enforcement officer performing such functions at the place of delivery, of the name and address of the consignee and the place of delivery, and withholds delivery to the consignee for such reasonable period of time designated in writing by such police commissioner, police chief or other law enforcement officer as such official may deem necessary for investigation as to whether the consignee may lawfully receive and possess such firearms.

(b) The transportation of such pistols or revolvers into, out of or within the city of New York may be done only with the consent of the police commissioner of the city of New York. To obtain such consent, the manufacturer must notify the police commissioner in writing of the name and address of the transporting manufacturer, or agent or employee of the manufacturer who is authorized in writing by such manufacturer to transport pistols or revolvers, the number, make and model number of the firearms to be transported and the place where the manufacturer regularly conducts business within the city of New York and such other information as the commissioner may deem necessary. The manufacturer must not transport such pistols and revolvers between the designated places of business for such reasonable period of time designated in writing by the police commissioner as such official may deem necessary for investigation and to give consent. The police commissioner may not unreasonably withhold his consent.

(10) Engaging in the business of gunsmith or dealer in firearms by a person to whom a valid license therefor has been issued pursuant to section 400.00.

(11) Possession of a pistol or revolver by a police officer or sworn peace officer of another state while conducting official business within the state of New York.

(b) At any time, any person who voluntarily delivers to a peace officer any weapon, instrument, appliance or substance specified in section 265.01, 265.02, 265.03, 265.04, or 265.05, under circumstances not suspicious, peculiar or involving the commission of any crime, shall not be arrested. Instead, the officer who might make the arrest shall issue or cause to be issued in a proper case a summons or other legal process to the person for investigation of the source of the weapon, instrument, appliance or substance.

(c) Section 265.01 shall not apply to possession of that type of billy commonly known as a "police baton" which is twenty-four to twenty-six inches in length and no more than one and one-quarter inches in thickness by members of an auxiliary police force of a city with a population in excess of one million persons when duly authorized by regulation or order issued by the police commissioner of such city. Such regulations shall require training in the use of the baton and instruction in the legal use of deadly physical force pursuant to article thirty-five of this chapter. Notwithstanding the provisions of this section or any other provision of law, possession of such baton shall not be authorized when used intentionally to strike another person except in those situations when the use of deadly physical force is authorized by such article thirty-five.

§ 5.00—Penal law not strictly construed

The general rule that a penal statute is to be strictly construed does not apply to this chapter, but the provisions herein must be construed according to the fair import of their terms to promote justice and effect the objects of the law.

§ 15.00—Culpability; definitions of terms

The following definitions are applicable to this chapter:

(1) "Act" means a bodily movement.

(2) "Voluntary act" means a bodily movement performed consciously as a result of effort or determination, and includes the possession of property if the actor was aware of his physical possession or control thereof for a sufficient period to have been able to terminate it.

(3) "Omission" means a failure to perform an act as to which a duty of performance is imposed by law.

(4) "Conduct" means an act or omission and its accompanying mental state.

(5) "To act" means either to perform an act or to omit to perform an act.

(6) "Culpable mental state" means "intentionally"or "knowingly" or "recklessly" or with "criminal negligence," as these terms are defined in section 15.05.

§ 15.05—Culpability; definitions of culpable mental states

The following definitions are applicable to this chapter:

(1) "Intentionally." A person acts intentionally with respect to a result or to conduct described by a statute defining an offense when his conscious objective is to cause such result or to engage in such conduct.

(2) "Knowingly." A person acts knowingly with respect to conduct or to a circumstance described by a statute defining an offense when he is aware that his conduct is of such nature or that such circumstance exists.

(3) "Recklessly." A person acts recklessly with respect to a result or to a circumstance described by a statute defining an offense when he is aware of and consciously disregards a substantial and unjustifiable risk that such result will occur or that such circumstance exists. The risk must be of such nature and degree that disregard thereof constitutes a gross deviation from the standard of conduct that a reasonable person would observe in the situation. A person who creates such a risk but is unaware thereof solely by reason of voluntary intoxication also acts recklessly with respect thereto.

(4) "Criminal negligence." A person acts with criminal negligence with respect to a result or to a circumstance described by a statute defining an offense when he fails to perceive a substantial and unjustifiable risk that such result will occur or that such circumstance exists. The risk must be of such nature and degree that the failure to perceive it constitutes a gross deviation from the standard of care that a reasonable person would observe in the situation.

§ 15.10—Requirements for criminal liability in general and for offenses of strict liability and mental culpability

The minimal requirement for criminal liability is the performance by a person of conduct which includes a voluntary act or the omission to perform an act which he is physically capable of performing. If such conduct is all that is required for commission of a particular offense, or if an offense or some material element thereof does not require a culpable mental state on the part of the actor, such offense is one of "strict liability." If a culpable mental state on the part of the actor is required with respect to every material element of an offense, such offense is one of "mental culpability."

§ 15.15—Construction of statutes with respect to culpability requirements

(1) When the commission of an offense defined in this chapter, or some element of an offense, requires a particular culpable mental state, such mental state is ordinarily designated in the statute defining the offense by use of the terms "intentionally," "knowingly," "recklessly" or "criminal negligence," or by use of terms, such as "with intent to defraud" and "knowing it to be false," describing a specific kind of intent or knowledge. When one and only one of such terms appears in a statute defining an offense, it is presumed to apply to every element of the offense unless an intent to limit its application clearly appears.

(2) Although no culpable mental state is expressly designated in a statute defining an offense, a culpable mental state may nevertheless be required for the commission of such offense, or with respect to some or all of the material elements thereof, if the proscribed conduct necessarily involves such culpable mental state. A statute defining a crime, unless clearly indicating a legislative intent to impose strict liability, should be construed as defining a crime of mental culpability. This subdivision applies to offenses defined both in and outside this chapter.

§ 15.20—Effect of ignorance or mistake upon liability

(1) A person is not relieved of criminal liability for conduct because he engages in such conduct under a mistaken belief of fact, unless:

(a) Such factual mistake negatives the culpable mental state required for the commission of an offense; or

(b) The statute defining the offense or a statute related thereto expressly provides that such factual mistake constitutes a defense or exemption; or

(c) Such factual mistake is of a kind that supports a defense of justification as defined in article thirty-five of this chapter.

(2) A person is not relieved of criminal liability for conduct because he engages in such conduct under a mistaken belief that it does not, as a matter of law, constitute an offense, unless such mistaken belief is founded upon an official statement of the law contained in:

(a) a statute or other enactment; or

(b) an administrative order or grant of permission; or

(c) a judicial decision of a state or federal court; or

(d) an interpretation of the statute or law relating to the offense, officially made or issued by a public servant, agency or body legally charged or empowered with the responsibility or privilege of administering, enforcing or interpreting such statute or law.

(3) Notwithstanding the use of the term "knowingly" in any provision of this chapter defining an offense in which the age of a child is an element thereof, knowledge by the defendant of the age of such child is not an element of any such offense and it is not, unless expressly so provided, a defense to a prosecution therefor that the defendant did not know the age of the child or believed such age to be the same as or greater than that specified in the statute.

Consolidated Laws of New York Annotated—Criminal Procedure Law (1977)

§ 1.20—Definitions of terms of general use in this chapter

Except where different meanings are expressly specified in subsequent provisions of this chapter, the term definitions contained in section 10.00 of the penal law are applicable to this chapter, and, in addition, the following terms have the following meanings:

(1) "Accusatory instrument" means an indictment, an information, a simplified information, a prosecutor's information, a superior court information, a misdemeanor complaint or a felony complaint. Every accusatory instrument, regardless of the person designated therein as accuser, constitutes an accusation on behalf of the state as plaintiff and must be entitled "the people of the state of New York" against a designated person, known as the defendant.

(2) "Local criminal court accusatory instrument" means any accusatory instrument other than an indictment or a superior court information.

(3) "Indictment" means a written accusation by a grand jury, more fully defined and described in article two hundred, filed with a superior court, which charges one or more defendants with the commission of one or more offenses, at least one of which is a crime, and which serves as a basis for prosecution thereof.

(3)-a. "Superior court information" means a written accusation by a district attorney more fully defined and described in articles one hundred ninety-five and two hundred, filed with a superior court pursuant to article one hundred ninety-five, which charges one or more defendants with the commission of one or more offenses, at least one of which is a crime, and which serves as a basis for prosecution thereof.

(4) "Information" means a verified written accusation by a person, more fully defined and described in article one hundred, filed with a local criminal court, which charges one or more defendants with the commission of one or more offenses, none of which is a felony, and which may serve both to commence a criminal action and as a basis for prosecution thereof.

(5) [See, also, subd. 5 below.] "Simplified traffic information" means a written accusation, more fully defined and described in article one hundred, by a police officer or other public servant authorized by law to issue same, filed with a local criminal court, which, being in a brief or simplified form prescribed by the commissioner of motor vehicles, charges a person with one or more traffic infractions or misdemeanors relating to traffic, and which may serve both to commence a criminal action for such offense and as a basis for prosecution thereof.

(5) [See, also, subd. 5 above.]

(a) "Simplified information" means a simplified traffic information, a simplified parks information, or a simplified environmental conservation information.

(b) "Simplified traffic information" means a written accusation by a police officer, or other public servant authorized by law to issue same, more fully defined and described in article one hundred, filed with a local criminal court, which, being in a brief or simplified form prescribed by the commissioner of motor vehicles, charges a person with one or more traffic infractions or misdemeanors relating to traffic, and which may serve both to commence a criminal action for such offense and as a basis for prosecution thereof.

(c) "Simplified parks information" means a written accusation by a police officer, or other public servant authorized by law to issue same, filed with a local criminal court, which, being in a brief or simplified form prescribed by the commissioner of parks and recreation, charges a person with one or more offenses, other than a felony, for which a uniform simplified parks information may be issued pursuant to the parks and recreation law and the navigation law, and which may serve both to commence a criminal action for such offense and as a basis for prosecution thereof.

(d) "Simplified environmental conservation information" means a written accusation by a police officer, or other public servant authorized by law to issue same, filed with a local criminal court, which being in a brief or simplified form prescribed by the commissioner of environmental conservation, charges a person with one or more offenses, other than a felony, for which a uniform simplified environmental conservation simplified information may be issued pursuant to the environmental conservation law, and which may serve both to commence a criminal action for such offense and as a basis for prosecution thereof.

(6) "Prosecutor's information" means a written accusation by a district attorney, more fully defined and described in article one hundred, filed with a local criminal court, which charges one or more defendants with the commission of one or more offenses, none of which is a felony, and which serves as a basis for prosecution thereof.

(7) "Misdemeanor complaint" means a verified written accusation by a person, more fully defined and described in article one hundred, filed with a local criminal court, which charges one or more defendants with the commission of one or more offenses, at least one of which is a misdemeanor and none of which is a felony, and which serves to commence a criminal action but which may not, except upon the defendant's consent, serve as a basis for prosecution of the offenses charged therein.

(8) "Felony complaint" means a verified written accusation by a person, more fully defined and described in article one hundred, filed with a local criminal court, which charges one or more defendants with the commission of one or more felonies and which serves to commence a criminal action but not as a basis for prosecution thereof.

(9) "Arraignment" means the occasion upon which a defendant against whom an accusatory instrument has been filed appears before the court in which the criminal action is pending for the purpose of having such court acquire and exercise control over his person with respect to such accusatory instrument and of setting the course of further proceedings in the action.

(10) "Plea," in addition to its ordinary meaning as prescribed in sections 220.10 and 340.20, means, where appropriate, the occasion upon which a defendant enters such a plea to an accusatory instrument.

(11) "Trial." A jury trial commences with the selection of the jury and includes all further proceedings through the rendition of a verdict. A non-jury trial commences with the first opening address, if there be any, and, if not, when the first witness is sworn, and includes all further proceedings through the rendition of a verdict.

(12) "Verdict" means the announcement by a jury in the case of a jury trial, or by the court in the case of a non-jury trial, of its decision upon the defendant's guilt or innocence of the charges submitted to or considered by it.

(13) "Conviction" means the entry of a plea of guilty to, or a verdict of guilty upon, an accusatory instrument other than a felony complaint, or to one or more counts of such instrument.

(14) "Sentence" means the imposition and entry of sentence upon a conviction.

(15) "Judgment." A judgment is comprised of a conviction and the sentence imposed thereon and is completed by imposition and entry of the sentence.

(16) "Criminal action." A criminal action (a) commences with the filing of an accusatory instrument against a defendant in a criminal court, as specified in subdivision seventeen; (b) includes the filing of all further accusatory instruments directly derived from the initial one, and all proceedings, orders and motions conducted or made by a criminal court in the course of disposing of any such accusatory instrument, or which, regardless of the court in which they occurred or were made, could properly be considered as a part of the record of the case by an appellate court upon an appeal from a judgment of conviction; and (c) terminates with the imposition of sentence or some other final disposition in a criminal court of the last accusatory instrument filed in the case.

(17) "Commencement of criminal action." A criminal action is commenced by the filing of an accusatory instrument against a defendant in a criminal court, and, if more than one accusatory instrument is filed in the course of the action, it commences when the first of such instruments is filed.

(18) "Criminal proceeding" means any proceeding which (a) constitutes a part of a criminal action or (b) occurs in a criminal court and is related to a prospective, pending or completed criminal action, either of this state or of any other jurisdiction, or involves a criminal investigation.

(19) "Criminal court" means any court defined as such by section 10.10.

(20) "Superior court" means any court defined as such by subdivision two of section 10.10.

(21) "Local criminal court" means any court defined as such by subdivision three of section 10.10.

(22) "Intermediate appellate court" means any court possessing appellate jurisdiction, other than the court of appeals.

(23) "Judge" means any judicial officer who is a member of or constitutes a court, whether referred to in another provision of law as a justice or by any other title.

(24) "Trial jurisdiction." A criminal court has "trial jurisdiction" of an offense when an indictment or an information charging such offense may properly be filed with such court, and when such court has authority to accept a plea to, try or otherwise finally dispose of such accusatory instrument.

(25) "Preliminary jurisdiction." A criminal court has "preliminary jurisdiction" of an offense when, regardless of whether it has trial jurisdiction thereof, a criminal action for such offense may be commenced therein, and when such court may conduct proceedings with respect thereto which lead or may lead to prosecution and final disposition of the action in a court having trial jurisdiction thereof.

(26) "Appearance ticket" means a written notice issued by a public servant, more fully defined in section 150.10, requiring a person to appear before a local criminal court in connection with an accusatory instrument to be filed against him therein.

(27) "Summons" means a process of a local criminal court, more fully defined in section 130.10, requiring a defendant to appear before such court for the purpose of arraignment upon an accusatory instrument filed therewith by which a criminal action against him has been commenced.

(28) "Warrant of arrest" means a process of a local criminal court, more fully defined in section 120.10, directing a police officer to arrest a defendant and to bring him before such court for the purpose of arraignment upon an accusatory instrument filed therewith by which a criminal action against him has been commenced.

(29) "Superior court warrant of arrest" means a process of a superior court directing a police officer to arrest a defendant and to bring him before such court for the purpose of arraignment upon an indictment filed therewith by which a criminal action against him has been commenced.

(30) "Bench warrant" means a process of a criminal court in which a criminal action is pending, directing a police officer, or a uniformed court officer, pursuant to paragraph b of subdivision two of section 530.70 of this chapter, to take into custody a defendant in such action who has previously been arraigned upon the accusatory instrument by which the action was commenced, and to bring him before such court. The function of a bench warrant is to achieve the court appearance of a defendant in a pending criminal action for some purpose other than his initial arraignment in the action.

(31) "Prosecutor" means a district attorney or any other public servant who represents the people in a criminal action.

(32) "District attorney" means a district attorney, an assistant district attorney or a special district attorney, and, where appropriate, the attorney general, an assistant attorney general, a deputy attorney general or a special deputy attorney general.

(33) "Peace officer." The following persons are peace officers:

(a) A police officer;

(b) An attendant, uniformed court officer or an official of the supreme court in the first and second departments;

(c) An attendant, uniformed court officer or other official attached to the county courts of Nassau and Suffolk counties;

(d) A marshal, clerk or attendant of a district court;

(e) A clerk, uniformed court officer or other official of the criminal court of the city of New York;

(f) A uniformed court officer or an official of the civil court of the city of New York;

(g) An attendant, clerk or uniformed court officer of the family court;

(h) An attendant, or an official, or guard of any state prison or of any penal correctional institution.

(i) A parole officer in the department of correctional services;

(j) A harbor master appointed by a county, city, town or village;

(k) An investigator of the office of the state commission of investigation;

(l) Onondaga county park rangers;

(m) An officer or agent of a duly incorporated society for the prevention of cruelty to animals and children;

(n) An inspector or investigator of the department of agriculture and markets;

(o) An employee of the department of taxation and finance assigned to enforcement of the tax on cigarettes imposed by article twenty of the tax law by the commissioner of taxation and finance;

(p) An employee of the New York City finance administration assigned to enforcement of the tax on cigarettes imposed by section D46–2.0 of the administrative code of the city of New York by the finance administrator;

(q) A constable or police constable of a city, county, town or village; or a bay constable of the town of Hempstead;

(r) Suffolk county park rangers;

(s) A probation officer;

(t) The sheriff, under-sheriff and deputy sheriffs of New York City;

(u) Long Island railroad police.

(34) "Police officer." The following persons are police officers:

(a) A sworn officer of the division of state police;

(b) Sheriffs, under-sheriffs and deputy sheriffs of counties outside of New York City;

(c) A sworn officer of an authorized county or county parkway police department;

(d) A sworn officer of an authorized police department or force of a city, town, village or police district;

(e) A sworn officer of an authorized police department of an authority or a sworn officer of the state regional park police in the office of parks and recreation;

(f) A sworn officer of the capital police force of the office of general services;

(g) An investigator employed in the office of a district attorney;

(h) An investigator employed by a commission created by an interstate compact who is, to a substantial extent, engaged in the enforcement of the criminal laws of this state;

(i) The chief and deputy fire marshals, the supervising fire marshals and the fire marshals of the bureau of fire investigation of the New York City fire department;

(j) A sworn officer of the division of law enforcement in the department of environmental conservation;

(k) A sworn officer of a police force of a public authority created by an interstate compact; (l) [See, also, par. (l) below] Long Island railroad police.

(l) [See, also, par. (l) above] An employee of the department of taxation and finance assigned to enforcement of the tax on cigarettes imposed by article twenty of the tax law by the commissioner of taxation and finance for the purpose of applying for and executing search warrants under article six hundred ninety of this chapter in connection with the enforcement of such tax on cigarettes.

(34)-a. "Geographical area of employment." The "geographical area of employment" of certain police officers is as follows:

    (a) New York state constitutes the "geographical area of employment" of any police officer employed as such by an agency of the state or by an authority which functions throughout the state;

    (b) A county, city, town or village, as the case may be, constitutes the "geographical area of employment" of any police officer employed as such by an agency of such political subdivision or by an authority which functions only in such political subdivision; and

    (c) Where an authority functions in more than one county, the "geographical area of employment" of a police officer employed thereby extends through all of such counties.

(35) "Commitment to the custody of the sheriff," when referring to an order of a court located in a county or city which has established a department of correction, means commitment to the commissioner of correction of such county or city.

(36) "County" ordinarily means (a) any county outside of New York City or (b) New York City in its entirety. Unless the context requires a different construction, New York City, despite its five counties, is deemed a single county within the meaning of the provisions of this chapter in which that term appears.

(37) "Lesser included offense." When it is impossible to commit a particular crime without concomitantly committing, by the same conduct, another offense of lesser grade or degree, the latter is, with respect to the former, a "lesser included offense." In any case in which it is legally possible to attempt to commit a crime, an attempt to commit such crime constitutes a lesser included offense with respect thereto.

(38) "Oath" includes an affirmation and every other made authorized by law of attesting to the truth of that which is stated.

(39) "Petty offense" means a violation or a traffic infraction.

(40) "Evidence in chief" means evidence, received at a trial or other criminal proceeding in which a defendant's guilt or innocence of an offense is in issue, which may be considered as a part of the quantum of substantive proof establishing or tending to establish the commission of such offense or an element thereof or the defendant's connection therewith.

C.   Current Law That Would Be Applied Were the Case Prosecuted Today

[Statutory changes are not relevant except for those noted below]

Consolidated Laws of New York—Criminal Procedure Law (2006)

§ 1.20—Definitions

Except where different meanings are expressly specified in subsequent provisions of this chapter, the term definitions contained in section 10.00 of the penal law are applicable to this chapter, and, in addition, the following terms have the following meanings:

    *   *   *

33.   "Peace officer" means *a person listed in section 2.10 of this chapter.*

34.   "Police officer." The following persons are police officers: [nine additional categories are added to the definitions of persons who are "police officers"]

. . .

§ 2.10—Persons designated as peace officers

Notwithstanding the provisions of any general, special or local law or charter to the contrary, only the following persons shall have the powers of, and shall be peace officers:

(1) Constables or police constables of a town or village, provided such designation is not inconsistent with local law.

(2) The sheriff, undersheriff and deputy sheriffs of New York city and sworn officers of the Westchester county department of public safety services appointed after January thirty-first, nineteen hundred eighty-three to the title of public safety officer and who perform the functions previously performed by a Westchester county deputy sheriff on or prior to such date.

(3) Investigators of the office of the state commission of investigation.

(4) Employees of the department of taxation and finance designated by the commissioner of taxation and finance as peace officers and assigned by the commissioner of taxation and finance

(a) to the enforcement of any of the criminal or seizure and forfeiture provisions of the tax law relating to (i) taxes imposed under or pursuant to the authority of article twelve-A of the tax law and administered by the commissioner of taxation and finance, (ii) taxes imposed under article twenty of the tax law, or (iii) sales or compensating use taxes relating to automotive fuel or cigarettes imposed under article twenty-eight or pursuant to the authority of article twenty-nine of the tax law and administered by the commissioner of taxation and finance or

(b) to the enforcement of any provision of the penal law relating to any of the taxes described in paragraph (a) of this subdivision and relating to crimes effected through the use of a statement or document filed with the department in connection with the administration of such taxes or

(c) as revenue crimes specialist and assigned to the enforcement of any of the criminal provisions of the tax law relating to taxes administered by the commissioner of taxation and finance other than those taxes set forth in paragraph (a) of this subdivision or any provision of the penal law relating to such taxes ... and those provisions of the penal law (i) relating to any of the foregoing taxes and (ii) relating to crimes effected through the use of a statement or document filed with the department in connection with the administration of such foregoing taxes or

(d) to the enforcement of any provision of law which is subject to enforcement by criminal penalties and which relates to the performance by persons employed by the department of taxation and finance of the duties of their employment.

Provided, however, that nothing in this subdivision shall be deemed to authorize any such employee designated as a peace officer after November first, nineteen hundred eighty-five to carry, possess, repair or dispose of a firearm unless the appropriate license therefor has been issued pursuant to section 400.00 of the penal law, and further provided that, prior to such designation by the commissioner each such employee shall have successfully completed the training requirements specified in section 2.30 of this article. ...

(5) Employees of the New York city department of finance assigned to enforcement of the tax on cigarettes imposed by title D of chapter forty-six of the administrative code of the city of New York by the commissioner of finance.

(6) Confidential investigators and inspectors, as designated by the commissioner, of the department of agriculture and markets, pursuant to rules of the department.

(7) Officers or agents of a duly incorporated society for the prevention of cruelty to animals.

(7)(a) Officers or agents of a duly incorporated society for the prevention of cruelty to children; provided, however, that nothing in this subdivision shall be deemed to authorize such officer or agent to carry, possess, repair, or dispose of a firearm unless the appropriate license therefor has been issued pursuant to section 400.00 of the penal law; and provided further that such officer or agent shall exercise the powers of a peace officer only when he is acting pursuant to his special duties.

(8) Inspectors and officers of the New York city department of health when acting pursuant to their special duties as set forth in section 564–11.0 of the administrative code of the city of New York; provided, however, that nothing in this subdivision shall be deemed to authorize such officer to carry, possess, repair or dispose of a firearm unless the appropriate license therefor has been issued pursuant to section 400.00 of the penal law.

(9) Park rangers in Suffolk county, who shall be authorized to issue appearance tickets, simplified traffic informations, simplified parks informations and simplified environmental conservation informations.

(10) Broome county park rangers who shall be authorized to issue appearance tickets, simplified traffic informations, simplified parks informations, and simplified environmental conservation informations; provided, however, that nothing in this subdivision shall be deemed to authorize such officer to carry, possess, repair or dispose of a firearm unless the appropriate license therefor has been issued pursuant to section 400.00 of the penal law.

(11) Park rangers in Onondaga and Cayuga counties, who shall be authorized to issue appearance tickets, simplified traffic informations, simplified parks informations and simplified environmental conservation informations, within the respective counties of Onondaga and Cayuga.

(12) Special policemen designated by the commissioner and the directors of in-patient facilities in the office of mental health pursuant to section 7.25 of the mental hygiene law, and special policemen designated by the commissioner and the directors of facilities under his jurisdiction in the office of mental retardation and developmental disabilities pursuant to section 13.25 of the mental hygiene law; provided, however, that nothing in this subdivision shall be deemed to authorize such officers to carry, possess, repair or dispose of a firearm unless the appropriate license therefor has been issued pursuant to section 400.00 of the penal law.

(13) Persons designated as special policemen by the director of a hospital in the department of health pursuant to section four hundred fifty-five of the public health law; provided, however, that nothing in this subdivision shall be deemed to authorize such officer to carry, possess, repair or dispose of a firearm unless the appropriate license therefor has been issued pursuant to section 400.00 of the penal law.

(14) [Repealed]

(15) Uniformed enforcement forces of the New York state thruway authority, when acting pursuant to subdivision two of section three hundred sixty-one of the public authorities law; provided, however, that nothing in this subdivision shall be deemed to authorize such officer to carry, possess, repair or dispose of a firearm unless the appropriate license therefor has been issued pursuant to section 400.00 of the penal law.

(16) Employees of the department of health designated pursuant to section thirty-three hundred eighty-five of the public health law; provided, however, that nothing in this subdivision shall be deemed to authorize such officer to carry, possess, repair or dispose of a firearm unless the appropriate license therefor has been issued pursuant to section 400.00 of the penal law.

(17) Uniformed housing guards of the Buffalo municipal housing authority.

(18) Bay constable of the city of Rye, the villages of Mamaroneck, South Nyack and bay constables of the towns of East Hampton, Hempstead, Oyster Bay, Riverhead, Southampton, Southold, Islip, Shelter Island, Brookhaven, Babylon, Smithtown, Huntington and North Hempstead; provided, however, that nothing in this subdivision shall be deemed to authorize the bay constables in the city of Rye, the village of South Nyack or the towns of Brookhaven, Babylon, Southold, East Hampton, Riverhead, Islip, other than a bay constable of the town of Islip who prior to April third, nineteen hundred and ninety eight, served as harbormaster for such town and whose position was reclassified as bay constable for such town prior to such date, Smithtown, Huntington and Shelter Island to carry, possess, repair or dispose of a firearm unless the appropriate license therefor has been issued pursuant to section 400.00 of the penal law.

(19) Harbor masters appointed by a county, city, town or village.

(20) Bridge and tunnel officers, sergeants and lieutenants of the Triborough bridge and tunnel authority.

(21)

    (a) Uniformed court officers of the unified court system.

    (b) Court clerks of the unified court system in the first and second departments.

    (c) Marshall, deputy marshall, clerk or uniformed court officer of a district court.

    (d) Marshalls or deputy marshalls of a city court, provided, however, that nothing in this subdivision shall be deemed to authorize such officer to carry, possess, repair or dispose of a firearm unless the appropriate license therefor has been issued pursuant to section 400.00 of the penal law.

    (e) Uniformed court officers of the city of Mount Vernon.

    (f) Uniformed court officers of the city of Jamestown.

(22) Patrolmen appointed by the Lake George park commission; provided however that nothing in this subdivision shall be deemed to authorize such officer to carry, possess, repair or dispose of a firearm unless the appropriate license therefor has been issued pursuant to section 400.00 of the penal law.

(23) Parole officers or warrant officers in the division of parole.

*　*　*

(24) Probation officers.

(25) Officials, as designated by the commissioner of the department of correctional services pursuant to rules of the department, and correction officers of any state correctional facility or of any penal correctional institution.

(26) Peace officers designated pursuant to the provisions of the New York state defense emergency act, as set forth in chapter seven hundred eighty-four of the laws of nineteen hundred fifty-one, as amended, when acting pursuant to their special duties during a period of attack or imminent attack by enemy forces, or during official drills called to combat natural or man-made disasters, or during official drills in preparation for an attack by enemy forces or in preparation for a natural or man-made disaster; provided, however, that nothing in this subdivision shall be deemed to authorize such officer to carry, possess, repair or dispose of a firearm unless the appropriate license therefor has been issued pursuant to section 400.00 of the penal law; and provided further, that such officer shall have the powers set forth in section 2.20 of this article only during a period of imminent or actual attack by enemy forces and

during drills authorized under section twenty-nine-b of article two-B of the executive law, providing for the use of civil defense forces in disasters. Notwithstanding any other provision of law, such officers shall have the power to direct and control traffic during official drills in preparation for an attack by enemy forces or in preparation for combating natural or man-made disasters; however, this grant does not include any of the other powers set forth in section 2.20 of this article.

(27) New York city special patrolmen appointed by the police commissioner pursuant to subdivision c or e of section 434a–7.0 or subdivision c or e of section 14–106 of the administrative code of the city of New York; provided, however, that nothing in this subdivision shall be deemed to authorize such officer to carry, possess, repair or dispose of a firearm unless the appropriate license therefor has been issued pursuant to section 400.00 of the penal law and the employer has authorized such officer to possess a firearm during any phase of the officers on-duty employment. Special patrolmen shall have the powers set forth in section 2.20 of this article only when they are acting pursuant to their special duties; provided, however, that the following categories of New York city special patrolmen shall have such powers whether or not they are acting pursuant to their special duties: school safety officers employed by the board of education of the city of New York; parking control specialists, taxi and limousine inspectors, urban park rangers and evidence and property control specialists employed by the city of New York; and further provided that, with respect to the aforementioned categories of New York city special patrolmen, where such a special patrolman has been appointed by the police commissioner and, upon the expiration of such appointment the police commissioner has neither renewed such appointment nor explicitly determined that such appointment shall not be renewed, such appointment shall remain in full force and effect indefinitely, until such time as the police commissioner expressly determines to either renew or terminate such appointment.

(28) All officers and members of the uniformed force of the New York city fire department as set forth and subject to the limitations contained in section 487a–15.0 of the administrative code of the city of New York; provided, however, that nothing in this subdivision shall be deemed to authorize such officer to carry, possess, repair or dispose of a firearm unless the appropriate license therefor has been issued pursuant to section 400.00 of the penal law.

(29) Special policemen for horse racing, appointed pursuant to the provisions of the pari-mutuel revenue law as set forth in chapter two hundred fifty-four of the laws of nineteen hundred forty, as amended; provided, however, that nothing in this subdivision shall be deemed to authorize such officer to carry, possess, repair or dispose of a firearm unless the appropriate license therefor has been issued pursuant to section 400.00 of the penal law.

(30) Supervising fire inspectors, fire inspectors, the fire marshal and assistant fire marshals, all of whom are full-time employees of the county of Nassau fire marshal's office.

* * *

(32) Investigators of the department of motor vehicles, pursuant to section three hundred ninety-two-b of the vehicle and traffic law; provided, however, that nothing in this subdivision shall be deemed to authorize such officer to carry, possess, repair or dispose of a firearm unless the appropriate license therefor has been issued pursuant to section 400.00 of the penal law.

(33) A city marshall of the city of New York who has received training in firearms handling from the federal bureau of investigation or in the New York city police academy, or in the absence of the available training programs from the federal bureau of investigation and the New York city police academy, from another law enforcement agency located in the state of New York, and who has received a firearms permit from the license division of the New York city police department.

(34) Waterfront and airport investigators, pursuant to subdivision four of section ninety-nine hundred six of the unconsolidated laws; provided, however, that nothing in this subdivision shall be deemed to authorize such officer to carry, possess, repair or dispose of a firearm unless the appropriate license therefor has been issued pursuant to section 400.00 of the penal law.

(35) Special investigators appointed by the state board of elections, pursuant to section 3–107 of the election law.

(36) Investigators appointed by the state liquor authority, pursuant to section fifteen of the alcoholic beverage control law; provided, however, that nothing in this subdivision shall be deemed to authorize such officer to carry, possess, repair or dispose of a firearm unless the appropriate license therefor has been issued pursuant to section 400.00 of the penal law.

(37) Special patrolmen of a political subdivision, appointed pursuant to section two hundred nine-v of the general municipal law; provided, however, that nothing in this subdivision shall be deemed to authorize such officer to carry, possess, repair or dispose of a firearm unless the appropriate license therefor has been issued pursuant to section 400.00 of the penal law.

(38) A special investigator of the New York city department of investigation who has received training in firearms handling in the New York police academy and has received a firearms permit from the license division of the New York city police department.

(39) Broome county special patrolman, appointed by the Broome county attorney; provided, however, that nothing in this subdivision shall be deemed to authorize such officer to carry, possess, repair or dispose of a firearm unless the appropriate license therefor has been issued pursuant to section 400.00 of the penal law.

(40) Special officers employed by the city of New York or by the New York city health and hospitals corporation; provided, however, that nothing in this subdivision shall be deemed to authorize such officer to carry, possess, repair or dispose of a firearm unless the appropriate license therefor has been issued pursuant to section 400.00 of the penal law. ...

(41) Fire police squads organized pursuant to section two hundred nine-c of the general municipal law, at such times as the fire department, fire company or an emergency rescue and first aid squad of the fire department or fire company are on duty, or when, on orders of the chief of the fire department or fire company of which they are members, they are separately engaged in response to a call for assistance pursuant to the provisions of section two hundred nine of the general municipal law; provided, however, that nothing in this subdivision shall be deemed to authorize such officer to carry, possess, repair or dispose of a firearm unless the appropriate license therefor has been issued pursuant to section 400.00 of the penal law.

(42) Special deputy sheriffs appointed by the sheriff of a county within which any part of the grounds of Cornell university or the grounds of any state institution constituting a part of the educational and research plants owned or under the supervision, administration or control of said university are located pursuant to section fifty-seven hundred nine of the education law; provided, however, that nothing in this subdivision shall be deemed to authorize such officer to carry, possess, repair or dispose of a firearm unless the appropriate license therefor has been issued pursuant to section 400.00 of the penal law. ...

(43) Housing patrolmen of the Mount Vernon housing authority, acting pursuant to rules of the Mount Vernon housing authority; provided, however, that nothing in this subdivision shall be deemed to authorize such officer to carry, possess, repair or dispose of a firearm unless the appropriate license therefor has been issued pursuant to section 400.00 of the penal law.

(44) The officers, employees and members of the New York city division of fire prevention, in the bureau of fire, as set forth and subject to the limitations contained in subdivision one of section 487a–1.0 of the administrative code of the city of New York; provided, however, that

nothing in this subdivision shall be deemed to authorize such officer to carry, possess, repair or dispose of a firearm unless the appropriate license therefor has been issued pursuant to section 400.00 of the penal law.

(45) Persons appointed and designated as peace officers by the Niagara frontier transportation authority, pursuant to subdivision thirteen of section twelve hundred ninety-nine-e of the public authorities law.

(46) Persons appointed as peace officers by the Sea Gate Association pursuant to the provisions of chapter three hundred ninety-one of the laws of nineteen hundred forty, provided, however, that nothing in this subdivision shall be deemed to authorize such officer to carry, possess, repair or dispose of a firearm unless the appropriate license therefor has been issued pursuant to section 400.00 of the penal law.

(47) Employees of the insurance frauds bureau of the state department of insurance when designated as peace officers by the superintendent of insurance and acting pursuant to their special duties; provided, however, that nothing in this subdivision shall be deemed to authorize such officer to carry, possess, repair or dispose of a firearm unless the appropriate license therefor has been issued pursuant to section 400.00 of the penal law.

(48) New York state air base security guards when they are designated as peace officers under military regulations promulgated by the chief of staff to the governor and when performing their duties as air base security guards pursuant to orders issued by appropriate military authority; provided, however, that nothing in this subdivision shall be deemed to authorize such guards to carry, possess, repair or dispose of a firearm unless the appropriate license therefor has been issued pursuant to section 400.00 of the penal law.

(49) Members of the army national guard military police and air national guard security personnel belonging to the organized militia of the state of New York when they are designated as peace officers under military regulations promulgated by the adjutant general and when performing their duties as military policemen or air security personnel pursuant to orders issued by appropriate military authority; provided, however, that nothing in this subdivision shall be deemed to authorize such military police or air security personnel to carry, possess, repair or dispose of a firearm unless the appropriate license therefor has been issued pursuant to section 400.00 of the penal law.

(50) Transportation supervisors in the city of White Plains appointed by the commissioner of public safety in the city of White Plains; provided, however, that nothing in this subdivision shall be deemed to authorize such officer to carry, possess, repair or dispose of a firearm unless the appropriate license therefor has been issued pursuant to section 400.00 of the penal law.

(51) Officers and members of the fire investigation division of the fire department of the city of Rochester, the city of Binghamton and the city of Utica, when acting pursuant to their special duties in matters arising under the laws relating to fires, the extinguishment thereof and fire perils; provided, however, that nothing in this subdivision shall be deemed to authorize such officer to carry, possess, repair or dispose of a firearm unless the appropriate license therefor has been issued pursuant to section 400.00 of the penal law.

(52) Security hospital treatment assistants, as so designated by the commissioner of the office of mental health while transporting persons convicted of a crime to court, to other facilities within the jurisdiction of the office of mental health, or to any state or local correctional facility; provided, however, that nothing in this subdivision shall be deemed to authorize such employee to carry, possess, repair or dispose of a firearm unless the appropriate license therefor has been issued pursuant to section 400.00 of the penal law.

(53) Authorized agents of the municipal directors of weights and measures in the counties of Suffolk, Nassau and Westchester when acting pursuant to their special duties as set

forth in section one hundred eighty-one of the agriculture and markets law; provided, however, that nothing in this subdivision shall be deemed to authorize such officer to carry, possess, repair or dispose of a firearm unless the appropriate license therefor has been issued pursuant to section 400.00 of the penal law.

(54) Special policemen appointed pursuant to section one hundred fifty-eight of the town law; provided, however, that nothing in this subdivision shall be deemed to authorize such officer to carry, possess, repair or dispose of a firearm unless the appropriate license therefor has been issued pursuant to section 400.00 of the penal law.

[55. Expired.]

(56) Dog control officers of the town of Brookhaven, who at the discretion of the town board may be designated as constables for the purpose of enforcing article twenty-six of the agriculture and markets law and for the purpose of issuing appearance tickets permitted under article seven of such law; provided, however, that nothing in this subdivision shall be deemed to authorize such officer to carry, possess, repair or dispose of a firearm unless the appropriate license therefor has been issued pursuant to section 400.00 of the penal law.

(57) Harbor Park rangers employed by the Snug Harbor cultural center in Richmond county and appointed as New York city special patrolmen by the police commissioner pursuant to subdivision c of section 14–106 of the administrative code of the city of New York. Notwithstanding any provision of law, rule or regulation, such officers shall be authorized to issue appearance tickets pursuant to section 150.20 of this chapter, and shall have such other powers as are specified in section 2.20 of this article only when acting pursuant to their special duties. Nothing in this subdivision shall be deemed to authorize such officers to carry, possess, repair or dispose of a firearm unless the appropriate license therefor has been issued pursuant to section 400.00 of the penal law and the employer has authorized such officer to possess a firearm during any phase of the officer's on-duty employment.

(57)(a) Seasonal park rangers of the Westchester county department of public safety while employed as authorized by the commissioner of public safety/sheriff of the county of Westchester; provided, however, that nothing in this subdivision shall be deemed to authorize such officer to carry, possess, repair or dispose of a firearm unless the appropriate license therefor has been issued pursuant to section 400.00 of the penal law.

(57)(b) Officers of the Westchester county public safety emergency force, when activated by the commissioner of public safety/sheriff of the county of Westchester; provided, however that nothing in this subdivision shall be deemed to authorize such officer to carry, possess, repair or dispose of a firearm unless the appropriate license therefor has been issued pursuant to section 400.00 of the penal law.

(58) Uniformed members of the security force of the Troy housing authority provided, however, that nothing in this subdivision shall be deemed to authorize such officer to carry, possess, repair or dispose of a firearm unless the appropriate license therefor has been issued pursuant to section 400.00 of the penal law.

(59) Officers and members of the sanitation police of the department of sanitation of the city of New York, duly appointed and designated as peace officers by such department; provided, however, that nothing in this subdivision shall be deemed to authorize such officer to carry, possess, repair or dispose of a firearm unless the appropriate license therefor has been issued pursuant to section 400.00 of the penal law. Provided, further, that nothing in this subdivision shall be deemed to apply to officers and members of the sanitation police regularly and exclusively assigned to enforcement of such city's residential recycling laws.

[60. Repealed.]

(61) Chief fire marshall, assistant chief fire marshall, fire marshall II and fire marshall I, all of whom are full-time employees of the Suffolk county department of fire, rescue and emergency services, when acting pursuant to their special duties in matters arising under the laws relating to fires, the extinguishment thereof and fire perils; provided, however, that nothing in this subdivision shall be deemed to authorize such officer to carry, possess, repair or dispose of a firearm unless the appropriate license therefor has been issued pursuant to section 400.00 of the penal law.

(61) Investigators employed by the criminal investigations bureau when assigned to such bureau by the superintendent of banks and acting pursuant to their special duties as set forth in article two-B of the banking law; provided, however, that nothing in this subdivision shall be deemed to authorize such officer to carry, possess, repair or dispose of a firearm unless the appropriate license therefor has been issued pursuant to section 400.00 of the penal law.

(62) Chief fire marshall, assistant chief fire marshall, fire marshall II and fire marshall I, all of whom are full-time employees of the town of Babylon, when acting pursuant to their special duties in matters arising under the laws relating to fires, the extinguishment thereof and fire perils; provided, however, that nothing in this subdivision shall be deemed to authorize such officer to carry, possess, repair or dispose of a firearm unless the appropriate license therefor has been issued pursuant to section 400.00 of the penal law.

(62) Employees of the division for youth assigned to transport and warrants units who are specifically designated by the director in accordance with section five hundred four-b of the executive law, provided, however, that nothing in this subdivision shall be deemed to authorize such employees to carry, possess, repair or dispose of a firearm unless the appropriate license therefor has been issued pursuant to section 400.00 of the penal law.

(63) Uniformed members of the fire marshal's office in the town of Southhampton, when acting pursuant to their special duties in matters arising under the laws relating to fires, the extinguishment thereof and fire perils; provided, however that nothing in this subdivision shall be deemed to authorize such officer to carry, possess, repair or dispose of a firearm unless the appropriate license therefor has been issued pursuant to section 400.00 of the penal law.

(63) Employees of the town court of the town of Greenburgh serving as a security officer; provided, however, that nothing in this subdivision will be deemed to authorize such officer to carry, possess, repair or dispose of a firearm unless the appropriate license therefor has been issued pursuant to section 400.00 of the penal law or to authorize such officer to carry or possess a firearm except while on duty.

(64) Cell block attendants employed by the city of Buffalo police department; provided, however, that nothing in this subdivision shall be deemed to authorize such officer to carry, possess, repair or dispose of a firearm unless the appropriate license therefor has been issued pursuant to section 400.00 of the penal law.

(65) Chief fire marshall, assistant chief fire marshall, fire marshall II and fire marshall I, all of whom are full-time employees of the town of Brookhaven, when acting pursuant to their special duties in matters arising under the laws relating to fires, the extinguishment thereof and fire perils; provided, however, that nothing in this subdivision shall be deemed to authorize such officer to carry, possess, repair or dispose of a firearm unless the appropriate license thereof has been issued pursuant to section 400.00 of the penal law.

(66) Employees of the village court of the village of Spring Valley serving as security officers at such village court; provided, however, that nothing in this subdivision shall be deemed to authorize such officer to carry, possess, repair or dispose of a firearm unless the appropriate license therefor has been issued pursuant to section 400.00 of the penal law.

(67) Employees of the town court of the town of Putnam Valley serving as a security officer; provided, however, that nothing in this subdivision will be deemed to authorize such

officer to carry, possess, repair or dispose of a firearm unless the appropriate license therefor has been issued pursuant to section 400.00 of the penal law or to authorize such officer to carry or possess a firearm except while on duty.

(68) Employees of the town court of the town of Southampton serving as uniformed court officers at such town court; provided, however, that nothing in this subdivision shall be deemed to authorize such officer to carry, possess, repair or dispose of a firearm unless the appropriate license therefor has been issued pursuant to section 400.00 of the penal law.

* * *

8.   THE CASE OF RAY EDWIN BILLINGSLEA (TEXAS, 1984)

A.   THE FACTS

It is 1984. Ray Edwin Billingslea lives in a small, two-story Dallas house owned by his mother, 94–year–old Hazel Billingslea, which saves him the cost of rent, utilities, and living expenses. 50 year-old Ray, with his common-law wife and his sons, has lived with his mother for the past 20 years. He has held menial jobs on and off, but does not currently work.

Figure 17. Ray Billingslea. (Dallas County Sheriff's Department)

Hazel Billingslea's granddaughter, Virginia, who is the daughter of Ray's sister, Katherine Jefferson, also lived at Hazel's house but moved out soon after she graduated from high school. Tired of being sexually harassed by Ray, she gets a judge to grant a peace bond, or injunction, against Ray to make him leave her alone. But Virginia stays close to her grandmother for the next several years, living 15 blocks away in the same Dallas neighborhood. She sees Hazel frequently, goes shopping for her, and brings her candy during her regular Saturday visits. Still, Ray runs the house his mother owns and does not get along with Virginia.

In March 1984, Hazel's health takes a downturn, and she becomes confined to her bed. For reasons unknown, Hazel's arm and jaw are broken, but Ray does not take the elderly woman to the hospital.

In recent weeks, Virginia has not seen her grandmother. She is frequently turned away at the door by Ray, who tells her that his mother is "asleep" and cannot be disturbed. Virginia persists and tries to reach her by telephone, but is twice threatened by Ray to "Keep your goddamned mother-fucking ass out of my and my mother's business or I will kill you."

Frustrated, Virginia finally calls her mother, Katherine, who moved to Albuquerque years earlier. After talking to her daughter, Katherine calls the Dallas Social Service Department with her suspicions that Ray is mistreating their mother. The Social Service office reports the complaint to Velma Mosley of the Adult Protective Services Section of the Department of Human Resources. Mosley, two police officers, and a police social services worker go to investigate the complaint, but when they arrive, Ray refuses to let them inside, telling them that it is too late at night.

The next day, April 24, 1984, they return to the Billingslea home, but Ray meets them in the front yard and objects to their entry into the house. After a long discussion, he acquiesces. Once inside, the group is overwhelmed by the strong, rancid odor of rotting flesh. Ray begins to berate the officers, demanding to know what "you mother-fuckers are doing in my house." The police officers and the social worker find their way upstairs to Hazel's bedroom. The elderly woman is lying in bed. "Oh, please help me," she exclaims when she sees Mosley. Mosley pulls back the sheets to examine her and finds Hazel naked from the waste down and in great pain. The smell of

Figure 18. Hazel Billingslea's house in Dallas. (Joel Sauer)

feces and rotting flesh is overpowering. She has bed sores on her buttocks and thighs, which are filled with maggots. One of the officers vomits from the sight and the smell. Paramedics are called.

The paramedics and social worker attempt to dress her, but she is in too much pain to be moved. The social worker vomits. The paramedics place a plastic bag over her—usually used as a body bag—to cover her and to contain the odor and maggots. She screams in pain as the paramedics move her to the stretcher. One of the paramedics vomits. Eventually, they get the elderly woman into an ambulance and take her to the hospital.

A doctor examining Hazel discovers that she has lost most of her muscle to deterioration and confirms that maggots are eating away at her flesh. The doctors x-ray her and discover broken bones. Hazel is disoriented and unable to feed herself. Her inner thighs are covered with second-degree burns and blisters from lying in pools of urine. The doctor believes her bedsores have taken four to six weeks to develop.

Earlier attention would have prevented the injuries to her and, even after the deterioration, earlier medical treatment could have reversed them. But it is determined that, in her present condition, nothing can be done for Hazel other than to administer large doses of antibiotics and pain killers.

When told that his mother requires medical care, Ray Billingslea responds, "Who will pay the utility here [at the house]?"

On May 5, 1984, eleven days after she is found by authorities, Hazel Billingslea dies. Ray continues to live in his mother's house after her death.

* * *

What liability and punishment, if any, would you impose on Ray for failing to care for his mother?

N	0	1	2	3	4	5	6	7	8	9	10	11
☐	☐	☐	☐	☐	☐	☐	☐	☐	☐	☐	☐	☐
no liability	liability but no punishment	1 day	2 wks.	2 mo.	6 mo.	1 yr.	3 yrs.	7 yrs.	15 yrs.	30 yrs.	life imprison- ment	death

B. THEN EXISTING LAW

Texas Penal Code (1984)

§ 1.07—Definitions

(a) In this code:

(1) "Act" means a bodily movement, whether voluntary or involuntary, and includes speech.

* * *

(7) "Bodily injury" means physical pain, illness, or any impairment of physical condition.

* * *

(8) "Conduct" means an act or omission and its accompanying mental state.

* * *

(23) "Omission" means failure to act.

* * *

(34) "Serious bodily injury" means bodily injury that creates a substantial risk of death or that causes death, serious permanent disfigurement, or protracted loss or impairment of the function of any bodily member or organ.

* * *

§ 19.01—Types of Criminal Homicide

(a) A person commits criminal homicide if he intentionally, knowingly, recklessly, or with criminal negligence causes the death of an individual.

(b) Criminal homicide is murder, capital murder, voluntary manslaughter, involuntary manslaughter, or criminally negligent homicide.

§ 19.05—Involuntary Manslaughter

(a) A person commits an offense if he:

(1) recklessly causes the death of an individual ...

* * *

(c) An offense under this section is a felony of the third degree.

§ 19.07—Criminally Negligent Homicide

(a) A person commits an offense if he causes the death of an individual by criminal negligence.

(b) An offense under this section is a Class A misdemeanor.

§ 22.04—Injury to a Child or an Elderly Individual

(a) A person commits an offense if he intentionally, knowingly, recklessly, or with criminal negligence, by act or omission, engages in conduct that causes to a child who is 14 years of age or younger or to an individual who is 65 years of age or older:

(1) serious bodily injury;

(2) serious physical or mental deficiency or impairment;

(3) disfigurement or deformity; or

(4) bodily injury.

(b) An offense under Subsection (a)(1), (2), or (3) of this section is a felony of the first degree when the conduct is committed intentionally or knowingly. When the conduct is engaged in recklessly it shall be a felony of the third degree.

(c) An offense under Subsection (a)(4) of this section is a felony of the third degree when the conduct is committed intentionally or knowingly. When the conduct is engaged in recklessly it shall be a Class A misdemeanor.

(d) An offense under Subsection (a) of this section when the person acts with criminal negligence shall be a Class A misdemeanor.

* * *

§ 6.01—Requirement of Voluntary Act or Omission

(a) A person commits an offense only if he voluntarily engages in conduct, including an act, an omission, or possession.

(b) Possession is a voluntary act if the possessor knowingly obtains or receives the thing possessed or is aware of his control of the thing for a sufficient time to permit him to terminate his control.

(c) A person who omits to perform an act does not commit an offense unless a statute provides that the omission is an offense or otherwise provides that he has a duty to perform the act.

§ 6.02—Requirement of Culpability

(a) Except as provided in subsection (b) of this section, a person does not commit an offense unless he intentionally, knowingly, recklessly, or with criminal negligence engages in conduct as the definition of the offense requires.

(b) If the definition of an offense does not prescribe a culpable mental state, a culpable mental state is nevertheless required unless the definition plainly dispenses with any mental element.

(c) If the definition of an offense does not prescribe a culpable mental state, but one is nevertheless required under subsection (b) of this section, intent, knowledge, or recklessness suffices to establish criminal responsibility.

(d) Culpable mental states are classified according to relative degrees, from highest to lowest, as follows:

(1) intentional;

(2) knowing;

(3) reckless;

(4) criminal negligence.

(e) Proof of a higher degree of culpability than that charged constitutes proof of the culpability charged.

§ 6.03—Definitions of Culpable Mental States

(a) A person acts intentionally, or with intent, with respect to the nature of his conduct or to a result of his conduct when it is his conscious objective or desire to engage in the conduct or cause the result.

(b) A person acts knowingly, or with knowledge, with respect to the nature of his conduct or to circumstances surrounding his conduct when he is aware of the nature of his conduct or that the circumstances exist. A person acts knowingly, or with knowledge, with respect to a result of his conduct when he is aware that his conduct is reasonably certain to cause the result.

(c) A person acts recklessly, or is reckless, with respect to circumstances surrounding his conduct or the result of his conduct when he is aware of but consciously disregards a substantial and unjustifiable risk that the circumstances exist or the result will occur. The risk must be of such a nature and degree that its disregard constitutes a gross deviation from the standard of care that an ordinary person would exercise under all the circumstances as viewed from the actor's standpoint.

(d) A person acts with criminal negligence, or is criminally negligent, with respect to circumstances surrounding his conduct or the result of his conduct when he ought to be aware of a substantial and unjustifiable risk that the circumstances exists or the result will occur. The risk must be of such a nature and degree that the failure to perceive it constitutes a gross deviation from the standard of care that an ordinary person would exercise under all the circumstances as viewed from the actor's standpoint.

§ 6.04—Causation: Conduct and Results

(a) A person is criminally liable if the result would not have occurred but for his conduct, operating either alone or concurrently with another cause, unless the concurrent cause was clearly sufficient to produce the result and the conduct of the actor clearly insufficient.

(b) A person is nevertheless responsible for causing a result if the only difference between what actually occurred and what he desired, contemplated or risked is that:

(1) a different offense was committed; or

(2) a different person or property was injured, harmed or otherwise affected.

Texas Family Code—Annotated (1984)

§ 12.04—Rights, Privileges, Duties, and Powers of Parent

Except as otherwise provided by judicial order or by an affidavit of relinquishment of parental rights executed under Section 15.03 of this code, the parent of a child has the following rights, privileges, duties, and powers:

(1) the right to have physical possession of the child and to establish its legal domicile;

(2) the duty of care, control, protection, moral and religious training, and reasonable discipline of the child;

(3) the duty to support the child, including providing the child with clothing, food, shelter, medical care, and education;

(4) the duty, except when a guardian of the child's estate has been appointed, to manage the estate of the child, including a power as an agent of the child to act in relation to the child's

estate if the child's action is required by a state, the United States, or a foreign government;

(5) the right to the services and earnings of the child;

(6) the power to consent to marriage, to enlistment in the armed forces of the United States, and to medical, psychiatric, and surgical treatment;

(7) the power to represent the child in legal action and to make other decisions of substantial legal significance concerning the child;

(8) the power to receive and give receipt for payments for the support of the child and to hold or disburse any funds for the benefit of the child;

(9) the right to inherit from and through the child; and

(10) any other right, privilege, duty, or power existing between a parent and child by virtue of law.

C. CURRENT LAW THAT WOULD BE APPLIED WERE THE CASE PROSECUTED TODAY

Texas Penal Code (2006)

§ 1.07—Definitions

* * *

(30) "Law" means the constitution or a statute of this state or of the United States, a written opinion of a court of record, a municipal ordinance, an order of a county commissioners court, or a rule authorized by and lawfully adopted under a statute.

§ 19.01—Types of Criminal Homicide

(a) A person commits criminal homicide if he intentionally, knowingly, recklessly, or with criminal negligence causes the death of an individual.

(b) Criminal homicide is murder, capital murder, manslaughter, or criminally negligent homicide.

§ 22.04—Injury to a Child, Elderly Individual, or Disabled Individual

(a) A person commits an offense if he intentionally, knowingly, recklessly, or with criminal negligence, by act or intentionally, knowingly, or recklessly by omission, causes to a child, elderly individual, or disabled individual:

(1) serious bodily injury;

(2) serious mental deficiency, impairment, or injury; or

(3) bodily injury.

(b) An omission that causes a condition described by Subsections (a)(1) through (a)(3) is conduct constituting an offense under this section if:

(1) the actor has a legal or statutory duty to act; or

(2) the actor has assumed care, custody, or control of a child, elderly individual, or disabled individual.

(c) In this section:

(1) "Child" means a person 14 years of age or younger.

(2) "Elderly individual" means a person 65 years of age or older.

(3) "Disabled individual" means a person older than 14 years of age who by reason of age or physical or mental disease, defect, or injury is substantially unable to protect himself from

harm or to provide food, shelter, or medical care for himself.

* * *

(d) The actor has assumed care, custody, or control if he has by act, words, or course of conduct acted so as to cause a reasonable person to conclude that he has accepted responsibility for protection, food, shelter, and medical care for a child, elderly individual, or disabled individual ...

(e) An offense under Subsection (a)(1) or (2) ... is a felony of the first degree when the conduct is committed intentionally or knowingly. When the conduct is engaged in recklessly, the offense is a felony of the second degree.

(f) An offense under Subsection (a)(3) ... is a felony of the third degree when the conduct is committed intentionally or knowingly. When the conduct is engaged in recklessly, the offense is a state jail felony.

(g) An offense under Subsection (a) is a state jail felony when the person acts with criminal negligence ...

* * *

§ 6.01—Requirement of Voluntary Act or Omission

(a) A person commits an offense only if he voluntarily engages in conduct, including an act, an omission, or possession.

(b) Possession is a voluntary act if the possessor knowingly obtains or receives the thing possessed or is aware of his control of the thing for a sufficient time to permit him to terminate his control.

(c) A person who omits to perform an act does not commit an offense unless a law as defined by Section 1.07 provides that the omission is an offense or otherwise provides that he has a duty to perform the act.

§ 12.35—State Jail Felony Punishment

(a) Except as provided by Subsection (c), an individual adjudged guilty of a state jail felony shall be punished by confinement in a state jail for any term of not more than two years or less than 180 days.

(b) In addition to confinement, an individual adjudged guilty of a state jail felony may be punished by a fine not to exceed $10,000.

* * *

9.   The Case of Linda Ruschioni (Massachusetts, 1993)

A.   The Facts

It is Monday night, July 19, 1993, in the Massachusetts town of Winchendon, which is 60 miles from Boston and near the New Hampshire state line. Winchendon is a typical New England town, home to 6,000 people. Many residents commute to Boston for work, but Winchendon has retained its small-town atmosphere and economy. Most people are considered middle class, and few live luxuriously. Paying the bills each month is a concern for nearly everyone.

Linda Ruschioni, a plaque maker, and her husband Ricci, a firefighter, live with their son Ricci Jr., 11, daughter Randi, 10, and daughter Traci, 8. This night, Linda and Traci go to the Family VideoLand store to rent a movie. They pick out a comedy, *Death Becomes Her*, and get in line to pay for the movie.

Linda Ruschioni pays for the movie and leaves with her daughter in tow. As they walk across the parking lot, Traci spots something on the ground. There are no cars around and no people in their particular part of the parking lot. She bends down and picks up two "Twin Spins" instant lottery tickets. The tickets are from a new game started one week earlier by the Massachusetts Lottery Commission. They cost $2 each and have the potential to pay from $1 to $20,000.

Traci yells, "Mom! Come here!" and hands her the tickets. Linda examines the tickets and sees that they are not scratched off. No one seems to be around looking for the tickets, so she puts them in her pocketbook, intending to play them later. Later that night, as Traci, her sister, and a friend watch the movie, Linda remembers the tickets and has Traci scratch them off. One of them is a $4 winner. The other scores $10,000, a 144,000–to–1 shot.

Linda cannot believe their luck. She grabs the children, packs them in the car, and heads for the nearest lottery dealer, a convenience store a few minutes from her house. Seconds later, she is in the store, jumping up and down as the children watch from the car. The clerk at the store verifies that both tickets are legitimate winners. Only the Lottery Commission itself can pay a $10,000 prize. Elated, Linda goes home.

The next morning, Linda, Ricci, and Traci show up at the lottery commission's regional office in Worcester and present the $10,000 ticket. Linda tells the Commission agent that her daughter found the ticket in a parking lot.

Figure 19. Traci Ruschioni, eight, holds a copy of the winning lottery ticket at home in Winchendon, Massachusetts. (John Bohn, Boston Globe)

Smiling and charmed by the child, the commission employee tells her that Traci is too young to cash the ticket, but it is perfectly okay for Linda to sign it and take the prize. After taxes, the ticket pays $6,700. The Commission determines that the winning ticket came from a book distributed to the Beverage Barn in Winchendon, next door to Family VideoLand.

Amazed by her daughter's good luck and thinking it is a wonderful story, Linda calls the local television station and tells them of Traci's find. The news station loves the story and airs it on the evening broadcast: the little girl who finds a $10,000 lottery ticket! Happy endings for all. Soon, stations and newspapers in Boston pick up the story, with national coverage close behind. A "Good Morning America" producer calls, and Linda goes on television.

After paying a dentist bill, car insurance, and splurging on a freezer, a new cage for Traci's birds, and a bicycle for Traci's sister, the Ruschionis plan to use the money to go back to Disney World, where they vacationed the year before.

*   *   *

Unbeknownst to the Ruschionis at the time, a Massachusetts statute requires persons finding property worth over $3 to turn it in to the local police station. The two tickets they find have a face value of $4, already over the statutory limit of $3, but in fact are worth much more, $10,004. However, at the time they "convert" the property to their use by cashing the tickets, the Ruschionis are unaware of their statutory duty to turn in the lost tickets. The Ruschionis hear of the laws only during their appearance on "Good Morning America."

"I didn't know about the law, of course not. Nobody knew it," Ricci Ruschioni later explains. "How many times has anybody walked down the street or found some change in a phone booth or found a few dollars on the street? How many of these people in the world would go back and give it to the police department? Most people would do what we did. You put it in your pocket and walk away."

*   *   *

Should Linda and Ricci Ruschioni be criminally liable for converting the lost ticket to their own use? If so, what amount of punishment would you impose?

N	0	1	2	3	4	5	6	7	8	9	10	11
☐	☐	☐	☐	☐	☐	☐	☐	☐	☐	☐	☐	☐
no liability	liability but no punishment	1 day	2 wks.	2 mo.	6 mo.	1 yr.	3 yrs.	7 yrs.	15 yrs.	30 yrs.	life imprisonment	death

B.   Then Existing Law

Laws of Massachusetts, Chapter 266—Crimes Against Property (1993)

§ 30—Larceny; general provisions and penalties

(1) Whoever steals, or with intent to defraud obtains by a false pretense, or whoever unlawfully, and with intent to steal or embezzle, converts, or secretes with intent to convert, the property of another as defined in this section, whether such property is or is not in his possession at the time of such conversion or secreting, shall be guilty of larceny, and shall ... if the value of the property stolen exceeds two hundred and fifty dollars, be punished by imprisonment in the state prison for not more than five years, or by a fine of not more than twenty-five thousand dollars and imprisonment in jail for not more than two years; or, if the value of the property stolen, other than a firearm as so defined, does not exceed two hundred and fifty dollars, shall be punished by

imprisonment in jail for not more than one year or by a fine of not more than three hundred dollars; ...

(2) The term "property", as used in the section, shall include money, personal chattels, a bank note, bond, promissory note, bill of exchange or other bill, order or certificate, a book of accounts for or concerning money or goods due or to become due or to be delivered, a deed or writing containing a conveyance of land, any valuable contract in force, a receipt, release or defeasance, a writ, process, certificate of title or duplicate certificate issued under chapter one hundred and eighty-five, a public record, anything which is of the realty or is annexed thereto, a security deposit received pursuant to section fifteen B of chapter one hundred and eighty-six, electronically processed or stored data, either tangible or intangible, data while in transit, and any domesticated animal, including dogs, or a beast or bird which is ordinarily kept in confinement.

. . .

Laws of Massachusetts, Chapter 134—Lost Goods and Stray Beasts (1993)

§ 1—Report of lost money or goods by finder

Any person who finds lost money or goods of the value of three dollars or more, the owner of which is unknown, shall within two days report the finding thereof to the officer in charge at a police station in the town where said property was found, or, if there is no police station, post notice thereof in two public places therein, or, instead of such report or posting, cause notice thereof to be advertised in a newspaper published therein.

§ 3—Restitution of property

If, within three months after the finding of stray beasts, or within one year after the finding of lost money or goods, the owner appears and, except as otherwise provided in section two, pays all reasonable expenses incurred by the finder in keeping such goods or beasts and in complying with this chapter, he shall have restitution of the money, goods or beasts.

[N.B.—Massachusetts's criminal code does not contain a general provision that reads in a minimum culpability requirement; nor does it contain a general mistake provision.]

Commonwealth v. Titus, 116 Mass. 42 (1874)

If the finder of lost goods, at the time of first taking the goods into his possession, has the intent to appropriate them to his own use and deprive the owner of them, and knows or has reasonable means of knowing who the owner is, he may be found guilty of larceny. But if the finder of lost goods takes them into his possession without any felonious intent at the time of taking, "a subsequent conversion of them to his own use, by whatever intent ... , will not constitute larceny." Defendant committed larceny when he appropriated the contents of a traveling bag found lying on a public highway and then discarded the bag in a remote wood lot.

Commonwealth v. Everson, 140 Mass. 292 (1885)

Ignorance of the law provided no defense for a man and a woman who sold liquor using an inkeeper's liquor license and not a liquor license for a public bar, as was required.

C.   CURRENT LAW THAT WOULD BE APPLIED WERE THE CASE PROSECUTED TODAY

[Statutes changes are not relevant]

CHAPTER 4.   THE SIGNIFICANCE OF RESULTING HARM: CAUSATION, ATTEMPT, AND IMPOSSIBILITY

10.   THE CASE OF JOSEPH B. WOOD (VERMONT, 1879)

A.   THE FACTS

It is 1874. Joseph B. Wood's daughter, Alma, a short, slight woman in her late twenties, marries Luman Smith, a farmer in Williston, Vermont. It is Alma's second marriage. To it, she brings Joseph, a child from her previous marriage who is named after his grandfather. Luman, 40, and Alma have two children together. Luman is devoted to the children.

Luman and Alma's relationship is not good, however, and they fight often. Alma leaves the home several times between 1874 and 1879. Tensions in the household are heightened by Alma's infidelity and prostitution, and by Luman's threats and occasional violence toward Alma. In 1879, Alma again leaves Luman, the farm, and the three children.

Luman soon realizes that he cannot run a farm and raise the three children by himself. The infant, in particular, requires constant attention. He goes to his estranged wife and begs her to return. She agrees, but

Figure 20. A typical Vermont farm of the period. (Vermont Historical Society)

only after he accepts three conditions. First, she is to be given her own room in the house where she can entertain guests without interruption from Luman. Second, her father is to move in with them. This arrangement helps her father and provides her with some degree of protection, if needed, as does the small revolver she has recently purchased. Finally, Luman signs most of his property over to her and agrees to allow her to use his horse when he is not using it.

After the deal is made and the property transferred, Alma nonetheless begins to plan to move west to Lincoln, Nebraska. Luman carries a good-sized dirk (a short, straight dagger) with him throughout the day. Fearing that Luman might use it against her, Alma steals the knife and hides it.

On October 23, just a few days after Alma and her father move back to the farm, Luman returns from a visit to the doctor in Essex Junction. Their daughter Helen runs to greet him at the gate, and they walk to the stable so Luman can hitch up his horse to go into town.

Wood enters the stable and objects to Luman hitching the horse, telling Luman he can no longer use it. Luman explains that the horse was not transferred to Alma with the other property, but Wood is undeterred. Before Luman can finish hitching the horse, Wood pulls a pistol on

Luman, who grabs the barrel and points it away. The two men struggle. Wood fires several shots at Luman but misses. Finally, Wood points the gun at Luman's abdomen and pulls the trigger. It is a lethal wound.

* * *

Would you convict Wood for the killing of Luman? If so, what amount of punishment would you impose?

N	0	1	2	3	4	5	6	7	8	9	10	11
☐	☐	☐	☐	☐	☐	☐	☐	☐	☐	☐	☐	☐
no	liability	1 day	2 wks.	2 mo.	6 mo.	1 yr.	3 yrs.	7 yrs.	15 yrs.	30 yrs.	life	death
liability	but										imprison-	
	no										ment	
	punishment											

* * *

In fact, Luman does not die immediately. Such a wound allows him to survive for some time and, at least for a period, with full mobility. But given the then current state of medical knowledge, all experts agree that he would have died from the wound within a week or two due to loss of blood and infection.

Alma, hearing the gun shots, runs out of the house with her revolver hidden in her apron. As she approaches, Luman sees the gun and grabs for it, but Alma holds tight. Luman begins choking Alma. Afraid for her life, she points the revolver at Luman and fires a round into his chest. Luman staggers away, saying "You need not shoot again, for I am a dead man." As Luman slumps, Alma and Wood go back to what they were doing before the shooting, showing neither concern nor remorse.

Luman and his daughter Helen make it to the home of Mr. and Mrs. Josiah Thompson, a neighboring farmer. Two doctors are called. Luman's lungs begin to fill with fluid from Alma's gunshot wound to his chest. He dies two days later from asphyxiation, having been suffocated by the fluid filling his lungs. Experts agree that he would have died from Wood's shot to the abdomen had he not first died from Alma's shot to the chest.

* * *

Would you impose criminal liability on Wood? If so, how much punishment would you impose?

N	0	1	2	3	4	5	6	7	8	9	10	11
☐	☐	☐	☐	☐	☐	☐	☐	☐	☐	☐	☐	☐
no	liability	1 day	2 wks.	2 mo.	6 mo.	1 yr.	3 yrs.	7 yrs.	15 yrs.	30 yrs.	life	death
liability	but										imprison-	
	no										ment	
	punishment											

B.   THEN EXISTING LAW

Vermont Statutes, Chapter 189 (1879)

§ 4086—Murder; degrees defined

Murder committed by means of poison, or by lying in wait, or by wilful, deliberate and premeditated killing, or committed in perpetrating or attempting to perpetrate arson, rape, robbery or burglary, shall be murder of the first degree. All other kinds of murder shall be murder of the second degree.

§ 4088—Punishment of murder

The punishment of murder in the first degree shall be death, and the punishment of murder in the second degree shall be imprisonment in the state prison for life.

§ 4089—Manslaughter

A person who commits manslaughter shall be imprisoned in the state prison for life or for not less than seven years, or be fined not more than one thousand dollars.

§ 4119—With intent to kill or murder, by one armed

A person who, armed with a dangerous weapon, assaults another with intent to kill or murder, shall be imprisoned in the state prison for life or for not less than five years.

Acts and Resolves of Vermont (1878)

No. 23—An Act for the Punishment of Attempts to Commit Offenses.

Sec. 1. Every person who shall attempt to commit an offense prohibited by law, punishable by death or imprisonment in the state prison, and in such attempt shall do any act toward the commission of such offense, but shall fail in the perpetration by reason of being interrupted or prevented in the execution of the same,—in case no express provision is made by law for the punishment of such attempt,—shall be punished, where the offense attempted to be committed is punishable with death or by imprisonment in the state prison for life, by imprisonment in the state prison for not more than ten years; and where any other of such offenses is so attempted to be committed, he shall be punished by imprisonment in the state prison, or in the county jail, or in the state workhouse, or by fine, respectively, as the offense so attempted to be committed is by law punishable; but in no case shall the punishment of such last mentioned attempt exceed one half the greatest punishment which might have been inflicted if the offense so attempted had been committed.

Sec. 2. Under an indictment or information charging any principal offense, the jury may, according as the proof may be, return a verdict that the respondent is not guilty of the principal offense of the character named in the preceding section charged, but is guilty of an attempt to commit the same, in the manner provided in the first section of this act.

State v. Tatro, 50 Vt. 483 (1878)

"To constitute murder of the first degree, the act must be done with malice forethought, and that malice must be actual, not constructive. ... Where the act is committed deliberately, with a deadly weapon, and is likely to be attended with dangerous consequences, the malice requisite to murder will be presumed. ... [I]ntent for an instant before the blow is sufficient to constitute malice."

State v. Scates, N.C. 420 (1858)

"If one man inflicts a mortal wound, of which the victim is languishing, and then a second kills the deceased by an independent act, we cannot imagine how the first can be said to have killed him, without involving the absurdity of saying that the deceased was killed twice. In such a case, the two persons could not be indicted as joint murderers, because there was no understanding, or connection between them. It is certain that the second person could be convicted of murder, if he killed with malice aforethought, and to convict the first would be assuming that he had also killed the same person at another time. Such a proposition cannot be sustained."

Commonwealth v. Webster, 59 Mass. (5 Cush.) 295, 307–08 (1850)

"The true nature of manslaughter is, that it is homicide mitigated out of tenderness to the frailty of human nature. Every man, when assailed with violence or great rudeness, is inspired with a sudden impulse of anger, which puts him upon resistance before time for cool reflection; and if, during that period, he attacks his assailant with a weapon likely to endanger life, and death ensues, it is regarded as done through heat of blood or violence of anger, and not through malice, or that coldblooded desire of revenge which more properly constitutes the feeling, emotion, or passion of malice."

C. Current Law That Would Be Applied Were the Case Prosecuted Today

Vermont Statutes, Title 13—Crimes & Criminal Procedure (2006)

§ 2301—Murder—Degrees defined

Murder committed by means of poison, or by lying in wait, or by wilful, deliberate and premeditated killing, or committed in perpetrating or attempting to perpetrate arson, sexual assault, aggravated sexual assault, robbery or burglary, shall be murder in the first degree. All other kinds of murder shall be murder in the second degree.

§ 2302—Determination of degree

The jury by whom a person is tried for murder, if it finds such person guilty thereof, shall state in its verdict whether it is murder in the first or in the second degree. If such person is convicted on confession in open court, the court, by examination of witnesses, shall determine the degree of the crime and give sentence accordingly.

§ 2303—Penalties for first and second degree murder

(a) The punishment for murder in the first degree shall be imprisonment for life and for a minimum term of 35 years unless the court finds that there are aggravating or mitigating factors which justify a different minimum term. If the court finds that the aggravating factors outweigh any mitigating factors, the minimum term may be longer than 35 years, up to and including life without parole. If the court finds that the mitigating factors outweigh any aggravating factors the minimum term may be set at less than 35 years but not less than 15 years.

(b) The punishment for murder in the second degree shall be imprisonment for life and for a minimum term of 20 years unless the court finds that there are aggravating or mitigating factors which justify a different minimum term. If the court finds that the aggravating outweigh any mitigating factors, the minimum term may be longer than 20 years, up to and including life without parole. If the court finds that the mitigating factors outweigh any aggravating factors, the minimum term may be set at less than 20 years but not less than 10 years.

· (c) Before sentencing a defendant for first or second degree murder, the court shall allow the parties to present arguments concerning aggravating and mitigating factors and sentence recommendations. The court shall enter written findings of fact, summarizing the offense and the defendant's participation in it. The court shall also enter specific written findings concerning aggravating and mitigating factors. These findings shall be based on the evidence taken at trial and at the sentence hearing, and on information from the presentence investigation report.

(d) Aggravating factors shall include the following:

(1) The murder was committed while the defendant was in custody under sentence of imprisonment.

(2) The defendant was previously convicted of a felony involving the use of violence to a person.

(3) The murder was committed while the defendant was engaged in the commission of, or in an attempt to commit, or in immediate flight after committing a felony.

(4) The victim of the murder was particularly weak, vulnerable or helpless.

(5) The murder was particularly severe, brutal or cruel.

(6) The murder involved multiple victims.

(7) The murder was random, predatory or arbitrary in nature.

(8) Any other factor that the state offers in support of a greater minimum sentence.

(e) Mitigating factors shall include the following:

(1) The defendant had no significant history of prior criminal activity before sentencing.

(2) The defendant was suffering from a mental or physical disability or condition that significantly reduced his or her culpability for the murder.

(3) The defendant was an accomplice in the murder committed by another person and his or her participation was relatively minor.

(4) The defendant, because of youth or old age, lacked substantial judgement in committing the murder.

(5) The defendant acted under duress, coercion, threat or compulsion insufficient to constitute a defense but which sufficiently affected his or her conduct.

(6) The victim was a participant in the defendant's conduct or consented to it.

(7) Any other factor that the defendant offers in support of a lesser minimum sentence.

§ 9—Attempts

(a) A person who attempts to commit an offense and does an act toward the commission thereof, but by reason of being interrupted or prevented fails in the execution of the same, shall be punished as herein provided unless other express provision is made by law for the punishment of the attempt. If the offense attempted to be committed is murder, aggravated murder, kidnaping, arson causing death, aggravated sexual assault or sexual assault, a person shall be punished as the offense attempted to be committed is by law punishable.

(b) If the offense attempted to be committed is a felony other than those set forth in subsection (a) of this section, a person shall be punished by the less severe of the following punishments:

(1) imprisonment for not more than ten years and fined not more than $10,000.00 or both; or

(2) as the offense attempted to be committed is by law punishable.

(c) If the offense attempted to be committed is a misdemeanor, a person shall be imprisoned or fined, or both, in an amount not to exceed one-half the maximum penalty for which the offense so attempted to be committed is by law punishable.

11. THE CASE OF LARRY EUGENE PHILLIPS (CALIFORNIA, 1993)

A. THE FACTS

On the night of October 30, 1993, Sergeant Ian Grimes is patrolling Glendale, a suburb northwest of Los Angeles, in an unmarked car. A Ford Thunderbird squeals its tires as it pulls out of a gas station and speeds north on Pacific Avenue toward the Ventura Freeway. Grimes pulls the car over for speeding before it reaches the freeway on-ramp. He approaches the passenger side and talks to the driver through the passenger window. The driver says that his name is "Dennis Franks," but has no license, claiming that he left it at home. In response to Grimes' questioning, the driver seems confused about his home address. The passenger explains that the car belongs to the driver's mother, but Grimes has already learned over his radio that it is a rental car from the airport. He directs the driver to step out and stand at the right rear of the car, where he can see both men as he talks to them. Both are big. The driver is six feet tall and weighs 210 pounds; the passenger is six feet and 340.

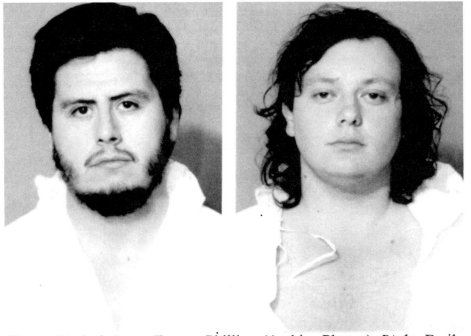

The driver stands in an odd way as he talks, holding his body at an angle. He claims not to be armed, but Grimes realizes the man's odd stance is designed to make his shirt hang over and hide the 9 mm Glock 17 semiautomatic handgun in his waistband. Grimes takes the weapon and backs up, taking cover behind a nearby planter on the sidewalk. The driver won't respond to Grimes' commands, nor for a moment will the passenger. Finally, Grimes hears a

Figure 21. *Left:* Larry Eugene Phillips. (Archive Photos). *Right:* Emil Matasareanu. (Archive Photos)

"clonk," which turns out to be the passenger dropping a Glock that he was holding. The passenger puts his hands out the window and Grimes holds the two in that position until back-up arrives.

A search of the car reveals:

- 1 Norinco folding-stock semiautomatic rifle
- 1 MAK 90 wood-stock semiautomatic rifle
- 1 Springfield Armory .45 pistol
- 1 Colt .45 pistol

Figure 22. The Glendale Police Department and bomb squad investigate the red Ford Thunderbird. (Gene Blevins, Los Angeles Daily News)

- 1,649 rounds of 7.62 x 39 mm ammunition, most loaded into 40–round magazines, taped three-together
- 3 seventy-five round drum magazines loaded with 7.62 x 39 mm ammunition
- 967 rounds of 9 x 19 mm jacketed hollow-point ammunition
- 357 rounds of .45 jacketed hollow-point ammunition
- 6 smoke bombs
- 2 improvised explosive devices
- 1 gas mask
- 2 sets National Body Armor Level III–A vests
- 2 200–channel, portable, programmable police radio scanners with earpieces
- Sunglasses, gloves, wigs, ski masks, and a stopwatch
- 2 spray cans of gray Studio Hair Color
- 3 different California automobile license plates
- $1,620 in cash.

The driver initially refuses to answer questions, but is subsequently identified as 23–year–old Larry Eugene Phillips. The passenger is 27–year–old Emil Dechebal Matasareanu.

At the station, the men explain their load of weapons by telling police they are on their way to a shooting range in the Angeles National Forest known as "Kentucky." It is October 30, 1993, the day before Halloween, "Devil's Night." The disguises and other material, they say, may be needed for a Halloween party after they leave the shooting range.

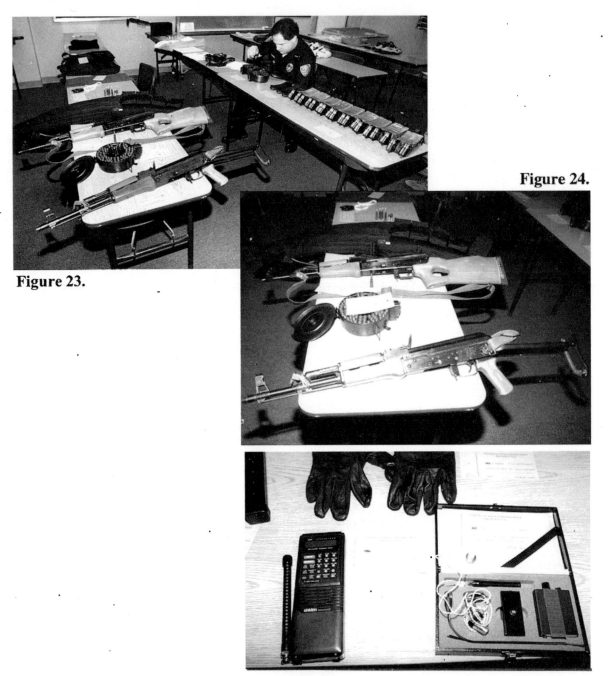

Figure 24.

Figure 23.

Figure 25. Weapons cache found in the red Ford Thunderbird that Larry Phillips was driving. (Gene Blevins, Los Angeles Daily News)

Further investigation leaves the police, and later the prosecutors with little doubt that the officer has stumbled onto two robbers on their way to a job. The supplies are a classic "bank robbery kit." But investigators are never able to determine what they planned to rob or exactly when.

Larry Eugene Phillips, born September 9, 1970, gets his first exposure to the life of crime on his sixth birthday, when the FBI knocks on the door of his family's home in Denver. Before Larry's eyes, they arrest his father, Larry, Sr., who has been a fugitive from a Colorado prison since his son's birth. A few years later, Larry's mother, Dorothy Clay, finalizes a divorce and moves with her son to a suburb of Los Angeles. His mother is no stranger to crime, having served 10 years for drug possession and stabbing a prison guard. At the age of 19, Phillips is arrested for the first time after stealing $400 from a Sears store in Alhambra, California.

Phillips and Matasareanu meet in 1989 and quickly become friends. They both enjoy weapons and like to go shooting together. Although four years the younger, Phillips is controlling and manipulative and soon becomes the duo's leader. "You can't imagine how manipulative my brother was," explains Phillips' half-brother later. "He tried to break your mind down and then build it up again so that you would become one of his crew."

Phillips, a bodybuilder, dreams incessantly of wealth, fantasizing about spending $100 bills by the handful. He idolizes 1980s robber-baron Michael Milken as well as Vito Corleone, the Godfather of big-screen fame. To pass the time, he sometimes drives around the chic neighborhoods of LA, watching the celebrities come and go, picturing himself living their lives.

Matasareanu, born in Romania on July 19, 1966, moves to California as a child and grows up in Altadena and other areas. Matasareanu's mother, a former singer who defected from the Romanian state opera, describes her son as a very intelligent boy, who she struggles to raise on her own. As a chubby boy, he is the butt of teasing from other children and classmates. The isolation of his youth turns him early to computers as an outlet. He gets computer training at the DeVry Institute. In his 20's, Matasareanu returns to Romania, marries, moves back to the United States, has a son, and starts a computer business. Not long after his wedding, a blocked artery in his brain causes him to begin suffering epileptic seizures that require surgery. Soon after, his computer business fails.

Phillips, at age 20, takes the California real estate test and passes. However, officials in the Department of Real Estate discover his 1989 theft conviction through a routine fingerprint check, and the state turns him down for a license because his application failed to disclose the conviction. About that time, Phillips, with no license, tells his probation officer that he is making a lot of money, about $2,000–$4,000 per transaction, as a real estate agent.

In 1991, Phillips, now 21, is arrested again, this time in Orange, California, on weapons charges, when a police officer spots a semiautomatic 9 mm pistol in his waistband and an extra clip of ammunition and a knife hidden inside a compartment in his BMW. He insists that he needs the gun for protection because he is going to pick up a large amount of cash from a real estate transaction. Detectives in the Orange Police Department, while investigating the weapons charges, link him to a real estate scam involving forged title documents.

Phillips also goes by the names Larry Franks, Dennis Franks, and Denis Rene. He regularly changes his address within the same city, and gives false addresses.

In 1992, Denver police link Phillips to a residential burglary and arrest him. He pleads guilty but skips the sentencing hearing and returns to California. Denver Police also link Phillips and Matasareanu to the robbery of an armored car, but by the time the DPD has gathered enough evidence to arrest the pair they have gone back to California.

Throughout the early 1990's, police and repossession agents search diligently but unsuccessfully for Phillips, repeatedly checking for him at a house he once rented in Altadena, a suburb 15 miles northeast of downtown Los Angeles. In 1993, Phillips, going by the name Larry Martinez, marries a woman he met while in Denver, Janette Teresa Federico, who is the mother of a young girl by another man. After the two move back to Los Angeles, they split up.

Then come the events of the night of October 30, 1993.

The two men are probably liable for at least some weapons offenses. (Their assault rifles are not at the time illegal in California, but there are registration requirements.) Should the two also be held criminally liable for attempted robbery? If so, what amount of punishment would you impose *for attempted robbery*?

N	0	1	2	3	4	5	6	7	8	9	10	11
☐	☐	☐	☐	☐	☐	☐	☐	☐	☐	☐	☐	☐
no liability	liability but no punishment	1 day	2 wks.	2 mo.	6 mo.	1 yr.	3 yrs.	7 yrs.	15 yrs.	30 yrs.	life imprison- ment	death

B. THEN EXISTING LAW

California Penal Code (1993)

§ 21(a)—Attempt to commit crime; specific intent and ineffectual act.

An attempt to commit a crime consists of two elements: a specific intent to commit the crime, and a direct but ineffectual act done toward its commission.

§ 664—Attempts; punishment

Every person who attempts to commit any crime, but fails, or is prevented or intercepted in the perpetration thereof, is punishable, where no provision is made by law for the punishment of such attempts, as follows:

(a) If the offense so attempted is punishable by imprisonment in the state prison, the person guilty of that attempt is punishable by imprisonment in the state prison for one-half the term of imprisonment prescribed upon a conviction of the offense so attempted; provided, however, that if the crime attempted is willful, deliberate, and premeditated murder, as defined in Section 189, the person guilty of that attempt shall be punishable by imprisonment in the state prison for life with the possibility of parole; provided, further, that if the crime attempted is any other one in which the maximum sentence is life imprisonment or death the person guilty of the attempt shall be punishable by imprisonment in the state prison for a term of five, seven, or nine years....

(b) If the offense so attempted is punishable by imprisonment in a county jail, the person guilty of such attempt is punishable by imprisonment in a county jail for a term not exceeding one-half the term of imprisonment prescribed upon a conviction of the offense so attempted.

(c) If the offense so attempted is punishable by a fine, the offender convicted of that attempt is punishable by a fine not exceeding one-half the largest fine which may be imposed upon a conviction of the offense so attempted.

* * *

§ 211—Robbery (defined)

Robbery is the felonious taking of personal property in the possession of another, from his person or immediate presence, and against his will, accomplished by means of force or fear.

§ 212—Fear (defined)

The fear mentioned in Section 211 may be either:

(1) The fear of an unlawful injury to the person or property of the person robbed, or of any relative of his or member of his family; or,

(2) The fear of an immediate and unlawful injury to the person or property of anyone in the company of the person robbed at the time of the robbery.

§ 212.5—Robbery; degrees

(a) Every robbery of any person who is performing his or her duties as an operator of any bus, taxicab, cable car, streetcar, trackless trolley, or other vehicle, including a vehicle operated on stationary rails or on a track or rail suspended in the air, and used for the transportation of persons for hire, every robbery of any passenger which is perpetrated on any of these vehicles, and every robbery which is perpetrated in an inhabited dwelling house, a vessel as defined in Section 21 of the Harbors and Navigation Code which is inhabited and designed for habitation, an inhabited floating home as defined in subdivision (d) of Section 18075.55 of the Health and Safety Code, a trailer coach as defined in the Vehicle Code which is inhabited, or the inhabited portion of any other building is robbery of the first degree.

(b) All kinds of robbery other than those listed in subdivisions (a) are of the second degree.

§ 213—Robbery; punishment

(a) Robbery is punishable as follows:

(1) Robbery of the first degree: by imprisonment in the state prison for three, four, or six years.

(2) Robbery of the second degree: by imprisonment in the state prison for two, three, or five years.

(b) Notwithstanding Section 664 [Punishment for unsuccessful attempt to commit crime: Attempted murder of peace officer or fire fighter], attempted robbery is punishable by imprisonment in the state prison.

§ 182—Conspiracy (definition); punishment; venue; evidence necessary to support conviction

(a) If two or more persons conspire:

(1) To commit any crime.

(2) Falsely and maliciously to indict another for any crime, or to procure another to be charged or arrested for any crime.

(3) Falsely to move or maintain any suit, action or proceeding.

(4) To cheat and defraud any person of any property, by any means which are in themselves criminal, or to obtain money or property by false pretenses or by false promises with fraudulent intent not to perform such promises.

(5) To commit any act injurious to the public health, to public morals, or to pervert or obstruct justice, or the due administration of the laws.

(6) To commit any crime against the person of the President or Vice President of the United States, the governor of any state or territory, any United States justice or judge, or the secretary of any of the executive departments of the United States.

They are punishable as follows:

When they conspire to commit any crime against the person of any official, ... they are guilty of a felony and are punishable by imprisonment in the state prison for five, seven, or nine years.

When they conspire to commit any other felony, they shall be punishable in the same manner and to the same extent as is provided for the punishment of that felony. If the felony is one for which different punishments are prescribed for different degrees, the jury or court which finds the defendant guilty thereof shall determine the degree of the felony defendant conspired to commit.

If the degree is not so determined, the punishment for conspiracy to commit the felony shall be that prescribed for the lesser degree, except in the case of conspiracy to commit murder, in which case the punishment shall be that prescribed for murder in the first degree.

If the felony is conspiracy to commit two or more felonies which have different punishments and the commission of those felonies constitute but one offense of conspiracy, the penalty shall be that prescribed for the felony which has the greater maximum term....

§ 183—Non-criminal conspiracies; no criminal punishment

No conspiracies, other than those enumerated in the preceding section, are punishable criminally.

§ 184—Overt act; venue

No agreement amounts to a conspiracy, unless some act, beside such agreement, be done within this state to effect the object thereof, by one or more of the parties to such agreement and the trial of cases of conspiracy may be had in any county in which any such act be done.

§ 12285—Registration; contents; fee; … possession of weapons; conditions; restrictions; forgiveness period

(a) Any person who lawfully possesses an assault weapon, as defined in Section 12276, prior to June 1, 1989, shall register the firearm by January 1, 1991, and any person who lawfully possessed an assault weapon prior to the date it was specified as an assault weapon pursuant to Section 12276.5 shall register the firearm within 90 days, with the Department of Justice pursuant to those procedures that the department may establish. The registration shall contain a description of the firearm that identifies it uniquely, including all identification marks, the full name, address, date of birth, and thumbprint of the owner, and any other information that the department may deem appropriate. The department may charge a fee for registration of up to twenty dollars ($20) per person but not to exceed the actual processing costs of the department. After the department establishes fees sufficient to reimburse the department for processing costs, fees charged shall increase at a rate not to exceed the legislatively approved annual cost-of-living adjustment for the department's budget or as otherwise increased through the Budget Act.

* * *

(c) A person who has registered an assault weapon under this section may possess it only under any of the following conditions unless a permit allowing additional uses is first obtained under Section 12286:

(1) At that person's residence, place of business, or other property owned by that person, or on property owned by another with the owner's express permission.

(2) While on the premises of a target range of a public or private club or organization organized for the purpose of practicing shooting at targets.

(3) While on a target range that holds a regulatory or business license for the purpose of practicing shooting at that target range.

(4) While on the premises of a shooting club which is licensed pursuant to the Fish and Game Code.

(5) While attending any exhibition, display, or educational project which is about firearms and which is sponsored by, conducted under the auspices of, or approved by a law enforcement agency or a nationally or state recognized entity that fosters proficiency in, or promotes education about, firearms.

(6) While on publicly owned land if the possession and use of a firearm described in Section 12276 is specifically permitted by the managing agency of the land.

(7) While transporting the assault weapon between any of the places mentioned in this subdivision, or to any licensed gun dealer, as defined in subdivision (c) of Section 12290, for servicing or repair pursuant to subdivision (b) of Section 12290, if the assault weapon is transported as required by Section 12026.1.

People v. Dillon, 668 P.2d 697 (Cal. 1983)

Seventeen-year-old defendant was convicted of attempted robbery after he and several armed schoolmates entered victim's marijuana farm with intent to steal marijuana. In determining whether the defendant's conduct constituted a "direct but ineffectual act done toward" the offense of robbery, the court declared that "mere preparation" is not punishable; the attempt statute requires "the actual commencement of the doing of the criminal deed." "Mere preparation, which may consist of planning the offense or of devising, obtaining or arranging the means for its commission, is not sufficient to constitute an attempt." Rather, the acts must "clearly indicate a certain, unambiguous intent to commit that specific crime, and, in themselves, [must be] an immediate step in the present execution of the criminal design."

People v. Lopez, 24 Cal. Rptr.2d 649 (1993)

Defendant was convicted of conspiracy to sell drugs where he bought chemicals used to make methamphetamine from an undercover officer and promised to sell the drug once made. "To sustain a conviction for conspiracy, the prosecution must show the conspirators intended to agree or conspire and intended to commit the offense which is the object of the conspiracy. The prosecution must also allege and prove that one or more of the parties to the agreement committed some overt act (besides the agreement itself) in furtherance of the conspiracy."

C.   CURRENT LAW THAT WOULD BE APPLIED WERE THE CASE PROSECUTED TODAY

[Statutory changes are not relevant]

12. THE CASE OF ROGER THOMAS (U.S. MILITARY, 1961)

A. THE FACTS

August 16, 1960 is a hot summer day in Pensacola, Florida. Two newly acquainted Airmen in the US Navy, Roger Thomas and Robert Abruzzese, spend most of the day at the house of two women Thomas knows in town. Nineteen year old Thomas, an adopted child whose stepfather is dead and whose mother lives in Hawaii, has been in the Navy since finishing the 9th grade in May, 1958. He has been married for about ten months, and his wife is pregnant. A few days ago, he was transferred to Pensacola. Abruzzese is eighteen years old and has been enlisted for eighteen months, sixteen of which he has spent in Pensacola. The two men are assigned to the same division.

After the men leave the women's house, they go back to Thomas' family living quarters on the U.S. Naval Air Station of Pensacola, known as Saufley Field. There, they make arrangements to meet later for an evening of "bar hopping." Abruzzese goes to the movies for the afternoon, returning to Thomas' around eight o'clock. Thomas' wife fixes the two some sandwiches for dinner. The men agree to meet again at a local bar called the Lamp Post at 9:30.

At 9:30, Abruzzese is at the Lamp Post as Thomas walks in with Dennis McClellan, another airman stationed at Saufley Field. McClellan is nineteen and married, and has been in the Navy as an apprentice parachute rigger for about two years. He has only recently met Thomas, and meets Abruzzese for the first time at the Lampost. The three men have a few beers at the Lampost, then decide to head over to a bar called Sleepy Hollow. Thomas and McClellan both have a few more beers at Sleepy Hollow, while Abruzzese has four. They agree the next place to hit is Taylor's Place, a bar on Pace Boulevard, known as a "pick-up place," or a "juke joint."

At Taylor's Place, Thomas and McClellan go directly into the bar while Abruzzese lingers in the parking lot. Abruzzese uses Thomas' ID to buy beer that night and doesn't want the doorman to notice him entering next to Thomas. Inside, McClellan spots two women sitting at a table. Feeling "lucky," he strolls over to ask Caryl Laverne Alvis to dance. She is a lively and bouncy nineteen year old who has been living in Pensacola for about three years. She married a sailor a year and a half after moving to Pensacola and now lives with him and her twenty-four month old son from a previous marriage in a trailer behind a police officer's house. At about 10:30 that night, she visited with the police officer and some of his guests, proudly showing off her son. Soon afterwards, she left her sleeping husband and walked over to Taylor's Place, which is not far from her trailer. She rarely goes out and has not previously been to Taylor's Place. When McClellan asks her to dance she agrees, but says she won't be able to dance well in her high heels.

As Abruzzese enters the bar, he sees McClellan drawing Alvis onto the dance floor. He orders a Falstaff beer. Before it comes, he notices Alvis begin to slump forward into McClellan. She slides down him and onto the floor, apparently unconscious. The dance floor crowd at Taylor's, probably having seen people fall down before, simply dance around Alvis. McClellan and Thomas pull her to the side of the dance floor, where somebody says she must be having a fit. Thomas, thinking she might swallow her tongue, replies, "I've got a wallet here, let's put it in the corner of her mouth."

McClellan suggests that the three take Alvis home. They carry her from the bar out into the parking lot, where they lay her across the back seat of McClellan's '54 Buick four door sedan. Abruzzese gets in the passenger seat, and Thomas climbs in next to Alvis. As they are leaving, a Pensacola Deputy Fire marshal approaches the car and asks the men what they are planning to do with Alvis. When they tell him, he says "You make sure you take her home, now."

McClellan begins driving east on Pace Blvd. Within a couple of blocks, he remarks, "Here's a chance to get an easy piece of ass." A discussion ensues as to whether the men should have sex with Alvis. McClellan says, "I'll go if you guys will." At first Thomas rejects the idea, but ultimately he expresses the same sentiment as McClellan, saying, "I am for it if you guys are." Thomas then touches Alvis' breasts, discovering that they are "falsies" (two pairs of panties inserted into Alvis' bra). He removes the falsies and remarks on how "flat-chested" Alvis is. McClellan then asks, "What color are her panties?" Thomas lifts up her dress and takes off Alvis' red panties. They reach a mutual agreement that they will all have sex with Alvis.

McClellan says he knows a secluded place on Santa Rosa island. He begins driving there, and the three start to argue about who should go first. McClellan claims that because he "picked up" Alvis, he should be first. The others seem to agree to this, but half way across the three mile Pensacola Bridge, McClellan and Abruzzese look into the back seat to find Thomas between Alvis' legs with his pants down, having sex with her. McClellan calls Thomas a "rabbit," and Thomas says "Turn around, you guys." By the time they get off the bridge, Thomas is putting his pants back on.

They cross over the Pensacola Beach Bridge and drive onto Santa Rosa Island for about a mile and a half before making a right turn toward the beach. McClellan stops the car and gets out, telling the others, "You guys take a walk." He starts to get undressed, and, when Abruzzese asks why, he says "I never make love to a woman with my clothes on." Abruzzese and Thomas walk about fifty or sixty feet down the road to smoke a cigarette. About five minutes later McClellan gets out of the car with just his socks on, having had sex with Alvis. Abruzzese, a virgin, then climbs into the backseat and begins to touch

Figure 26. Beach on Santa Rosa Island. (Corbis/David Muench)

Alvis, who is warm and whose limbs he can move freely. He does not successfully have sex with Alvis; he is "in the right position" but does not penetrate. He does ejaculate.

When Abruzzese gets out of the car, Thomas and McClellan are down by the water "washing off." They all get back into the car and head towards town. Abruzzese asks to be let off at the USO in Pensacola so that he can catch the bus back to the base; he goes on duty early the next morning. Thomas and McClellan agree, and the three concoct a story about not being able to find Alvis' address in order to cover up the block of time during which they had sex with her.

* * *

Would you convict Thomas for rape? If so, what amount of punishment would you impose?

N	0	1	2	3	4	5	6	7	8	9	10	11
☐	☐	☐	☐	☐	☐	☐	☐	☐	☐	☐	☐	☐
no	liability	1 day	2 wks.	2 mo.	6 mo.	1 yr.	3 yrs.	7 yrs.	15 yrs.	30 yrs.	life	death
liability	but										imprison-	
	no										ment	
	punishment											

Would you convict Abruzzese for attempted rape? If so, what amount of punishment would you impose?

N	0	1	2	3	4	5	6	7	8	9	10	11
☐	☐	☐	☐	☐	☐	☐	☐	☐	☐	☐	☐	☐
no liability	liability but no punishment	1 day	2 wks.	2 mo.	6 mo.	1 yr.	3 yrs.	7 yrs.	15 yrs.	30 yrs.	life imprisonment	death

*   *   *

As they reach Pensacola, the men become concerned that Alvis has not regained consciousness. Abruzzese checks for a pulse and says he can't find one. McClellan, on the other hand, insists that he heard her snoring as he was having sex with her and that he can now detect a pulse. Thomas and McClellan drop Abruzzese off at the USO and then start to drive Alvis to her house.

Before they get far, however, Thomas and McClellan decide Alvis needs medical attention. At about 12:30 a.m., they pull into Glenn's Gas Station and make a call to the police. Soon afterwards, a police officer arrives and sees the woman who rents the trailer behind his house lying in the back seat of McClellan's car.

The officer checks the woman's pulse and determines that she is dead. A subsequent autopsy shows that she suffered a heart attack caused by acute interstitial myocarditis, an inflammation of the heart muscles. The coroner determines that she died at the moment she collapsed on the dance floor at Taylor's Place.

*   *   *

Knowing the complete facts, would you convict Thomas for his having intercourse with Alvis' body? If so, for what offense? What amount of punishment would you impose?

N	0	1	2	3	4	5	6	7	8	9	10	11
☐	☐	☐	☐	☐	☐	☐	☐	☐	☐	☐	☐	☐
no liability	liability but no punishment	1 day	2 wks.	2 mo.	6 mo.	1 yr.	3 yrs.	7 yrs.	15 yrs.	30 yrs.	life imprisonment	death

Knowing the complete facts, would you convict Abruzzese for attempting but failing to have intercourse with Alvis' body? If so, what amount of punishment would you impose?

N	0	1	2	3	4	5	6	7	8	9	10	11
☐	☐	☐	☐	☐	☐	☐	☐	☐	☐	☐	☐	☐
no liability	liability but no punishment	1 day	2 wks.	2 mo.	6 mo.	1 yr.	3 yrs.	7 yrs.	15 yrs.	30 yrs.	life imprisonment	death

B. Then Existing Law

Uniform Code of Military Justice (1961)

Art. 80—Attempts

(a) An act, done with specific intent to commit an offense under this code, amounting to more than mere preparation and tending but failing to effect its commission, is an attempt to commit that offense.

(b) Any person subject to this code who attempts to commit any offense punishable by this code shall be punished as a court-martial may direct, unless otherwise specifically prescribed.

(c) Any person subject to this code may be convicted of an attempt to commit an offense although it appears on the trial that the offense was consummated.

Art. 81—Conspiracy

Any person subject to this code who conspires with any other person or persons to commit an offense under this code shall, if one or more of the conspirators does an act to effect the object of the conspiracy, be punished as a court-martial may direct.

Art. 120—Rape and carnal knowledge

(a) Any person subject to this code who commits an act of sexual intercourse with a female not his wife, by force and without her consent, is guilty of rape and shall be punished by death or such other punishment as a court-martial may direct.

(b) Any person subject to this code who, under circumstances not amounting to rape, commits an act of sexual intercourse with a female not his wife who has not attained the age of sixteen years, is guilty of carnal knowledge and shall be punished as a court-martial may direct.

(c) Penetration, however slight, is sufficient to complete these offenses.

Art. 128—Assault

(a) Any person subject to this code who attempts or offers with unlawful force or violence to do bodily harm to another person, whether or not the attempt or offer is consummated, is guilty of assault and shall be punished as a court-martial may direct.

(b) Any person subject to this code who–

(1) commits an assault with a dangerous weapon or other means or force likely to produce death or grievous bodily harm; or

(2) commits an assault and intentionally inflicts grievous bodily harm with or without a weapon; is guilty of aggravated assault and shall be punished as a court martial may direct.

Art. 134—General article

Though not specifically mentioned in this code, all disorders and neglects to the prejudice of good order and discipline in the armed forces, all conduct of a nature to bring discredit upon the armed forces, and crimes and offenses not capital, of which persons subject to this code may be guilty, shall be taken cognizance of by a general or special or summary court-martial, according to the nature and degree of the offense, and punished at the discretion of such court.

C. Current Law That Would Be Applied Were the Case Prosecuted Today

[Statutory changes are not relevant except the following:]

Uniform Code of Military Justice (2006)

[Prospective amendment effective October 1, 2007]

Art. 120—Rape, sexual assault, and other sexual misconduct

(a) Rape. Any person subject to this chapter [10 USCS §§ 801 et seq.] who causes another person of any age to engage in a sexual act by—

(1) using force against that other person;

(2) causing grievous bodily harm to any person;

(3) threatening or placing that other person in fear that any person will be subjected to death, grievous bodily harm, or kidnaping;

(4) rendering another person unconscious; or

(5) administering to another person by force or threat of force, or without the knowledge or permission of that person, a drug, intoxicant, or other similar substance and thereby substantially impairs the ability of that other person to appraise or control conduct;

is guilty of rape and shall be punished as a court-martial may direct.

*   *   *

(c) Aggravated sexual assault. Any person subject to this chapter [10 USCS §§ 801 et seq.] who—

(1) causes another person of any age to engage in a sexual act by—

(A) threatening or placing that other person in fear (other than by threatening or placing that other person in fear that any person will be subjected to death, grievous bodily harm, or kidnapping); or

(B) causing bodily harm; or

(2) engages in a sexual act with another person of any age if that other person is substantially incapacitated or substantially incapable of—

(A) appraising the nature of the sexual act;

(B) declining participation in the sexual act; or

(C) communicating unwillingness to engage in the sexual act;

is guilty of aggravated sexual assault and shall be punished as a court-martial may direct.

*   *   *

(e) Aggravated sexual contact. Any person subject to this chapter [10 USCS §§ 801 et seq.] who engages in or causes sexual contact with or by another person, if to do so would violate subsection (a) (rape) had the sexual contact been a sexual act, is guilty of aggravated sexual contact and shall be punished as a court-martial may direct.

*   *   *

(h) Abusive sexual contact. Any person subject to this chapter [10 USCS §§ 801 et seq.] who engages in or causes sexual contact with or by another person, if to do so would violate subsection (c) (aggravated sexual assault) had the sexual contact been a sexual act, is guilty of abusive sexual contact and shall be punished as a court-martial may direct.

*   *   *

(k) Indecent act. Any person subject to this chapter [10 USCS §§ 801 et seq.] who engages in indecent conduct is guilty of an indecent act and shall be punished as a court-martial may direct.

* * *

(m) Wrongful sexual contact. Any person subject to this chapter [10 USCS §§ 801 et seq.] who, without legal justification or lawful authorization, engages in sexual contact with another person without that other person's permission is guilty of wrongful sexual contact and shall be punished as a court-martial may direct.

(n) Indecent exposure. Any person subject to this chapter [10 USCS §§ 801 et seq.] who intentionally exposes, in an indecent manner, in any place where the conduct involved may reasonably be expected to be viewed by people other than members of the actor's family or household, the genitalia, anus, buttocks, or female areola or nipple is guilty of indecent exposure and shall by punished as a court-martial may direct.

* * *

(r) Consent and mistake of fact as to consent. Lack of permission is an element of the offense in subsection (m) (wrongful sexual contact). Consent and mistake of fact as to consent are not an issue, or an affirmative defense, in a prosecution under any other subsection, except they are an affirmative defense for the sexual conduct in issue in a prosecution under subsection (a) (rape), subsection (c) (aggravated sexual assault), subsection (e) (aggravated sexual contact), and subsection (h) (abusive sexual contact).

(s) Other affirmative defenses not precluded. The enumeration in this section of some affirmative defenses shall not be construed as excluding the existence of others.

(t) Definitions. In this section:

(1) Sexual act. The term "sexual act" means—

(A) contact between the penis and the vulva, and for purposes of this subparagraph contact involving the penis occurs upon penetration, however slight; or

(B) the penetration, however slight, of the genital opening of another by a hand or finger or by any object, with an intent to abuse, humiliate, harass, or degrade any person or to arouse or gratify the sexual desire of any person.

(2) Sexual contact. The term "sexual contact" means the intentional touching, either directly or through the clothing, of the genitalia, anus, groin, breast, inner thigh, or buttocks of another person, or intentionally causing another person to touch, either directly or through the clothing, the genitalia, anus, groin, breast, inner thigh, or buttocks of any person, with an intent to abuse, humiliate, or degrade any person or to arouse or gratify the sexual desire of any person.

(3) Grievous bodily harm. The term "grievous bodily harm" means serious bodily injury. It includes fractured or dislocated bones, deep cuts, torn members of the body, serious damage to internal organs, and other severe bodily injuries. It does not include minor injuries such as a black eye or a bloody nose. It is the same level of injury as in section 928 (article 128) of this chapter [10 USCS § 928], and a lesser degree of injury than in section 2246(4) of title 18 [18 USCS § 2246(4)].

(4) Dangerous weapon or object. The term "dangerous weapon or object" means—

(A) any firearm, loaded or not, and whether operable or not;

(B) any other weapon, device, instrument, material, or substance, whether animate or inanimate, that in the manner it is used, or is intended to be used, is known to be capable of producing death or grievous bodily harm; or

(C) any object fashioned or utilized in such a manner as to lead the victim under the circumstances to reasonably believe it to be capable of producing death or grievous bodily harm.

(5) Force. The term "force" means action to compel submission of another or to overcome or prevent another's resistance by—

(A) the use or display of a dangerous weapon or object;

(B) the suggestion of possession of a dangerous weapon or object that is used in a manner to cause another to believe it is a dangerous weapon or object; or

(C) physical violence, strength, power, or restraint applied to another person, sufficient that the other person could not avoid or escape the sexual conduct.

* * *

(8) Bodily harm. The term "bodily harm" means any offensive touching of another, however slight.

* * *

(10) Lewd act. The term "lewd act" means—

(A) the intentional touching, not through the clothing, of the genitalia of another person, with an intent to abuse, humiliate, or degrade any person, or to arouse or gratify the sexual desire of any person; or

(B) intentionally causing another person to touch, not through the clothing, the genitalia of any person with an intent to abuse, humiliate or degrade any person, or to arouse or gratify the sexual desire of any person.

(11) Indecent liberty. The term "indecent liberty" means indecent conduct, but physical contact is not required. It includes one who with the requisite intent exposes one's genitalia, anus, buttocks, or female areola or nipple to a child. An indecent liberty may consist of communication of indecent language as long as the communication is made in the physical presence of the child. If words designed to excite sexual desire are spoken to a child, or a child is exposed to or involved in sexual conduct, it is an indecent liberty; the child's consent is not relevant.

(12) Indecent conduct. The term "indecent conduct" means that form of immorality relating to sexual impurity which is grossly vulgar, obscene, and repugnant to common propriety, and tends to excite sexual desire or deprave morals with respect to sexual relations. Indecent conduct includes observing, or making a videotape, photograph, motion picture, print, negative, slide, or other mechanically, electronically, or chemically reproduced visual material, without another person's consent, and contrary to that other person's reasonable expectation of privacy, of—

(A) that other person's genitalia, anus, or buttocks, or (if that other person is female) that person's areola or nipple; or

(B) that other person while that other person is engaged in a sexual act, sodomy (under section 925 (article 125)), or sexual contact.

* * *

(14) Consent. The term "consent" means words or overt acts indicating a freely given agreement to the sexual conduct at issue by a competent person. An expression of lack of consent through words or conduct means there is no consent. Lack of verbal or physical resistance or submission resulting from the accused's use of force, threat of force, or placing another person in fear does not constitute consent. A current or previous dating relationship by itself or the manner of dress of the person involved with the accused in the sexual conduct at issue shall not constitute consent. A person cannot consent to sexual activity if—

(A) under 16 years of age; or

(B) substantially incapable of—

(i) appraising the nature of the sexual conduct at issue due to—

(I) mental impairment or unconsciousness resulting from consumption of alcohol, drugs, a similar substance, or otherwise; or

(II) mental disease or defect which renders the person unable to understand the nature of the sexual conduct at issue;

(ii) physically declining participation in the sexual conduct at issue; or

(iii) physically communicating unwillingness to engage in the sexual conduct at issue.

* * *

13.   THE CASE OF JOSEPH A. BAILEY (VIRGINIA, 1983)

A.   THE FACTS

A burst of static erupts from a citizens' band radio in Roanoke, Virginia on the night of Saturday, May 21, 1983. Rebel, a local CB operator, broadcasts a message for all to hear, although it is directed at one man in particular: "I know where you at, know how to get at you. Now don't worry me, boy, because I guarantee you, you ain't man enough to walk out on the damn front porch and do your thing.... I's going to meet you down there with my hands tied behind me and kick the shit out of you with my feet, 'cause you be one of them 'ole Army faggots, just like George S. Patton. [I'll] come over personally and put a pineapple [grenade] up your ass and pill the pin on it. How about that?"

Black Panther answers back, telling Rebel: "You ain't got guts enough to come over here and see me, you understand that, Rebel? You think you so damn big on the goddamn radio and you can whip every damn son of a bitch on the radio ... I'm gonna tell you one thing. I'm gonna take care of you. Please don't come, please don't do it, 'cause I don't want to do what I'm gonna have to do.... but the Black Panther be waiting on you. You're nothing but a damn yellow-back son of a bitch. That's all."

Rebel, incensed, yells into his microphone: "Back up, boy, 'cause I'm going to get your ass. You hear me? Talk and listen, 'cause I'm going to come up there in a blue and white car and I'm going to kick the shit out of you, boy.... You get your 357 Magnum out there on your front porch and you just have it in your hands, just awaiting for me, and I'll be there in just a minute. So don't worry about it, just get out there on the porch. Get on the porch, because I want a piece of your ass, boy."

The radio goes silent as Black Panther goes to sit on his front porch, gun in hand. It is around 10:45 p.m.

* * *

Figure 27. Gordon Edward Murdock. (Roanoke Times)

Black Panther and Rebel are better known as George Edward Murdock and Joseph A. Bailey, both residents of the Roanoke area and rancorous enemies over the airwaves. For three years, the two have traded verbal blows a few nights per week, often generating complaints from other area CB users. Interestingly, the two have met once before—Bailey came to Murdock's house on Conway Street years ago, in order to help fix a broken microphone wire on Murdock's radio.

Murdock himself is a retired 70–year-old veteran of World War II, who has been living alone since the death of his wife a few years before. Though he can see shape and colors, his eyesight has deteriorated to the point that he has been declared legally blind. In January 1983, an optometrist reports that Murdock has 20/1,300 vision—meaning that text that a normal person could read from 1,300 feet away can be read by Murdock only if it were 20 feet or closer. In addition to his vision problems, Murdock suffers from a quick temper, exacerbated by his increasingly impaired mental function—a result of advanced age.

Bailey, almost thirty years younger than Murdock, is a truck driver from Vinton, Virginia and a longtime CB radio operator. As is normal in CB circles, he has a large group of over-the-air friends with whom he talks on a regular basis. The CB radio community around Roanoke is large and active, though it is not as large as it was in the 1970s. Nonetheless, both Rebel and Black Panther are recognizable names around Roanoke, and are notorious characters both on and off the air. Murdock, in particular, is known to the police as a cranky old man with a history of drinking problems. In the past, he has called the police dozens of times, usually complaining about trespassers on his lawn. On one occasion, he fired his pistol at suspected prowlers.

On the afternoon of May 21, 1983, Bailey receives a phone call from his sister, who tells him that she caught her husband molesting her seventeen year old daughter that morning. Bailey is extremely upset and decides to deal with his anger as best he knows how—by purchasing a twelve-pack of beer from his local convenience store. Over the course of the afternoon, Bailey drinks all twelve beers, and finishes off a fifth of liquor, in the process becoming quite inebriated. Across town, Murdock is following suit, drinking until he reaches a .271% blood alcohol level; this is almost three times the limit at which one would be arrested for DUI if caught driving.

Bailey, already angered by the afternoon's events, decides to take out some frustration on Murdock via the CB radio. Almost immediately upon signing on and hearing Murdock talk, Bailey tells Murdock, "Here you are showing your ignorance again and you're in that bottle again real heavy running your mouth." Murdock, recognizing the voice of his long-time sparring partner, launches into a diatribe, railing against Bailey, his relatives, and life in general. Bailey decides to push him, accusing General George S. Patton (who Murdock idolizes) of being a homosexual. The argument escalates from there, becoming increasingly more personal as the two decide to have a duel on the front porch of Murdock's suburban residence. Bailey tells Murdock that he will arrive in a blue and white car, ready to fight, and that Bailey should be on his porch with his gun.

Figure 28. Joseph A. Bailey. (Roanoke Times)

* * *

Figure 29. The house on Conway Street where Murdock waited on his porch for Bailey's arrival. (Joshua Nowocin)

Rather than traveling to Murdock's house, however, Bailey dials 9–1–1, telling the dispatcher that a man is standing on his porch at the intersection of Conway and Baldwin streets waving a gun in the air. Bailey doesn't give his name or address, but tells the dispatcher "Maybe you oughta go see him." Police are dispatched and are on the way to Murdock's house when Bailey makes another call, this one nine minutes after the first. This time, he tells the dispatcher Murdock's name, and says "He's talking about shooting anything that moves." The dispatcher takes the call more seriously this time, assuring him that police are on the way. Again, Bailey refuses to tell the dispatcher his name or address.

Officer Willie Chambers of the Roanoke Police Department pulls to the side of the road, a few yards away from Murdock's house. A few minutes after he and his partner arrive, he sees a man walk out to the porch and sit down, taking an object out of his pocket and setting it beside him. Another police car pulls up, this one carrying Officers Turner and Beavers, who wait in the car as Chambers watches the scene for about five minutes. In that time, Murdock makes no threatening movements, but Chambers worries that the man may have made the threats reported to the emergency dispatcher. After conferring with the other officers, Chambers decides to get out of his car and approach the man.

With the other officers waiting a few yards from the house, Chambers approaches Murdock. It becomes obvious that the object laying on the porch is a gun, and Chambers orders Murdock to leave the gun alone and walk down the stairs. Chambers does not identify himself as an officer; he believes that the blue and white police cars and police uniforms on the men should make it obvious that he is a member of the force. Chambers does not know that Murdock is blind, nor is he aware of his intoxication. He does, however, know that Murdock has a history of reported mental problems.

Murdock curses at Chambers and reaches for his gun, prompting Chambers to draw his own gun and retreat to safety. Officer Beavers, who by this point has moved into position on the street in front of the house, yells: "Willie, he's got a gun!" A second later, shots ring out as Murdock shoots toward the area where Chambers had been standing seconds before.

Seeing the muzzle flash, Officer Beavers returns fire, shooting six times and hitting Murdock twice. One bullet enters his leg, and another enters his chest. Murdock immediately falls to the porch floor, gasping for breath. As Chambers checks to be sure that he has not been shot, Beavers approaches Murdock, laying on the floor. He looks up at he police officer and whispers "You shot me." Thirty seconds later, he says "I didn't know you was the police."

An ambulance arrives to take Murdock to Roanoke Community Hospital, where he is admitted in critical condition. He dies a few hours later, early in the morning of Sunday, May 22.

* * *

Would you convict Bailey for the death of Murdock? If so, what amount of punishment would you impose?

N	0	1	2	3	4	5	6	7	8	9	10	11
□	□	□	□	□	□	□	□	□	□	□	□	□
no liability	liability but no punishment	1 day	2 wks.	2 mo.	6 mo.	1 yr.	3 yrs.	7 yrs.	15 yrs.	30 yrs.	life imprison- ment	death

B. THEN EXISTING LAW

Code of Virginia (1983)

§ 18.2–32—First and second degree murder defined; punishment

Murder, other than capital murder, by poison, lying in wait, imprisonment, starving, or by any willful, deliberate, and premeditated killing, or in the commission of, or attempt to commit, arson, rape, forcible sodomy, inanimate object sexual penetration, robbery, burglary or abduction, except as provided in § 18.2–31, is murder of the first degree, punishable as a Class 2 felony.

All murder other than capital murder and murder in the first degree is murder of the second degree and is punishable as a Class 3 felony.

§ 18.2–33—Felony homicide defined; punishment

The killing of one accidentally, contrary to the intention of the parties, while in the prosecution of some felonious act other than those specified in §§ 18.2–31 and 18.2–32, is murder of the second degree and is punishable as a Class 3 felony.

§ 18.2–35—How voluntary manslaughter punished

Voluntary manslaughter is punishable as a Class 5 felony.

§ 18.2–36—How involuntary manslaughter punished

Involuntary manslaughter is punishable as a Class 5 felony.

§ 18.2–461—Giving false reports to police officers

It shall be unlawful for any person knowingly to give a false report as to the commission of any crime to any law-enforcement official with intent to mislead. Violation of the provisions of this section shall be punishable as a Class 1 misdemeanor.

Harris v. Commonwealth, 114 S.E. 597, 599–600 (Va. 1922)

Every unlawful homicide is either murder or manslaughter; whether it is murder or manslaughter depends entirely on whether it was done with malice, either express or implied. A reasonable provocation is always necessary to reduce a felonious homicide from murder to manslaughter. Words alone, however insulting or contemptuous, are never a sufficient provocation, where a deadly weapon is used, to have that effect.

Pugh v. Commonwealth, 292 S.E.2d 339 (Va. 1982)

Murder is a homicide committed with malice, either express or implied. Express malice is present when "one person kills another with a sedate, deliberate mind, and formed design."

Implied malice exists when any "purposeful, cruel act is committed by one individual against another without any, or without great provocation." If the crime is significantly out of proportion to the provocation, malice is presumed.

Albert v. Commonwealth, 27 S.E.2d 177, 178 (Va. 1943)

"This in substance is the law on this subject as administered in Virginia: 'Involuntary manslaughter is the killing of one accidentally, contrary to the intention of the parties, in the prosecution of some unlawful, but not felonious, act; or in the improper performance of a lawful act.' 1 East. P.C., ch. 12, sec. 1."

Collins v. Commonwealth, 307 S.E.2d 884, 890 (Va. 1983)

"[A] defendant may not escape criminal responsibility for a crime which he arranges to have committed by an unwitting agent."

C.   CURRENT LAW THAT WOULD BE APPLIED WERE THE CASE PROSECUTED TODAY

[Statutory changes are not relevant]

CHAPTER 5. CAN THERE BE CRIMINAL LIABILITY WITHOUT PROVING THAT THE DEFENDANT SATISFIES THE ELEMENTS OF AN OFFENSE? DOCTRINES OF IMPUTATION

14. THE CASE OF KEITH MONDELLO (NEW YORK, 1989)

A. THE FACTS

Bensonhurst is a predominantly white, working-class neighborhood in Brooklyn, New York with roughly 150,000 residents. Half of the residents are Italian immigrants, most of whom emigrated from Sicily and southern Italy. Of the remaining half, a majority are second- or third-generation Italian–American. While Bensonhurst has a sizable Hispanic population, the black population is small, approximately 7,000. The dominant Italian presence is evident in the many Italian language street signs and store window advertisements.

The cultural influence of its southern Italian and Sicilian residents creates a unique environment in Bensonhurst. Moving two or three blocks away is considered moving "out of the neighborhood." The neighborhood is often described as "a big family." Bensonhurst residents take pride in their neighborhood, where family life is very important. Perhaps in an attempt to replicate the village environment of the home country, a sense of defensive protection against intrusion exists in which outsiders are perceived as threats. Many landlords do not rent to otherwise qualified non-Italians.

In private social clubs scattered throughout Bensonhurst, one can find older men drinking cups of darkly brewed espresso. Italian pastry, pasta, and pork shops, many of which import their merchandise from Italy, are located on Bensonhurst streets, as are 2- and 3-story well-kept homes. A number of homes have religious statues in the front yard, often of the Virgin Mary. Young men and teenagers often gather on street corners where they drink, smoke, and talk in a local form of macho slang.

Each night, one such group gathers outside the "Snacks and Candies" store, on the corner of 68th Street and 20th Avenue. One of the group's leaders is 18-year-old Keith Mondello, who is one-half Italian (his mother is Jewish but converted to Catholicism). Mondello has spent all of his life in Bensonhurst. He lives across the street from the candy store and works as a construction supervisor at Digi Enterprises.

Above the candy store lives Gina Feliciano, a 17-year-old woman with a history of drug use who at one time was on friendly terms with Mondello. They dated for about a week in junior high school. Lately, however, the relationship between Mondello and Feliciano has deteriorated into a feud. Many Bensonhurst residents dislike Feliciano because she dates black and dark-skinned Latino men. Feliciano, who is half Puerto Rican and half Italian, feels "more comfortable" around black and Latino men than around the men in her neighborhood. The Feliciano apartment has no phone.

Late Monday, August 22, 1989, some black and Hispanic men Gina knows have a run-in with Keith Mondello and his crowd. Gina's friends had been playing music and goofing off in front of her building. Mondello tells them to leave, and after a little argument, they do. Feliciano then tells Mondello that she is going to invite her black and Puerto Rican friends to her apartment the following day for her 18th birthday party. Mondello tells her that blacks do not belong in the neighborhood, and that they might get hurt if they come to Bensonhurst. In response, Feliciano tells Mondello and his friends that about 30 of her black and Puerto Rican friends are coming the next day to beat them up.

Joey Fama, a 17-year-old Bensonhurst resident of Italian descent, is one of Mondello's friends. Fama dropped out of school in the 8th grade and now lives with his family at 1773 71st Street. At the age of 3, Fama was involved in an automobile accident that may have caused mental impairment. Prone to violence, he has a lower than normal IQ, reduced memory and cognitive flexibility, and a "fund of knowledge appropriate for an 8 or 9-year-old." Such symptoms are consistent with early-age brain damage.

Figure 30. Joey Fama. (Bettmann/Corbis)

Yusuf K. Hawkins, a black 16-year-old, lives in the predominantly black and Hispanic East New York section of Brooklyn. Hawkins is a good student who maintains an 85 average and has received many academic awards. He is a good basketball player and is beginning to master the slam dunk. Hawkins wants to be a technical engineer and is about to begin his studies at the East New York High School of Transit Technology, which is affiliated with the city's transit authority. He does not do drugs. Hawkins has two brothers, Freddy and Amir, 19 years old and 15 years old, respectively. Yusuf and Amir, are very close and do many things together. Hawkins plans to attend Transit Technology's three-day orientation on August 28, 1991. Excited about beginning school, Hawkins tells his mother, 36-year-old Diane Hawkins, "Mom, I can't wait till Monday comes." Hawkins' father, 35-year-old Moses Stewart, has purchased new clothes for his son to wear at his new school. Stewart describes Hawkins as pursuing "the American Dream." Hawkins does not know Gina Feliciano, and is unaware of the exchange between her and Mondello.

At 5:30 p.m. on Wednesday night, August 23, 1989, Sal "the Squid" Mannino, owner of the candy store where Mondello and his friends hang out, repeats to Mondello that Gina has threatened to bring her black and Hispanic friends to her 18th birthday party that night for a fight with the neighborhood crowd. At 7:30 p.m. Mondello begins to gather most of his friends in the schoolyard of Public School 205, next to the candy store. Included in the crowd are Bensonhurst residents 18-year-old Steven Curreri, 20-year-old Joseph Serrano, John Vento, 19-year-old Pasquale Raucci, 18-year-old Brian O'Donnell, and 24-year-old John Patino.

Mondello also reaches out to some people he knows over on 18th Avenue. That group, which includes Joey Fama, is older and tougher than the 68th Street boys. According to neighborhood lore, the young thugs from 18th Avenue are connected with the Mafia.

Joseph Gibbons, an African–American Bensonhurst resident and friend of Mondello's, helps his best friend Charles Stressler gather a box of eight "Big Man" baseball bats from Stressler's house. They bring the bats to the gathering and distribute them to the crowd, which by 8:30–9:00 p.m. has grown to about 30. Other members of the crowd have brought their own bats. Joey Fama has brought a gun. As the crowd gathers, Fama mentions that he is "carrying." Mondello is not present at the time Fama says this.

The young men posture, flexing their muscles and stretching their adolescent egos. As they wait, they talk about sports, women, and cars and pass the bats around, taking practice swings. Racial epithets, including "nigger" are used while the group waits. The young men in the crowd call back and forth such things as "Hey, let me see your bat!" and, "Yeah, that's a good bat."

Strains of "Happy Birthday" filter down from Gina's apartment, but it doesn't seem like much of a party. Only Gina, her mother, an aunt and a few others are there. Gina's own sister, Dawn, refuses to go. The only black or Hispanic within blocks is Gibbons, who helped bring the bats. The crowd numbers around 30, at least four times the number of those at the party. Gina pokes her head out the window a few times to mock Mondello and his friends. "You're all jealous because the black guys are getting all the white meat," she says at one

Figure 31. Yusuf Hawkins. (Bettmann/Corbis)

point. Later she shouts, "It's because you guys are all dead in bed." Then, around 9:00 p.m., the mood of the crowd changes. Their adrenaline has already peaked, and they begin to doubt that Gina's friends will show.

In East New York, Hawkins, his long-time friend Luther Sylvester, a 17-year-old student at Automotive High School, and another youth have spent most of the afternoon sitting on a stoop, talking about buying new sneakers. In the evening, Hawkins and Sylvester go to the home of their friend Claude Stanford to watch "Mississippi Burning," the movie based on the murder of three civil-rights activists in the 1960s. Stanford is an 18-year-old hardware store clerk.

Hawkins, Sylvester, and Stanford are joined at Stanford's home by another friend, Troy Banner, an 18-year-old high school graduate who works as an orderly at Brookdale Hospital. Earlier in the day, Banner telephoned Bensonhurst resident Nicholas Hadzinas in response to a newspaper classified advertisement offering Hadzinas' 1983 Pontiac G-200 for sale. Banner and Hadzinas have agreed that Banner will come that evening to Hadzinas' home at 1965 69th Street (also known as Bay Ridge Avenue) to see the car. Hawkins, Sylvester, and Stanford agree to accompany Banner.

Hadzinas directs Banner to take the "N" train to the 20th Avenue stop, and to walk several blocks up 20th Avenue to Hadzinas' home. After mistakenly boarding the "N" train travelling in the wrong direction, Hawkins and his friends transfer onto the correct train. At 9:20 p.m., they get off the train at 20th Avenue and 64th Street and walk into Bensonhurst, looking for the address where the car is located. Hawkins and his friends have never been to Bensonhurst and are unfamiliar with the neighborhood. Uncertain which way to go, Banner asks a passerby on 20th Avenue how to reach 69th Street. The group stops briefly at a nearby newsstand to buy batteries, film, and candy.

Walking east on 20th Avenue, the group stops again to ask a man directions to Bay Ridge Avenue. They continue on through the neighborhood, Banner clutching the piece of paper with the address. As they pass 67th Street, they are noticed by Chris Lomuto, who yells, "They're here!" Because blacks are rare in Bensonhurst, Mondello and the crowd believe Hawkins and his friends are the people Feliciano described. The group pours out of the schoolyard. Joseph Gibbons stays behind, saying he wants to guard the radio he brought along.

With Mondello and Fama in the lead, the group pursues Hawkins and his friends. Mondello brandishes a bat, while Fama runs clutching something in his hand. Unaware that the Bensonhurst group is approaching from behind, Hawkins and his friends turn left onto Bay Ridge Avenue. The whites, responding to the rallying cry, move around the corner in waves.

With the mob following them, Stressler, Patino, Fama and Mondello catch up and surround the blacks. Sylvester and Standford are stopped several yards up the block, while Hawkins is stopped nearest to the corner. Mondello stands next to Sylvester. John Vento shouts, "Is it them?" Backing up against a building adjacent to the sidewalk, Hawkins tells the crowd that he is looking for an address. Some of the Bensonhurst youths realize that Hawkins and his friends are not Feliciano's friends and back off.

Fama, standing on the curb about 12 feet to the left of Mondello and near Hawkins, pulls a chrome-plated .32 caliber semi-automatic pistol from his waistband. Hawkins screams "Oh shit! Oh shit! Oh shit!" Someone yells for Fama not to shoot, but he fires four shots at Hawkins from a distance of seven feet. Hawkins is backing away from Fama when two shots strike him in the chest and one hits him in the left hand. The two shots that enter the left side of Hawkins' chest, about one inch apart, pass through his lungs and heart. The bullets perforate his stomach and spleen. Hawkins staggers 15 yards and collapses on the sidewalk.

Figure 32. Keith Mondello after his arrest. (Bettmann/Corbis)

After seeing Hawkins fall, Mondello puts his hands over his head and takes off running with Stressler up 69th Street toward 21st Avenue, throwing the bats onto a lawn. The others also flee the scene, leaving Hawkins bleeding on the sidewalk. As Fama runs away, he gives the gun to Serrano (one of the Bensonhurst crowd). The weapon is never recovered. Elizabeth Galarza, a neighborhood woman, rushes to Hawkins, yells for someone to call 911, and holds the dying Hawkins' hand. Hawkins' friends, shaking, stand by Hawkins. An anonymous male caller phones 911 to report the shooting, and an ambulance arrives four minutes later. Hawkins is rushed to Maimonides Medical Center, but is pronounced dead on arrival at 9:39 p.m. There are no drugs or alcohol in Hawkins' system at the time of his death.

After the shooting, Mondello, Curreri, and Raucci go to Chris Lumoto's house, where they drink and watch a baseball game and rap videos. Later, Mondello goes to his girlfriend's house, where the police arrest him early the next day.

* * *

Would you convict Fama for the death of Hawkins? If so, what amount of punishment would you impose?

N	0	1	2	3	4	5	6	7	8	9	10	11
☐	☐	☐	☐	☐	☐	☐	☐	☐	☐	☐	☐	☐
no liability	liability but no punishment	1 day	2 wks.	2 mo.	6 mo.	1 yr.	3 yrs.	7 yrs.	15 yrs.	30 yrs.	life imprisonment	death

Would you convict Mondello for complicity in the death of Hawkins? If so, what amount of punishment would you impose?

N	0	1	2	3	4	5	6	7	8	9	10	11
☐	☐	☐	☐	☐	☐	☐	☐	☐	☐	☐	☐	☐
no liability	liability but no punishment	1 day	2 wks.	2 mo.	6 mo.	1 yr.	3 yrs.	7 yrs.	15 yrs.	30 yrs.	life imprisonment	death

B.   THEN EXISTING LAW

Consolidated Laws of New York (1989)

§ 15.05—Culpability; definitions of culpable mental states

The following definitions are applicable to this chapter:

(1) "Intentionally." A person acts intentionally with respect to a result or to conduct described by a statute defining an offense when his conscious objective is to cause such result or to engage in such conduct.

(2) "Knowingly." A person acts knowingly with respect to conduct or to a circumstance described by a statute defining an offense when he is aware that his conduct is of such nature or that such circumstance exists.

(3) "Recklessly." A person acts recklessly with respect to a result or to a circumstance described by a statute defining an offense when he is aware of and consciously disregards a substantial and unjustifiable risk that such result will occur or that such circumstance exists. The risk

must be of such nature and degree that disregard thereof constitutes a gross deviation from the standard of conduct that a reasonable person would observe in the situation. A person who creates such a risk but is unaware thereof solely by reason of voluntary intoxication also acts recklessly with respect thereto.

(4) "Criminal negligence." A person acts with criminal negligence with respect to a result or to a circumstance described by a statute defining an offense when he fails to perceive a substantial and unjustifiable risk that such result will occur or that such circumstance exists. The risk must be of such nature and degree that the failure to perceive it constitutes a gross deviation from the standard of care that a reasonable person would observe in the situation.

§ 20.00—Criminal liability for conduct of another

When one person engages in conduct which constitutes an offense, another person is criminally liable for such conduct when, acting with the mental culpability required for the commission thereof, he solicits, requests, commands, importunes, or intentionally aids such person to engage in such conduct.

§ 125.25—Murder in the second degree

A person is guilty of murder in the second degree when:

(1) With intent to cause the death of another person, he causes the death of such person or of a third person; except that in any prosecution under this subdivision, it is an affirmative defense that:

    (a) The defendant acted under the influence of extreme emotional disturbance for which there was a reasonable explanation or excuse, the reasonableness of which is to be determined from the viewpoint of a person in the defendant's situation under the circumstances as the defendant believed them to be. Nothing contained in this paragraph shall constitute a defense to a prosecution for, or preclude a conviction of, manslaughter in the first degree or any other crime; ...

        *   *   *

(2) Under circumstances evincing a depraved indifference to human life, he recklessly engages in conduct which creates a grave risk of death to another person, and thereby causes the death of another person; ...

Murder in the second degree is a class A–1 felony.

§ 125.20—Manslaughter in the first degree

A person is guilty of manslaughter in the first degree when:

(1) With intent to cause serious physical injury to another person, he causes the death of such person or of a third person; or

(2) With intent to cause the death of another person, he causes the death of such person or of a third person under circumstances which do not constitute murder because he acts under the influence of extreme emotional disturbance, as defined in paragraph (a) of subdivision one of section 125.25. The fact that homicide was committed under the influence of extreme emotional disturbance constitutes a mitigating circumstance reducing murder to manslaughter in the first degree and need not be proved in any prosecution initiated under this subdivision; ...

Manslaughter in the first degree is a class B felony.

§ 125.15—Manslaughter in the second degree

A person is guilty of manslaughter in the second degree when:

(1) He recklessly causes the death of another person; or

*   *   *

Manslaughter in the second degree is a class C felony.

§ 125.10—Criminally negligent homicide

A person is guilty of criminally negligent homicide when, with criminal negligence, he causes the death of another person.

Criminally negligent homicide is a class E felony.

§ 120.25—Reckless endangerment in the first degree

A person is guilty of reckless endangerment in the first degree when, under circumstances evincing a depraved indifference to human life, he recklessly engages in conduct which creates a grave risk of death to another person.

Reckless endangerment in the first degree is a class D felony.

§ 120.20—Reckless endangerment in the second degree

A person is guilty of reckless endangerment in the second degree when he recklessly engages in conduct which creates a substantial risk of serious physical injury to another person.

Reckless endangerment in the second degree is a class A misdemeanor.

§ 70.00—Sentence of imprisonment for felony

(1) Indeterminate sentence. Except as provided in subdivision four, a sentence of imprisonment for a felony shall be an indeterminate sentence. When such a sentence is imposed, the court shall impose a maximum term in accordance with the provisions of subdivision two of this section and the minimum period of imprisonment shall be as provided in subdivision three of this section.

(2) Maximum term of sentence. The maximum term of an indeterminate sentence shall be at least three years and the term shall be fixed as follows:

(a) For a class A felony, the term shall be life imprisonment;

(b) For a class B felony, the term shall be fixed by the court, and shall not exceed twenty-five years ...

(c) For a class C felony, the term shall be fixed by the court, and shall not exceed fifteen years;

(d) For a class D felony, the term shall be fixed by the court, and shall not exceed seven years; and

(e) For a class E felony, the term shall be fixed by the court and shall not exceed four years.

(3) Minimum period of imprisonment. The minimum period of imprisonment under an indeterminate sentence shall be at least one year and shall be fixed as follows:

(a) In the case of a class A felony, the minimum period shall be fixed by the court and specified in the sentence.

(i) For a class A–1 felony, such minimum period shall not be less than fifteen years nor more than twenty-five years.

(ii) For a class A–II felony, such minimum period shall not be less than three years nor more than eight years four months....

(b) Where the sentence is for a class B or class C violent felony offense ... the minimum period shall be fixed by the court pursuant to subdivision four of section 70.02. Where the sentence is for a class B felony offense specified in subdivision two of section 220.44, the minimum period must be fixed by the court at one-third of the maximum term imposed and must be specified in the sentence. Where the sentence is for any other felony, the minimum period shall be fixed by the court and specified in the sentence and shall be not less than one year nor more than one-third of the maximum term imposed....

(4) Alternative definite sentence for class D, E, and certain class C felonies. When a person, other than a second or persistent felony offender, is sentenced for a class D or class E felony, or to a class C felony specified in article two hundred twenty or article two hundred twenty-one, and the court, having regard to the nature and circumstances of the crime and the history and character of the defendant, is of the opinion that a sentence of imprisonment is necessary but that it would be unduly harsh to impose an indeterminate sentence, the court may impose a definite sentence of imprisonment and fix a term of one year or less.

C.   Current Law That Would Be Applied Were the Case Prosecuted Today

[Statutory changes are not relevant]

15. THE CASE OF JORDAN WEAVER (INDIANA, 1991)

A. THE FACTS

During the late afternoon of April 2, 1991 in Indianapolis, Jordan Weaver takes two "triple-dipped" paper blotter "hits" of a particularly potent batch of lysergic acid diethylamide (LSD, or "acid"). Later in the day, Weaver's girlfriend of fifteen months, Wendy Waldman, picks him up to go out to eat. The two had planned a "special night" together at Renee's Restaurant in Broad Ripple because 17-year-old Wendy is leaving for her spring break vacation in Florida. Jordan and Wendy's relationship has been a stormy one—a type of "fatal attraction" affair. Friends and relatives question why two people with such dissimilar interests have stayed together for so long. Wendy's parents have even forbidden her from seeing Jordan, although she continues to be drawn to his "exciting" personality. Wendy is a serious student, deeply involved with her family. She "morally" disapproves of drug use and drinking and driving.

Jordan, on the other hand, dropped out of high school in his junior year and is the product of a broken home, troubled by drug abuse and alcoholism. His parents divorced and both moved to Texas in August 1990, so he now lives with his twenty-year-old sister, her husband, and her two young children. His

Figure 33. Jordan Weaver. (Richard Miller, Indianapolis Star)

drug use began at age 12, when he got drunk for the first time, and continued with the use of marijuana at age 13, LSD at 15, and peyote, opium, and cocaine. Jordan has also "huffed" gasoline at other times. Within the last two years, he has "dropped acid" at least 15 times.

Before they leave for the restaurant, Jordan tells Wendy that he is tripping so hard that he is not sure he should go out. Usually when he takes acid he tries to remain with close friends in a secluded space so that he can "keep the trip under control." Upon Wendy's insistence, they decide to go out anyway. At the restaurant Jordan cannot read the menu due to the effects of the LSD, and he and Wendy argue about his drug use. Jordan ends up handing the waitress some money before they have ordered, then saying he is not hungry. Wendy makes up a story to explain the strange behavior, and the two quickly exit the restaurant. Outside, Jordan begins to say bizarre things: he asks Wendy if he is dead, tells her that he is Jesus Christ, and professes his love for another woman. This last comment sparks another argument, one that the couple has had repeatedly throughout their relationship. According to friends, Wendy is a jealous person who has "gone off the deep end" whenever Jordan has tried to break up with her.

Jordan and Wendy go back to his sister's apartment so that he can change his shirt. There, he sees the walls start to breathe and close in on him, watches random objects float through the air, and observes trails of light following objects in motion. He is shocked to see his sister's face begin to melt and distort. The couple leaves the apartment to go to Broad Ripple Park, where they meet their friends Kris Hettle, Tracie Glanzman, Jessica Godley, and Kurt Steigerwald. As Jordan begins to trip harder, Jordan's whole body becomes numb and he feels like "a slimy mold is crawling around" in his brain, and that "something is eating through his stomach." Jordan begins to act erratically in the park. The group decides to take him to the deserted Alverna Retreat Center, a former Franciscan monastery in the quiet far northside area of Indianapolis.

Figure 34. Alverna Retreat Center parking lot. (Marion County Superior Court Records)

At the Retreat Center, Wendy and the other friends try to get Jordan, who is acting increasingly agitated, to sit down on the blanket they have spread on the ground. Jordan refuses to sit down, and bites Wendy on her hand and fingers. Wendy then offers to have sex with Jordan, but he begins to wrestle Kurt to the ground and to lick and kiss Kurt's neck. Kris comes to help, but Weaver hits Kurt in the eye and escapes from both of them. He heads for Kurt's car, where Jessica is sitting. Jordan gets into the car, seizes Jessica by the throat, and begins to kiss her. When she resists, Jordan begins strangling her, and shouts at her, calling her "Wendy." Kurt and Kris grab a tire iron from the trunk of Kurt's car and hit Weaver twice in the head in an attempt to stop him from choking Jessica. The blows have no effect. They then throw a blanket over him and attempt to choke him. They eventually succeed in getting Weaver off of Jessica. As he seems to be in a completely irrational state, the group decides to put Jordan in the trunk of the car to take him to the hospital. When they fail to get him in the trunk, they think about hitting him with the car in order to stop his attacks.

Figure 35. Wendy Waldman's car after Weaver's wreck. (Marion County Superior Court Records)

Weaver then goes after Wendy. He lifts her body up and hurls her head-first onto the pavement of the Center's parking lot. He begins slamming her head and face into the concrete. He pulls her head up by the hair and repeatedly punches her face. He "savagely" kicks her limp body while she lies on the ground. By the end of the beating, Wendy's face is a "bloody pulp" with no distinguishable features—her nose is smashed in, both her upper and lower jaw are shattered, her ears are "inside her head," she has lost five teeth, her chin is torn off, her eyes are swollen shut, many bones in her face are broken, and her brain is bruised. A state trooper who finds her later will have to clear teeth and blood from her throat so that she can breathe. Kurt, Kris, Jessica, and Tracy, who have been attempting to distract Weaver, drive away to get help.

Wendy is left comatose and lying face-down in a pool of blood on the pavement. Weaver jumps in her car and attempts to drive off, but does not make it far. Soon after he gets the Honda Civic rolling, Jordan hits a bush, causing the car to roll over on its side. Thinking that his spaceship has crashed and that he must break through its force field in order to get air to breathe, Weaver kicks through the windshield to escape. The Far Northside neighborhood that he walks into next is described by some as the "most quiet neighborhood in [Indianapolis]."

On the 8100 block of Round Hill Court, Weaver smashes through a closed bay window into the kitchen of Barbara and Michael Blickman. Michael Blickman, an attorney, races into the kitchen after hearing the glass shatter and is confronted with the "crazed" Weaver, who is covered with fresh blood. Fearing for his family's safety, Blickman smashes a chair over Weaver's head, then begins to wrestle with him in an effort to get him out of the house. During the scuffle, which lasts several minutes, Weaver shoves his hand and fingers into Blickman's mouth, choking Blickman. In response, Blickman bites down hard enough to draw blood. During the melee, Barbara Blickman screams and beats Weaver with a leg of the broken chair. Her screams are heard by the Blickmans' neighbors, sixty-four year old Jerome Sweeney, his wife, and their visiting twenty-six year old son Brian. Minutes earlier, Brian had heard Wendy's "blood-curdling" screams from the Retreat Center and realized that a girl "was either being killed or raped." He notified the sheriff's department. When the Sweeneys hear Barbara Blickman screaming that a man is in her house fighting with her husband, they rush outside just in time to see the sheriff's deputies arrive.

Figures 36 & 37. Michael Blickman and the broken window through which Weaver entered his kitchen. (Marion County Superior Court Records)

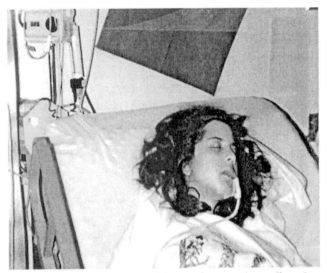

Figure 38. Wendy Waldman in a coma after the attack. (Marion County Superior Court Records)

Jerome Sweeney runs with two sheriff's deputies towards his back yard to show them a gap in the fence through which he thinks Jordan might have escaped. Jerome, however, had suffered a heart attack fifteen years earlier which left his heart in a weakened condition. The adrenalin rush of the chaos proves too much for the elderly steel company representative, and he collapses in his backyard from cardiac arrest. The two sheriff's deputies try to administer CPR until the paramedics arrive, but it is apparent that Jerome has "just dropped dead."

Meanwhile, Michael Blickman has managed to drag Weaver out of his house and into the driveway, where it takes five sheriff's deputies to subdue him. As he wrestles with the officers, Weaver repeatedly screams, "Get off me, pigs!"

* * *

Would you convict Jordan Weaver for his attack of Wendy Waldman? If so, what amount of punishment would you impose?

N	0	1	2	3	4	5	6	7	8	9	10	11
☐	☐	☐	☐	☐	☐	☐	☐	☐	☐	☐	☐	☐
no	liability	1 day	2 wks.	2 mo.	6 mo.	1 yr.	3 yrs.	7 yrs.	15 yrs.	30 yrs.	life	death
liability	but										imprison-	
	no										ment	
	punishment											

Would you convict Weaver for the death of Jerome Sweeney? If so, what amount of punishment would you impose?

N	0	1	2	3	4	5	6	7	8	9	10	11
☐	☐	☐	☐	☐	☐	☐	☐	☐	☐	☐	☐	☐
no	liability	1 day	2 wks.	2 mo.	6 mo.	1 yr.	3 yrs.	7 yrs.	15 yrs.	30 yrs.	life	death
liability	but										imprison-	
	no										ment	
	punishment											

B. THEN EXISTING LAW

Indiana Code (1991)

§ 35–42–1–1—Murder

Sec. 1. A person who:

(1) knowingly or intentionally kills another human being;

(2) kills another human being while committing or attempting to commit arson, burglary, child molesting, consumer product tampering, criminal deviate conduct, kidnaping, rape, robbery; or

* * *

commits murder, a felony.

§ 35–42–1–5—Reckless homicide

Sec. 5. A person who recklessly kills another human being commits reckless homicide, a Class C felony.

§ 35–42–1–4—Involuntary manslaughter

Sec. 4. A person who kills another human being while committing or attempting to commit:

(1) a Class C or Class D felony that inherently poses a risk of serious bodily injury;

(2) a Class A misdemeanor that inherently poses a risk of serious bodily injury; or

(3) battery;

commits involuntary manslaughter, a Class C felony. However, if the killing results from the operation of a vehicle, the offense is a Class D felony.

§ 35–42–2–1—Battery

(a) A person who knowingly or intentionally touches another person in a rude, insolent, or angry manner commits battery, a Class B misdemeanor. However, the offense is:

(1) a Class A misdemeanor if it results in bodily injury to any other person, or if it is committed against a law enforcement officer or against a person summoned and directed by the officer while the officer is engaged in the execution of his official duty.

(2) a Class D felony if it results in bodily injury to:

(A) a law enforcement officer or a person summoned and directed by a law enforcement officer while the officer is engaged in the execution of his official duty;

(B) a person less than fourteen (14) years of age and is committed by a person at least eighteen (18) years of age;

(C) a person of any age who is mentally or physically disabled and is committed by a person having the care of the mentally or physically disabled person, whether the care is assumed voluntarily or because of a legal obligation;

(D) the other person and the person who commits the battery was previously convicted of a battery in which the victim was the other person;

(E) an endangered adult (as defined by IC 35–46–1–1);

(F) an employee of the department of correction while the employee is engaged in the execution of the employee's official duty;

(3) a Class C felony if it results in serious bodily injury to any other person or if it is committed by means of a deadly weapon.

§ 35–42–2–2—Criminal recklessness

(a) A person who recklessly, knowingly or intentionally performs an act that creates a substantial risk of bodily injury to another person commits criminal recklessness, a Class B misdemeanor. However, the offense is a:

(1) Class A misdemeanor if the conduct includes the use of a vehicle; or

(2) Class D felony if it is committed while armed with a deadly weapon.

(b) A person who recklessly, knowingly or intentionally inflicts serious bodily injury on another person commits criminal recklessness, a Class D felony. However, the offense is a Class C felony if committed by means of a deadly weapon.

§ 35–41–1–4—"Bodily injury" defined

"Bodily injury" means any impairment of physical condition, including physical pain.

§ 35–41–1–25—"Serious bodily injury" defined

"Serious bodily injury" means bodily injury that creates a substantial risk of death or that causes serious permanent disfigurement, unconsciousness, extreme pain, or permanent or protracted loss or impairment of the function of a bodily member or organ.

§ 35–41–2–2—Culpability

(a) A person engages in conduct "intentionally" if, when he engages in the conduct, it is his conscious objective to do so.

(b) A person engages in conduct "knowingly" if, when he engages in the conduct, he is aware of a high probability that he is doing so.

(c) A person engages in conduct "recklessly" if he engages in the conduct in plain, conscious, and unjustifiable disregard of harm that might result and the disregard involves a substantial deviation from acceptable standards of conduct.

(d) Unless the statute defining the offense provides otherwise, if a kind of culpability is required for commission of an offense, it is required with respect to every material element of the prohibited conduct.

§ 35–41–3–5—Intoxication

(a) It is a defense that the person who engaged in the prohibited conduct did so while he was intoxicated, if the intoxication resulted from the introduction of a substance into his body:

(1) without his consent; or

(2) when he did not know that the substance might cause intoxication.

(b) Voluntary intoxication is a defense only to the extent that it negates an element of an offense referred to by the phrase "with intent to" or "with intention to."

§ 35–41–5–1—Attempt

(a) A person attempts to commit a crime when, acting with the culpability required for commission of the crime, he engages in conduct that constitutes a substantial step toward commission of the crime. An attempt to commit a crime is a felony or misdemeanor of the same class as the crime attempted. However, an attempt to commit murder is a Class A felony.

(b) It is no defense that, because of a misapprehension of the circumstances, it would have been impossible for the accused person to commit the crime attempted.

Zickefoose v. Indiana, 270 Ind. 618, 388 N.E.2d 507 (1979)

Defendant was found guilty of attempted murder where he severely beat a woman using a deadly weapon and continued the attack even after she lost consciousness and fell down. "The emphasis in [the Indiana] statute is on what the defendant has already done toward committing the crime and not on what remains to be done."

Rhode v. State, 181 Ind. App. 265, 391 N.E.2d 666 (Ind. Ct. App. 1979)

Indiana's attempt law, § 35–41–5–1, does not permit an offense of "attempted reckless homicide." Citing the Model Penal Code commentary, the Court ruled that, despite the attempt statute's language that only "the culpability required for the commission of the offense" is required, a "specific intent" must be proven, since the very definition of attempt is "to try."

Terry v. State, 465 N.E.2d 1085 (Ind. 1984)

Section 35–41–3–5(b) violates the state constitution and is therefore invalid, since "the attempt by the legislature to remove [voluntary intoxication as a defense] goes against [the] firmly ingrained principle [that] intoxication may be offered to negate capacity to formulate intent. ... Any factor which serves as a denial of the existence of *mens rea* must be considered by a trier of fact before a guilty finding is entered."

C.   Current Law That Would Be Applied Were the Case Prosecuted Today

[Statutory changes not relevant, except the following:]

Indiana Code (2006)

§ 35–41–2–5—Intoxication

Intoxication is not a defense in a prosecution for an offense and may not be taken into consideration in determining the existence of a mental state that is an element of the offense unless the defendant meets the requirements of IC 35–41–3–5.

§ 35–41–3–5—Intoxication

(a) It is a defense that the person who engaged in the prohibited conduct did so while he was intoxicated, only if the intoxication resulted from the introduction of a substance into his body:

    (1) without his consent; or

    (2) when he did not know that the substance might cause intoxication.

~~(b) Voluntary intoxication is a defense only to the extent that it negates an element of an offense referred to by the phrase "with intent to" or "with intention to."~~

Sanchez v. State of Indiana, 749 N.E.2d 509 (Ind. 2001)

The court notes that in 1996, the United States Supreme Court held, in *Montana v. Egelhoff*, 518 U.S. 37 (1996), that the Fourteenth Amendment Due Process Clause is not offender by a statute that bars the use of evidence of voluntary intoxication to negate a culpable state of mind required by an offense definition. In response, the Indiana Legislature enacted Section 35–41–2–5. Relying on *Egelhoff* as to the federal constitution and reaching a similar conclusion with regard to their state constitution, the court held that *Terry v. State* was no longer good law and that the new statute was constitutional. [In *Egelhoff*, a plurality of the Court concluded that due process is offended only if an exclusion of evidence "offends some principle of justice so rooted in the traditions and conscience of our people as to be ranked as fundamental."]

CHAPTER 6. CAN COMMITTING A CRIME BE DOING THE RIGHT THING? JUSTIFICATION DEFENSES

16. THE CASE OF JOHN CHARLES GREEN (MISSOURI, 1967)

A. THE FACTS

John Charles Green is 19 years old, 5 feet 9 inches tall, and weighs 155 pounds. He has never known his father, and was separated from his mother as a child and placed in various foster homes. He does not know where any of his relatives live.

Green is convicted of burglary in the Circuit Court of Adair County, Missouri, on November 1, 1966, and is sentenced to three years imprisonment. The Department of Corrections receives him on November 4, and a month later he enters the Missouri Training Center for Men, a medium security prison in Moberly, Missouri.

MTC has a population of about 600 inmates. Most of the inmates are second offenders over 25 years old, a number of whom are serving life terms. During the night shift, two guards are assigned to each main building, each of which houses 300 inmates celled in four separate wings. Three case workers serve about 200 inmates each. There is one nurse and one chaplain. No "jail-house lawyers" are allowed. No legal services for indigent inmates are provided. The library contains only a set of the Missouri statutes.

Figure 39. Aerial view of the Missouri Training Center for Men at Moberly. (Missouri Department of Corrections)

It is commonly known that same-sex rapes occur within the prison. The Missouri Training Center has a procedure for dealing with complaints by one prisoner against another. When an inmate complains to a guard, the guard may take no action or may pass the complaint on for investigation. A prisoner also may complain directly to the prison administration, bypassing the guards, by sending a note through the prison mail. But such "snitch-kites," as they are known, are frequently examined by prisoners working in the prison mail system. Most prisoners are hesitant to use snitch-kites for fear of retaliation. Prison policy does not permit investigation of complaints or transfers unless the victim divulges the name of his assailant. Usually, the prisoner is left among his fellow inmates during the investigation, unless the guard witnesses the alleged assault. If an attack is investigated and confirmed, the victim can be given protective custody in "the hole," a special cell normally used to discipline prisoners.

On December 16, 1966, a few days after his arrival at MTC, Green appears before the disciplinary board for fighting, the result of fending off sexual advances by other prisoners. On January 2, 1967, after lights out, two men pick the lock on Green's cell—an easy and common practice. One man is about Green's size. The other is approximately six feet tall, weighing 200 pounds. Green yells for a guard, but the guard on duty is separated from the wing by a heavy door and does not respond. Green tries to push the first man aside but the second man grabs him, holds a knife to his throat, and threatens to stab him if he does not "cooperate" with them. Green then submits to rape by both men.

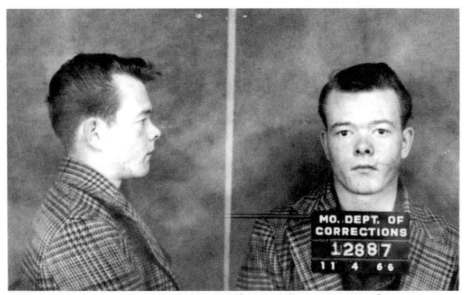

Figure 40. John Charles Green. (Missouri Department of Corrections)

Figure 41. The administrative staff of the Missouri Training Center for Men at Moberly in the 1960's, from left: Major Wilbur Morgan, Donald Hartness, Jerry Heming, Lew Walker, Superintendent Edward Haynes, Vern Baker, John Kozlowski, and Ernest McNealy. (Missouri Department of Corrections)

Green then submits to rape by both men.

Several minutes after the assailants leave, Green slits his own arm in order to get removed from the inmate population, then goes for a guard. He is taken to the prison hospital, where he is kept for several days. Green reports the incident to Donald Hartness, the Assistant Superintendent of Treatment, and asks to be moved from the general population in order to avoid further attacks. Green refuses to name his attackers for fear that he will be killed. Hartness tells him he must resolve his own problems and suggests that he go back and fight it out. Despite his objections, Green is returned to his old cell.

Several days later, again after lights out, three men pick Green's lock and enter his cell. Green attempts to run, but is knocked out. He wakes up later with anal pain and discovers "grease" in his anal area. Realizing that he has been raped again, he feigns having swallowed glass so that he can talk to an official without the other inmates knowing, and asks a guard to hospitalize him.

The next day, Green is brought before the disciplinary board and charged with self-destruction. The disciplinary board is composed of Mr. Baldwin (the Assistant Superintendent of Custody), Mr. Hartness, and a guard. Green describes the assaults and asks for protective custody. He again refuses to give his attackers' names. Mr. Baldwin tells Green that the best he can do is to arrange a wing change. He advises Green to "fight it out, submit to the assaults, or go over the fence." The Board assigns no punishment for the violation charged. The Superintendent of the center, Edward Haynes, reviews the hearing's record and approves Green's cell change to an adjoining wing.

Edward E. Haynes   A. H. Baldwin

Figure 42. Moberly prison officials. (Missouri Department of Corrections)

When Green is moved to the new wing, other prisoners taunt him. He also is propositioned for sex by a guard, named Petre. He reports this to Captain Chapman, and the guard is transferred.

At noon on April 14, 1967, five inmates come to Green's cell and tell him that they will come for him that night to gang rape him, and that he will be their "punk" (the person who is penetrated in male same-sex intercourse) for the remainder of his time in prison. They threaten to seriously injure or to kill him if he does not cooperate.

As before, the lock in Green's cell can easily be picked. Because his past reports have been futile, Green decides not to tell authorities of the threat of gang rape, but to escape instead. Around 6:00 p.m. that day, he quietly climbs over the fence near the power house on the west side of the institution and walks down a railroad track for a short distance, across several fields, and along a nearby highway.

At the 10:00 p.m. bed check, he is reported missing and a search begins.

Around 4:00 a.m., Green comes across a car in the driveway of William Wagner, Jr., north of Yates. The keys are in the car, so he starts the engine and begins maneuvering the car out of the driveway, but with some difficulty. Wagner, awakened by the engine, yells at him from the house, and Green runs off. Wagner notifies the police. Early that afternoon, Trooper Roy Robinson comes across Green, who is sitting beside the road looking at a highway map. He takes Green into custody without incident and returns him to Moberly. Green is charged with escape.

*   *   *

Would you convict Green of escape? If so, what amount of punishment would you impose?

N	0	1	2	3	4	5	6	7	8	9	10	11
☐	☐	☐	☐	☐	☐	☐	☐	☐	☐	☐	☐	☐
no liability	liability but no punishment	1 day	2 wks.	2 mo.	6 mo.	1 yr.	3 yrs.	7 yrs.	15 yrs.	30 yrs.	life imprisonment	death

B. Then Existing Law

Missouri Statutes (1967)

§ 557.351—Escapes or attempts to escape from state institutions or custody, penalty

Any person sentenced to the state division of corrections upon conviction of escaping or attempting to escape from any state institution in which he was lawfully confined or from the lawful custody of any person or willfully failing to remain within the extended limits of confinement or to return to an institution or facility designated by the director of the division of corrections when permitted to go at large shall be sentenced to the division of corrections for a term of not less than two and not exceeding five years.

State v. King, 372 S.W.2d 857 (Mo. App. 1963)

Defendant appealed his conviction for attempt to escape a penitentiary by claiming that his underlying conviction of robbery was unlawful and that his solitary confinement in the penitentiary was cruel and unusual punishment. The court affirmed the conviction and held that "an attempt to escape is not justifiable because the conditions of imprisonment were intolerable or inhumane."

State v. St. Clair, 262 S.W.2d 25 (Mo. 1953)

The court allowed defendant to raise a duress defense to a charge of robbery, based on allegations that two men displayed a shotgun and threatened to kill him if he did not commit the offense. "To constitute a defense to a criminal charge, the coercion must be present, imminent, and impending and of such a nature as to induce a well grounded apprehension of death or serious bodily injury if the act is not done. Threat of future injury is not enough. Nor can one who has a reasonable opportunity to avoid doing the act without undue exposure to death or serious bodily injury invoke the doctrine as an excuse."

People v. Richards, 269 Cal. App.2d 768 (1969)

Defendant was denied a duress and a necessity defense for escaping from a state correctional facility after he had been repeatedly sexually assaulted, received no help from prison officials, and learned that inmates planned to kill him within a few days. "In order for duress or fear produced by threats or menace to be a valid ... excuse, ... the act must have been done under such threats or menaces as show that the life of the person threatened or menaced was in danger.... The danger must not be one of future violence, but of present and immediate violence at the time of the commission of the forbidden act. The danger of death at some future time" will not excuse. The defense of necessity was denied since "this is not a case where the prisoner departed from the limits of his custody while pursued by those who would take his life ... or by those who sought by force and violence to have him submit to sodomy.... The evil sought to be prevented is not only the escape of the prisoner in question, but also ... the destruction of the general discipline of the prison."

C. Current Law That Would Be Applied Were the Case Prosecuted Today

Missouri Statutes (2006)

§ 575.210—Escape or attempted escape from confinement

1. A person commits the crime of escape or attempted escape from confinement if, while being held in confinement after arrest for any crime, while serving a sentence after conviction for

any crime, or while at an institutional treatment center operated by the department of corrections as a condition of probation or parole, he escapes or attempts to escape from confinement.

2. Escape or attempted escape from confinement in the department of corrections is a class B felony.

3. Escape or attempted escape from confinement in a county or city correctional facility is a class D felony except that it is:

(1) A class A felony if it is effected or attempted by means of a deadly weapon or dangerous instrument or by holding any person as hostage;

(2) A class C felony if escape or attempted escape is facilitated by striking or beating any person.

§ 558.011—Sentence of imprisonment, terms—conditional release

1. The authorized terms of imprisonment, including both prison and conditional release terms, are:

(1) For a class A felony, a term of years not less than ten years and not to exceed thirty years, or life imprisonment;

(2) For a class B felony, a term of years not less than five years and not to exceed fifteen years;

(3) For a class C felony, a term of years not to exceed seven years;

(4) For a class D felony, a term of years not to exceed four years;

(5) For a class A misdemeanor, a term not to exceed one year;

(6) For a class B misdemeanor, a term not to exceed six months;

(7) For a class C misdemeanor, a term not to exceed fifteen days.

§ 562.071—Duress

1. It is an affirmative defense that the defendant engaged in the conduct charged to constitute an offense because he was coerced to do so, by the use of, or threatened imminent use of, unlawful physical force upon him or a third person, which force or threatened force a person of reasonable firmness in his situation would have been unable to resist.

2. The defense of "duress" as defined in subsection 1 is not available:

(1) As to the crime of murder;

(2) As to any offense when the defendant recklessly places himself in a situation in which it is probable that he will be subjected to the force or threatened force described in subsection 1.

§ 563.026—Justification generally

1. Unless inconsistent with other provisions of this chapter defining justifiable use of physical force, or with some other provision of law, conduct which would otherwise constitute any crime other than a class A felony or murder is justifiable and not criminal when it is necessary as an emergency measure to avoid an imminent public or private injury which is about to occur by reason of a situation occasioned or developed through no fault of the actor, and which is of such gravity that, according to ordinary standards of intelligence and morality, the desirability of avoiding the injury outweighs the desirability of avoiding the injury sought to be prevented by the statute defining the crime charged.

2. The necessity and justifiability of conduct under subsection 1 may not rest upon considerations pertaining only to the morality and advisability of the statute, either in its general applica-

tion or with respect to its application to a particular class of cases arising thereunder. Whenever evidence relating to the defense of justification under this section is offered, the court shall rule as a matter of law whether the claimed facts and circumstances would, if established, constitute a justification.

    3.   The defense of justification under this section is an affirmative defense.

City of St. Louis v. Klocker, 637 S.W.2d 174 (Mo. Ct. App. 1982)

The defense of necessity generally contains three elements: "1) the act charged must have been done to prevent a significant (harm); 2) there must have been no adequate alternative; 3) the harm caused must not have been disproportionate to the harm avoided ... The accepted norms of society determine the relative harmfulness of the two alternatives."

17. THE CASE OF JOHANN SCHLICHT (GERMANY, 1919)

A. THE FACTS

In early November 1918, conditions in Germany are difficult. Four years of sustained conflict in World War I have left the country's infrastructure in shambles. The government's emphasis on industrial war production, its ill-advised agricultural policies, and the Allied embargo have all conspired to make food shortages and rising prices commonplace. Popular morale is low. Malnourishment is common. The shortages and price increases prompt protests and strikes, and occasionally riots. A revolution starts with a mutiny at the naval base at Kiel on November 3, and soon spreads to the civilian populace, culminating in the abdication of the Kaiser on November 10, 1918. The next day, World War I comes to an end as Germany surrenders.

Figures 43 & 44. Civil unrest in the streets of Berlin after the armistice. (Archive Photos)

While 1919 brings peace, it does not bring stability. In January 1919, food prices are 2.6 times higher than they were in 1913, before the war. The country endures the failed "Sparticist Revolt" in January, in which left-wing socialists, mostly workers and former soldiers, try to take over Berlin but are crushed by volunteer units loyal to the Social Democratic government. In April, local communists attempt to create a republic in Munich, but this also fails. The food shortages, price jumps, and the accompanying protests continue. By December 1919, food prices are 4.5 times higher than they were in 1913.

Tension between residents of the urban and of the rural regions has existed for some time and is greatly exacerbated by the food shortages. Urban residents resent that rural dwellers have more food. Rural farmers resent the government price controls, perceived as governmental bias favoring urban interests. One writer describes the situation this way:

> Thefts of farmers' crops by a hungry urban population provide country dwellers with all the proof they need of the dangerous and depraved nature of the inhabitants of Germany's cities. Such thefts reach epidemic proportion in the aftermath of the War. An undernourished urban population, which has suffered for years from inadequate food-rations and extortionate black-market prices for food, make self-service expeditions into farmers' fields, as the ability of the police ... to control lawbreaking plummets.

This is the situation that faces Johann Schlicht, the owner of a fruit orchard in Reindorf, in the Bavarian region. The police are wholly ineffective at stemming recurring thievery. Schlicht tries passive means of protecting his livelihood such as erecting fences around the orchard, but all measures prove ineffective. It becomes clear that the only effective means of protection will be the force of arms.

Neither the thieves nor Schlicht need the fruit to avoid starvation. The thieves want to have food without having to pay the inflated prices. Schlicht depends on selling the fruit to make a living and support his family.

Schlicht keeps watch at night, sitting in a shed amidst his fruit trees. He is armed with a loaded rifle and accompanied by his dog. In the early morning, two men sneak into the orchard and begin stealing fruit from the trees. Schlicht shouts at them to drop the fruit and threatens to shoot. They nonetheless begin running away with the fruit. As the only means left to him to prevent the thievery, Schlicht fires buckshot in their direction and seriously injures one of them, who is lucky not to be killed.

Schlicht is charged with intentional assault. He notes that law enforcement authorities have proven completely ineffective at stemming the thefts and that his less harmful attempts at protecting his fruit have all failed. His injury of the thief was the only means available to him to effectively protect his property.

*   *   *

Would you convict Schlicht for his assault of the thief? If so, what amount of punishment would you impose?

N	0	1	2	3	4	5	6	7	8	9	10	11
☐	☐	☐	☐	☐	☐	☐	☐	☐	☐	☐	☐	☐
no liability	liability but no punishment	1 day	2 wks.	2 mo.	6 mo.	1 yr.	3 yrs.	7 yrs.	15 yrs.	30 yrs.	life imprisonment	death

B. THEN EXISTING LAW

[none—a case of first impression]

C. Current Law That Would Be Applied Were the Case Prosecuted Today

Federal Republic of Germany—Penal Code (2002)

§ 22—Attempt

Whoever, in accordance with his understanding of the act, takes an immediate step towards the realization of the elements of the offense, attempts to commit a crime.

§ 23—Punishability of an Attempt

(1) The attempt to commit a felony is always punishable, while an attempt to commit a misdemeanor only is punishable if expressly provided by law.

(2) The attempt may be punished more leniently than the completed act (Section 49, subsection 1).

. . .

§ 211—Murder

(1) The murderer shall be punished with imprisonment for life.

(2) A murderer is, whoever kills a human being out of murderous lust, to satisfy his sexual desires, from greed or otherwise base motives, treacherously or cruelly or with means dangerous to the public or in order to make another crime possible or cover it up.

§ 212—Manslaughter

(1) Whoever kills a human being without being a murderer, shall be punished for manslaughter with imprisonment for not less than five years.

(2) In especially serious cases imprisonment for life shall be imposed.

§ 213—Less Serious Case of Manslaughter

If the person committing manslaughter was provoked to rage by maltreatment inflicted on him or a relative or a serious insult by the person killed and was thereby immediately torn to commit the act, or in the event of an otherwise less serious case, the punishment shall be imprisonment from one year to ten years.

§ 223—Bodily Injury

(1) Whoever physically maltreats or harms the health of another person, shall be punished with imprisonment for not more than five years or a fine.

(2) An attempt shall be punishable.

§ 224—Dangerous Bodily Injury

(1) Whoever commits bodily harm:

    1.   through the administration of poison or other substances dangerous to health;

    2.   by means of a weapon or other dangerous tool;

    3.   by means of a sneak attack;

    4.   jointly with another participant; or

    5.   by means of a treatment dangerous to life,

shall be punished with imprisonment from six months to ten years, in less serious cases with imprisonment from three months to five years.

(2) An attempt shall be punishable.

§ 226—Serious Bodily Injury

(1) If the bodily injury has, as a result, that the injured person:

    1. loses his sight in one eye or in both eyes, his hearing, his speech or his procreative capacity;

    2. loses or permanently can no longer use an important bodily member;

    3. is permanently disfigured in a substantial way or becomes infirm, paralyzed, mentally ill or disabled, then the punishment shall be imprisonment from one year to ten years.

(2) If the perpetrator intentionally or knowingly causes one of the results indicated in subsection (1), then the punishment shall be imprisonment for not less than three years.

(3) In less serious cases under subsection (2), imprisonment from six months to five years shall be imposed, in less serious cases under subsection (2), imprisonment from one year to ten years.

§ 229—Negligent Bodily Injury

Whoever negligently causes bodily injury to another person shall be punished with imprisonment for not more than three years or a fine.

§ 242—Theft

(1) Whoever takes moveable property not his own away from another with the intent of unlawfully appropriating the property for himself or a third person, shall be punished with imprisonment for not more than five years or a fine.

(2) An attempt shall be punishable.

§ 16—Mistake about Circumstances of the Act

(1) Whoever upon commission of the act is unaware of a circumstance which is a statutory element of the offense does not act intentionally. Punishability for negligent commission remains unaffected.

(2) Whoever upon commission of the act mistakenly assumes the existence of circumstances which would satisfy the elements of a more lenient norm, may only be punished for intentional commission under the more lenient norm.

§ 17—Mistake of Law

If upon commission of the act the perpetrator lacks the appreciation that he is doing something wrong, he acts without guilt if he was unable to avoid this mistake. If the perpetrator could have avoided the mistake, the punishment may be mitigated pursuant to Section 49 subsection (1).

§ 32—Necessity Defense

(1) Whoever commits an act, required as necessary defense, does not act unlawfully.

(2) Necessary defense is the defense which is required to avert an imminent unlawful assault from oneself or another.

§ 33—Excessive Necessity Defense

If the perpetrator exceeds the limits of necessary defense due to confusion, fear or fright, then he shall not be punished.

§ 34—Necessity as Justification

Whoever, faced with an imminent danger to life, limb, freedom, honor, property or another legal interest which cannot otherwise be averted, commits an act to avert the danger from himself or another, does not act unlawfully, if, upon weighing the conflicting interests, in particular the affected legal interests and the degree of danger threatening them, the protected interest substantially outweighs the one interfered with. This shall apply, however, only to the extent that the act is a proportionate means to avert the danger.

§ 35—Necessity as Excuse

(1) Whoever, faced with an imminent danger to life, limb or freedom which cannot otherwise be averted, commits an unlawful act to avert the danger from himself, a relative or person close to him, acts without guilt. This shall not apply to the extent that the perpetrator could be expected under the circumstances to assume the risk, in particular, because he himself caused the danger or stood in a special legal relationship; however the punishment may be mitigated pursuant to Section 49 subsection (1), if the perpetrator was not required to assume the risk with respect to a special legal relationship.

(2) If upon commission of the act the perpetrator mistakenly assumes that circumstances exist, which would excuse him under subsection (1), he will only be punished, if he could have avoided the mistake. The punishment shall be mitigated pursuant to Section 49 subsection (1).

§ 49—Special Statutory Mitigating Circumstances

(1) If mitigation is prescribed or permitted under this provision, then the following shall apply to such mitigation:

    1. Imprisonment for not less than three years shall take the place of imprisonment for life;

    2. In cases of imprisonment for a fixed term, at most three-fourths of the maximum term provided may be imposed. In case of a fine the same shall apply to the maximum number of daily rates;

    3. An increased minimum term of imprisonment shall be reduced:

in the case of a minimum term of ten or five years, to two years;

in case of a minimum term of three or two years, to six months;

in case of a minimum term of one year, to three months;

in other cases to the statutory minimum.

. . .

18. THE CASE OF WOLFGANG DASCHNER (GERMANY, 2002)

A. THE FACTS

Jakob von Metzler, eleven years old, is the son of Friedrich von Metzler, a banker living in Frankfurt, Germany. Jakob attends the Carl-Schurz School, a prestigious English-language institution in Frankfurt. On September 27th, 2002, Jakob does not get home from school at the usual time. At 12:40 p.m., a caretaker at von Metzler's home finds a ransom letter informing them of Jakob's kidnapping. The kidnapper demands €1,000,000, to be delivered to the Oberschweinstiege bus stop by Sunday night. The kidnapper assures the family that Jakob will be returned safely if his demands are met. Police are immediately informed, and an investigation begins that afternoon.

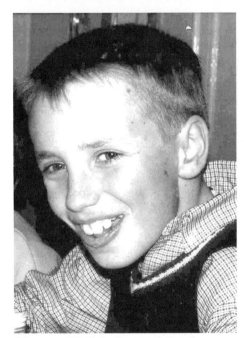

Figure 45. Jakob von Metzler. (AFP/Getty Images)

The director of the Frankfurt police force is on vacation, leaving Wolfgang Daschner, who at 59 is a long-time police veteran, as the highest ranking police officer in the city. He activates the police emergency plan and orders that a special squad be formed to deal with the kidnapping.

The squad's primary goal is to protect Jakob's life and well-being. A police psychologist reports that the ransom letter's phrasing gives reasonable hope that Jakob is still alive. Unfortunately, none of the police department's initial leads pan out. Daschner and the other assigned officers decide to put the ransom in place at the bus station, keeping the location under constant surveillance.

On Monday the 30th at 1:10am, officers watching the bus stop observe a person picking up the ransom money. He is followed and watched constantly by police, and is soon identified as 27 year old Magnus Gäfgen.

Gäfgen is no stranger to Jakob von Metzler. Gäfgen's 16-year old girlfriend attends the same college as Jakob's sister. Gäfgen is a calm and highly intelligent law school student who lacks confidence and social skills, and has a history of trying to impress others via displays of wealth. His friends are mostly the children of rich parents. However, by 2002, he is more than €10,000 in debt.

After picking up the ransom money, Gäfgen deposits money at various bank branches, test-drives a Mercedes and ultimately buys the car. He then picks up his girlfriend and books a vacation to the island of Fuerteventura for both of them, and goes shopping. The police notice that Gäfgen does not contact any accomplices, nor does he show any signs of having to take care of the child.

Police begin to worry that Jakob is in danger; some fear that Gäfgen is happy to have him die to avoid being identified later on by his victim. Out of growing fear for Jakob von Metzler's life, and with no hint of where the child might be, police arrest Gäfgen at 4:20 p.m. on the 30th. At the same time, the police begin investigating his friends, family, and acquaintances. Search efforts are intensified to try to locate Jakob before it is too late.

Beginning at 6:20 p.m., Gäfgen is interrogated by a police officer with special interrogation expertise. The officer uses a technique that involves trying to befriend Gäfgen. Initially, Gäfgen claims that he has nothing to do with any kidnapping; he claims to have been asked by a stranger to pick up the money in exchange for €20,000. The officer does not believe the story.

Police enter and search Gäfgen's apartment, finding half of the ransom money in addition to a checklist with items such as "Inspect the driving route," "Inspect the boardwalk," "Backpacks," "Letter," "Test delivery of letter," and "Axe." Police conclude that Gäfgen is unlikely to have had accomplices.

At the police station, Gäfgen is told of these findings. He admits that he deposited the money at various banks, bought a car and booked a vacation. He continues to evade all questions regarding the location of the child, and ultimately asks for legal counsel.

The officer continues interrogating Gäfgen, offering him a piece of paper with alternatives and demanding that Gäfgen check the box next to what he has done. Gäfgen places a check next to the box marked "Someone else is looking after [Jakob] somewhere." A police psychologist watching this part of the interrogation concludes that Gäfgen did not answer substantively, but was only seeking to waste time.

Figure 46. Magnus Gäfgen. (AFP/Getty Images)

At 8:00p.m., Daschner is updated on the state of the investigation. He says over the phone that "force" can be used from this point forward. The officer giving the report does not see this as an order, but rather as a suggestion to think about.

In a meeting held minutes later at the police station, members of the special squad agree that Gäfgen is at least an accomplice to the kidnapping. One officer asks how Gäfgen would react to the use of force. A police psychologist says that because Gäfgen has already shown his willingness to be evasive in order to waste time, he would do so again in the face of pressure, rendering force useless as an interrogation tool. The psychologist suggests that the police instead confront Gäfgen with Jakob's siblings, who Gäfgen has tried to befriend in the past. The officers then create a plan to expose Gäfgen to Jakob's siblings and then to his parents in an effort to get Gäfgen to tell the police where Jakob is being held. At 11:30 p.m., Daschner is told of the new plan via phone and agrees with its use.

After speaking with his attorney, Gäfgen tells the police that Jakob is being held in a shack by a lake in Langen, a small suburb of Frankfurt. He does not give sufficient details to give police the location of the cabin, but is convincing enough that the police consider it to be a real lead. Police again believe that Gäfgen may have accomplices, based on his statement and his answer in the earlier investigation. Gäfgen names two friends as accomplices later in his interrogation.

On September 1st, 1,000 police officers and 60 dogs are sent to the lake in Langen to search. SWAT-teams enter the accomplices' apartments. They arrest one at 6:02 a.m., and the other at 6:26

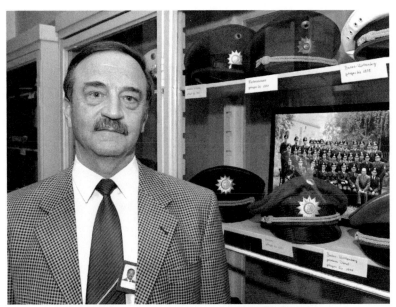

Figure 47. Wolfgang Daschner. (AFP/Getty Images)

a.m., both at home. No trace of Jakob is be found in either apartment.

After receiving another briefing at 6:30, Daschner decides that Jakob's life is in danger, and Gäfgen needs to be forced to disclose Jakob's location. Daschner orders that Gäfgen be interrogated again, first by threatening and then actually using the application of force, under the supervision of a medical doctor and without actually causing physical injury. Daschner explains to his subordinates that he considers this to be lawful action because to have Jakob die would be a greater evil.

Later, police conclude that the two "accomplices" were wholly unconnected to the kidnapping. The same morning, Daschner's lieutenants meet to discuss their orders. Though they do not approve of what they consider to be

Figure 48. German police officers search the area surrounding the lake for any sign of Jakob von Metzler. (AFP/Getty Images)

torture, all agree that Daschner's plan should be used if the "family confrontation" plan fails. All agree to circumvent Daschner's orders for the time being.

At 8:00 a.m., Daschner calls his lieutenant into his office and asks why his order has not been executed. The Frankfurt SWAT commander expresses his concerns about torture and says that he only knows of one police officer who could safely administer the force. The officer, an instructor in martial arts, is currently on vacation. Daschner orders that the officer be brought by helicopter immediately. Meanwhile, the unit investigating the lake reports that a sleeping bag with red stains on it was found in a shack matching the one Gäfgen described.

At 8:40, Daschner's lieutenant enters the room where Gäfgen is being interrogated. He tells Gäfgen that there are no doubts regarding his involvement in the kidnapping of Jakob von Metzler. The police fear for Jakob's life, and if Gäfgen continues to lie or to remain silent, the police will extract a confession by inflicting pain, without injury, under a medical doctor's supervision. The lieutenant tells Gäfgen that "a special officer is on a helicopter on its way here, and he can inflict pain on you which you will never forget." The lieutenant makes a motion with his hands to imitate a helicopter closing in on Gäfgen.

Within a few minutes, Gäfgen reveals that he has hidden Jakob below a boardwalk near a lake in Birstein—a different lake than he had previously said—approximately 40 miles from Frankfurt. The lieutenant runs out of the office, shouting for a map of that area. Two other police officers familiar with that area enter the interrogation room and get details of the location from Gäfgen.

Police proceed immediately to Birstein, taking Gäfgen to with them. By his direction, they find Jakob.

* * *

Would you convict Wolfgang Daschner for ordering his lieutenant to torture Gäfgen? If so, what amount of punishment would you impose?

N	0	1	2	3	4	5	6	7	8	9	10	11
☐	☐	☐	☐	☐	☐	☐	☐	☐	☐	☐	☐	☐
no liability	liability but no punishment	1 day	2 wks.	2 mo.	6 mo.	1 yr.	3 yrs.	7 yrs.	15 yrs.	30 yrs.	life imprison-ment	death

B. Then Existing Law

Federal Republic of Germany—Penal Code (2002)

§ 240—Coercion

(1) Whoever unlawfully with force or threat of an appreciable harm compels a human being to commit, acquiesce in or omit an act, shall be punished with imprisonment for not more than three years or a fine.

(2) The act shall be unlawful if the use of force or the threat of harm is deemed reprehensible in relation to the desired objective.

(3) An attempt shall be punishable.

(4) In especially serious cases the punishment shall be imprisonment from six months to five years. An especially serious case exists as a rule, if the perpetrator:

    1. coerces another person to commit a sexual act;

2. coerces a pregnant woman to terminate the pregnancy; or

3. abuses his powers or position as a public official.

§ 343—Extortion of Testimony

(1) Whoever, as a public official charged with participation in:

1. a criminal proceeding, a proceeding to order custody of a public authority;

2. a proceeding to impose a civil penalty; or

3. a disciplinary proceeding, disciplinary court or professional disciplinary proceeding,

physically maltreats another, otherwise uses force against him, threatens him with force or torments him emotionally, in order to coerce him to testify to or declare something in the proceeding or to fail to do so, shall be punished with imprisonment from one year to ten years.

(2) In less serious cases the punishment shall be imprisonment from six months to five years.

§ 357—Subornation of a Subordinate to Commit a Crime

(1) A superior who suborns or undertakes to suborn a subordinate to commit an unlawful act in public office or allows such an unlawful act of his subordinate to happen, has incurred the punishment provided for this unlawful act.

(2) The same rule shall be applied to a public official, to whom supervision or control over the official business of another public official has been transferred to the extent that the unlawful act committed by the latter public official concerns the business subject to the supervision or control.

§ 16—Mistake about Circumstances of the Act

(1) Whoever upon commission of the act is unaware of a circumstance which is a statutory element of the offense does not act intentionally. Punishability for negligent commission remains unaffected.

§ 17—Mistake of Law

If upon commission of the act the perpetrator lacks the appreciation that he is doing something wrong, he acts without guilt if he was unable to avoid this mistake. If the perpetrator could have avoided the mistake, the punishment may be mitigated pursuant to Section 49(1) [which specifies the number of years to be taken off of each sentence when mitigated].

§ 32—Necessity Defense

(1) Whoever commits an act, required as necessary defense, does not act unlawfully.

(2) Necessary defense is the defense which is required to avert an imminent unlawful assault from oneself or another.

§ 34—Necessity as Justification

Whoever, faced with an imminent danger to life, limb, freedom, honor, property or another legal interest which cannot otherwise be averted, commits an act to avert the danger from himself or another, does not act unlawfully, if, upon weighing the conflicting interests, in particular the affected legal interests and the degree of danger threatening them, the protected interest substantially outweighs the one interfered with. This shall apply, however, only to the extent that the act is a proportionate means to avert the danger.

§ 35—Necessity as Excuse

(1) Whoever, faced with an imminent danger to life, limb or freedom which cannot otherwise be averted, commits an unlawful act to avert the danger from himself, a relative or person close to

him, acts without guilt. This shall not apply to the extent that the perpetrator could be expected under the circumstances to assume the risk, in particular, because he himself caused the danger or stood in a special legal relationship; however the punishment may be mitigated pursuant to Section 49 subsection (1), if the perpetrator was not required to assume the risk with respect to a special legal relationship.

(2) If upon commission of the act the perpetrator mistakenly assumes that circumstances exist, which would excuse him under subsection (1), he will only be punished, if he could have avoided the mistake. The punishment shall be mitigated pursuant to Section 49 subsection (1).

§ 11—Terms Relating to Persons and Subject Matter

(1) Within the meaning of this law:

* * *

2. a public official is whoever, under German law:

(a) is a civil servant or judge;

(b) otherwise has an official relationship with public law functions or;

(c) has been appointed to a public authority or other agency or has been commissioned to perform duties of public administration without prejudice to the organizational form chosen to fulfill such duties;

Federal Republic of Germany—Criminal Procedure Code (2002)

§ 136a—Prohibited Methods of Examination

(1) The accused's freedom to make up his mind and to manifest his will shall not be impaired by ill-treatment, induced fatigue, physical interference, administration of drugs, torment, deception or hypnosis. Coercion may be used only as far as this is permitted by criminal procedure law. Threatening the accused with measures not permitted under its provisions or holding out the prospect of an advantage not envisaged by statute shall be prohibited.

(2) Measures which impair the accused's memory or his ability to understand shall not be permitted.

(3) The prohibition under subsections (1) and (2) shall apply irrespective of the accused's consent. Statements which were obtained in breach of this prohibition shall not be used, even if the accused agrees to their use.

Hessian Law on Security and Public Order (2002)

§ 6—Liability for the Acts of Persons

(1) If a person causes a risk he is liable for it.

§ 12—Interrogation and Duty of Disclosure

(1) The Police and Public Order Authorities may interrogate a person if there are factual indications to support the presumption that the person can give helpful information relating to a police or security matter.

* * *

(4) Section 136a of the Criminal Procedure Code is applicable to this section.

§ 56—Acting on Orders

(1) Police Officers must use force if ordered to do so by a superior. This is not required if the order is incompatible with human dignity....

(2) An order may not be executed if it were criminal to do so. If it is executed nonetheless, a Police Officer is only culpable if he or she perceives or if it the circumstances make it obvious to him or her that it is a crime to execute this order.

C.   CURRENT LAW THAT WOULD BE APPLIED WERE THE CASE PROSECUTED TODAY

[Statutory changes are not relevant]

19. THE CASE OF MOTTI ASHKENAZI (ISRAEL, 1997)

A. THE FACTS

Motti Ashkenazi, a thin, 30–year-old man from a poor, crime-ridden South Tel Aviv neighborhood, strolls along the crowded beach between Tel Aviv and Jaffa on a hot Friday afternoon in June 1997. A drug addict and petty thief who only a week ago was arrested after bungling a car burglary, Ashkenazi has been thinking about getting off drugs and putting his life together for a while. But the going has been tough, even with the support of his family.

As he walks, he sees that someone has left a black backpack unattended. Ashkenazi looks around and sees no one watching. He picks up the backpack and quickly sneaks off, pleased by his good fortune. Without opening the backpack, he walks down nearby Geula Street and into the stairwell of an abandoned apartment building. There, he unzips the backpack to inspect his loot. He finds a clock with wires connected to a cookie tin, with loose nails surrounding the contraption. Ashkenazi quickly realizes he has just stolen a terrorist's bomb.

Panicked but in control, he runs to the nearby Savoy Hotel and tells the reception desk clerk what he found. The clerk calls the police. The bomb squad arrives in minutes and begins trying to deactivate the bomb in the apartment building stairwell. Meanwhile, Ashkenazi stands outside the building, keeping the street clear of passersby. He warns a group of children to stay away. Police halt traffic in the area and evacuate residents from the neighboring buildings. The bomb squad finds that the bomb is packed with nearly three kilograms of explosives. After an hour's work, they use a robot to shoot the backpack in a way that neutralizes the bomb.

Figure 49. Ashkenazi pointing to the spot where he found the knapsack. (Wolston/Maariv)

Police officers search the crowded nearby beach for more bombs, but find none. Considering the volume of explosive and the number of people on the beach, police conclude that many would have been killed. A major terrorist attack has been averted.

In the midst of the police activity, Ashkenazi slips away. He is well known to the police, however, and detectives easily track him down for questioning. At first, Ashkenazi lies to the police and tells them he found the backpack in the apartment building stairwell where he had gone to urinate, but later confesses to having stolen the backpack from the beach.

* * *

Figure 50. Police disarm the terrorist bomb Ashkenazi brought from the crowded beach. (Motti Kimchi/Ha-aretz Daily)

Would you convict Ashkenazi for his theft of the backpack? If so, what amount of punishment would you impose?

N	0	1	2	3	4	5	6	7	8	9	10	11
☐	☐	☐	☐	☐	☐	☐	☐	☐	☐	☐	☐	☐
no liability	liability but no punishment	1 day	2 wks.	2 mo.	6 mo.	1 yr.	3 yrs.	7 yrs.	15 yrs.	30 yrs.	life imprison-ment	death

B.   THEN EXISTING LAW
Israeli Penal Law (1997)

§ 383—Definition of Theft

(a) A person commits theft—

1) if he takes and carries away—without the owner's consent, fraudulently, and without claiming a right in good faith—a thing capable of being stolen, with the intention—when he takes it—of permanently depriving its owner;

2) if he—while having lawful possession of a thing capable of being stolen, being its bailee or part owner—fraudulently converts it to his own use or to the use of another person who is not the owner.

(b) In respect of theft under subsection (a), it is immaterial that the person who takes or converts the object in question is a director or officer of a body corporate which is its owner, provided that the aggregate of other circumstances amounts to stealing—

(c) For the matter of stealing—

1) "taking" includes obtaining possession—

a) by a trick;

b) by intimidation;

c) by a mistake on the owner's part, the person who takes the object knowing that the possession has been so obtained;

d) by finding, if the finder at that time believes that the owner can be discovered by reasonable means;

2) "carrying away" includes the removal of a thing from the place which it occupies, but in the case of an attached object, only if it has been completely detached;

3) "ownership" includes part ownership, possession, a right to possession and control;

4) "thing capable of being stolen"—a thing which has value and is the property of a person, but if the thing is attached to an immovable object, only if it has been detached from it.

§ 384—Punishment for Theft

If a person commits theft, he is liable to three years imprisonment, unless some other punishment is provided in view of the circumstances of the theft or of the nature of the stolen object.

§ 34J—Defensive Force

No person shall bear criminal responsibility for an act that was immediately necessary in order to repel an unlawful attack, which posed real danger to his own or another person's life, freedom, bodily welfare or property; however, a person is not acting in self defense when his own wrongful conduct caused the attack, the possibility of such a development having been foreseen by himself.

§ 34K—Necessity

No person shall bear criminal responsibility for an act that was immediately necessary in order to save his own or another person's life, freedom, bodily welfare or property from a real danger of severe injury, due to the conditions prevalent at the time the act was committed, there being no alternative but to commit the act.

§ 34M—Justification

No person shall bear criminal responsibility for an act, which he committed under any of the following circumstances:

(1) he was lawfully obligated or authorized to commit it;

(2) he committed it under the order of a competent authority, which he lawfully was obligated to obey, unless the order is obviously unlawful;

(3) in respect of an act which lawfully requires consent, when the act was immediately necessary in order to save a person's life or his bodily welfare, or to prevent severe injury to his health, if, under the circumstances, he was not able to obtain the consent;

(4) he committed it on a person with lawful consent, in the course of a medical procedure or treatment, the objective of which was that person's or another person's benefit.

(5) he committed it in the course of a sports activity or of a sports game, such as are not prohibited by law and do not conflict with public order, in accordance with rules customary for them.

§ 34P—Unreasonableness

The provisions of sections 34J, 34K, and 34L shall not apply, if, under the circumstances, the act was not a reasonable one for the prevention of the injury.

§ 34R—Misinterpretation of situation

(a) If a person commits an act, while imagining a situation that does not exist, he shall not bear criminal responsibility, except to the extent that he would have had to bear it, had the situation really been as he imagined it.

(b) Subsection (a) shall also apply to an offense of negligence, on condition that the mistake was reasonable, and to an offense of strict liability, …

§ 25—What constitutes an attempt

A person attempts to commit an offense if he, with intent to commit the offense, does an act that constitutes more than mere preparation and the offense is not completed.

§ 26—Commission of the offense is impossible

For the purpose of attempt, it shall be immaterial if the commission of the offense was impossible because of circumstances of which the person attempting the offense was not aware and of which the person was mistaken.

§ 27—Special penalty for attempt

If a provision sets a mandatory or minimum penalty for offense, it shall not apply to an attempt to commit the offense.

§ 28—Exemption because of remorse

If a person attempts to commit an offense, he shall not bear criminal responsibility for it if he proves that, of own free will and out of remorse, he stopped its commission or substantially contributed to the prevention of results upon which completion of the offense depends; however, this shall not derogate from his criminal liability for another completed offense connected to the same act.

C. Current Law That Would Be Applied Were the Case Prosecuted Today

[Statutory changes are not relevant]

Chapter 7. Is Wrongdoing Ever Blameless? Excuse Defenses

20. The Case of Janice Leidholm (North Dakota, 1981)

A. The Facts

It is August 1981. Janice Leidholm, 42, and her husband Chester Leidholm, 45, live on a farm about 13 miles from Washburn, North Dakota, near the Missouri River. The couple have been married for 23 years and are the parents of five adult children. The youngest two, Sandra and Neil, are ages 20 and 21. Sandra lives at home, as does Neil, who sleeps in an old converted bus parked on the property. The older three are married and live on their own. The Leidholms live and support themselves off the farm and from money Chester earns when he takes an occasional construction job at area power plants.

The Leidholms' bleak marriage is dominated by alcohol abuse by both Janice and Chester and by the physical abuse of Janice by Chester. At times, his beatings leave her black-and-blue for three or four days. When the pain is too much to bear, she goes to her daughters' homes in the morning and has them rub her badly bruised back. During one of the beatings, Chester sits on top of her and strangles her, stopping only as she begins to lose consciousness. The beatings are regularly followed by apologies and Chester's promises never to hit her again. To hide the bruises, Janice often wears long-sleeved dresses. She seeks medical treatment only for the worst beatings.

On several occasions, the family tries to help Janice leave Chester— even if only for a brief respite. One daughter gives Janice money to visit her brother in Chicago, which she does and then returns home. At

Figure 51. Chester Leidholm enjoying a cigarette on July 19, 1981. (Family Photo)

another time, Janice appeals to Chester's brother Lloyd, who talks to Chester about the violence. Several times Janice tries to convince Chester to go with her to a marriage counselor. She also asks the sheriff's office about getting into a shelter. On several occasions, Janice tries to kill herself, one time stabbing herself with a kitchen knife. When their children try to step in to stop the beatings, Chester warns them against interfering in the marriage.

On August 6, 1981, Janice spends the day at home while Chester drives to the nearby town of Underwood to pick up some parts for their combine harvester. He returns around 4:30 p.m., slurring his words and smelling of liquor. He is still angry from a previous argument over his suspicions that Janice is having an affair. A while later, the two leave for a gun club picnic at a park in

Figure 52. The Leidholms at their daughter's wedding. (Family Photo)

Washburn. Chester gives Janice the silent treatment on the way, which he frequently does when upset.

Janice and Chester drink heavily at the picnic and are soon drunk. They begin to argue, this time about new friends Janice has begun seeing—a young couple from Dunseith, a small North Dakota town about 120 miles away. Chester is also upset because he thinks that his wife pays too much attention to a man at the picnic. As the picnic winds down, Janice says that she wants to stay in town with her daughter Laurie, but Chester insists that she come home. Afraid of being alone with Chester, Janice convinces her daughter Sandra, who has joined them at the picnic, to come home with them rather than stay with her sister as was planned.

Chester and Janice fight constantly on the trip home. Chester accuses her of spending too much time with the man at the party. Janice reminds him of an affair he had with another woman. She says she wants to return to Washburn to spend the night at Laurie's house. Chester again refuses and in his anger, reaches across to the passenger side door, opens it, and with the truck moving at 45 m.p.h., tries to push Janice out. Sandra, who is sitting between the two, pulls her mother back in and closes the door. Sometime later, Janice says she wants to get out and tries to open the door while the truck is moving. Sandra pulls her back into the truck. Chester tells Janice to leave in the morning if she wants to.

When they arrive home just after midnight, they discover a problem with the water system. Sandra checks around the house to find the problem. Fearing that her parents may try to drive while intoxicated, Sandra checks the family cars for keys and removes the ones she finds. The argument between Chester and Janice continues. Janice goes into the house and tries to call a deputy sheriff she knows for help, but Chester pushes her to the floor. Each time she tries to stand and get to the phone, he pushes her back to the floor. Chester is now shouting, and Janice is crying.

Janice walks out of the house to get away from Chester, but Chester, who is much bigger, catches up with her and throws the 5′ 1″, 150–pound Janice to the ground. During the fight, Chester takes away her wedding rings and tells her that she is a drunk and does not deserve to be married anymore. Chester repeatedly pushes his crying wife to the ground. When Chester begins to tire and insists they go into the house and go to sleep, Janice refuses to go with him. He picks her up and drags her inside.

In the living room, the argument continues. They argue about their drinking. They talk about divorce. There is discussion about her moving to Minot the following week to live with their daughter, Wanda. Eventually, Chester goes to bed while Janice remains in the living room. Later, Chester comes into the living room and tells her to go to bed. She does not. Chester then comes back out to the living room, picks her up, drags her across the floor into the bedroom, and throws her onto the bed. She eventually removes her clothes, puts on her nightgown, and lies in bed next to him.

Sometime before 1:00 a.m., Chester falls asleep. Janice, lying beside him, is still awake. She slips out of bed, goes to kiss Sandra goodnight, and heads for the kitchen. Although Sandra has tried to hide all the knives out of fear that her mother might try again to hurt herself, Janice finds a butcher's knife and walks back to the bedroom, careful not to wake Chester. As he sleeps, Janice stabs Chester twice in the right side of his chest. Chester struggles out of bed and crawls to the living room. He calls Sandra, and when she comes to the top of the stairs, Chester screams, "Get Neil. Mom stabbed me." Sandra runs to him and helps him sit down on the couch, then rushes to get her brother who is sleeping in the old bus parked on the property.

Neil and Sandra return to the house to find their father lying on the floor bleeding, with the knife on the floor beside his head. Neil puts his hand over the wound to try to stop the bleeding and cradles his father's head in his arms. Within minutes, Chester dies from blood loss and shock.

Janice calls her brother-in-law Roy Leidholm, and tells him "Roy, I just killed Chester." Janice tells him to call an ambulance, which he does. It is now 1:15 a.m., and her next call is to the deputy sheriff she knows. She is nearly hysterical and her words come out in unintelligible sobs. Finally she manages to tell him just to come out to the farm, but cannot give more details. Janice calls the information line to get the sheriff's number. She calls him too, and manages to tell him that she killed her husband.

Paramedics pronounce Chester dead when they arrive. Janice tells a paramedic, "I couldn't take it anymore."

As she waits for deputies to arrive, Janice washes up and changes clothes. Deputies arrest Janice at 3:30 a.m. and charge her with first-degree murder.

*   *   *

Would you convict Janice Leidholm for killing her husband? If so, what amount of punishment would you impose?

N	0	1	2	3	4	5	6	7	8	9	10	11
☐	☐	☐	☐	☐	☐	☐	☐	☐	☐	☐	☐	☐
no liability	liability but no punishment	1 day	2 wks.	2 mo.	6 mo.	1 yr.	3 yrs.	7 yrs.	15 yrs.	30 yrs.	life imprison-ment	death

B. THEN EXISTING LAW

North Dakota Century Code (1981)

§ 12.1–16–01—Murder

A person is guilty of murder, a class AA felony, if he:

(1) Intentionally or knowingly causes the death of another human being;

(2) Causes the death of another human being under circumstances manifesting extreme indifference to the value of human life; or

(3) Acting either alone or with one or more other persons, commits or attempts to commit treason, robbery, burglary, kidnaping, felonious restraint, arson, gross sexual imposition, or escape and, in the course of and in furtherance of such crime or of immediate flight therefrom, he, or another participant, if there be any, causes the death of any person; except that in any prosecution under this subsection in which the defendant was not the only participant in the underlying crime, it is an affirmative defense that the defendant:

(a) Did not commit the homicidal act or in any way solicit, command, induce, procure, counsel, or aid the commission thereof; and

(b) Was not armed with a firearm, destructive device, dangerous weapon, or other weapon which under the circumstances indicated a readiness to inflict serious bodily injury; and

(c) Reasonably believed that no other participant was armed with such a weapon; and

(d) Reasonably believed that no other participant intended to engage in conduct likely to result in death or serious bodily injury. Subsections (1) and (2) shall be inapplicable in the circumstances covered by subsection 2 of section 12.1–16–02.

§ 12.1–16–02—Manslaughter

A person is guilty of manslaughter, a class B felony, if he

(1) recklessly causes the death of another human being; or

(2) causes the death of another human being under circumstances which would be class AA felony murder, except that the person causes the death under the influence of extreme emotional disturbance for which there is reasonable excuse. The reasonableness of the excuse must be determined from the viewpoint of a person in his situation under the circumstances as he believes them to be. An extreme emotional disturbance is excusable, within the meaning of this subsection only, if it is occasioned by substantial provocation, or a serious event, or situation for which the offender was not culpably responsible.

§ 12.1–16–03—Negligent homicide

A person is guilty of a class C felony if he negligently causes the death of another human being.

§ 12.1–32.01—Classifications of Offenses—Penalties

Offenses are divided into seven classes, which are denominated and subject to maximum penalties, as follows:

(1) Class AA felony, for which a maximum penalty of life imprisonment may be imposed. Notwithstanding the provisions of section 12–59–05 [consideration by board], a person found guilty of a class AA felony shall not be eligible to have his sentence considered by the parole board for thirty years, less sentence reduction earned for good conduct, after his admission to the penitentiary.

(2) Class A felony, for which a maximum penalty of twenty years' imprisonment, a fine of ten thousand dollars, or both, may be imposed.

(3) Class B felony, for which a maximum penalty of ten years' imprisonment, a fine of ten thousand dollars, or both, may be imposed.

(4) Class C felony, for which a maximum penalty of five years imprisonment, a fine of five thousand dollars, or both, may be imposed.

§ 12.1–02–02—Requirements of culpability

(1) For the purposes of this title, a person engages in conduct:

(a) "Intentionally" if, when he engages in the conduct, it is his purpose to do so.

(b) "Knowingly" if, when he engages in the conduct, he knows or has a firm belief, unaccompanied by substantial doubt, that he is doing so, whether or not it is his purpose to do so.

(c) "Recklessly" if he engages in the conduct in conscious and clearly unjustifiable disregard of a substantial likelihood of the existence of the relevant facts or risks, such disregard involving a gross deviation from acceptable standards of conduct, except that, as provided in section 12.1–04–02, awareness of the risk is not required where its absence is due to self-induced intoxication.

(d) "Negligently" if he engages in the conduct in unreasonable disregard of a substantial likelihood of the existence of the relevant facts or risks, such disregard involving a gross deviation from acceptable standards of conduct.

(e) "Willfully" if he engages in the conduct intentionally, knowingly, or recklessly.

(2) If a statute or regulation thereunder defining a crime does not specify any culpability and does not provide explicitly that a person may be guilty without culpability, the culpability that is required is willfully.

(3)

(a) Except as otherwise expressly provided, where culpability is required, that kind of culpability is required with respect to every element of the conduct and to those attendant circumstances specified in the definition of the offense, except that where the required culpability is "intentionally", the culpability required as to an attendant circumstance is "knowingly".

(b) Except as otherwise expressly provided, if conduct is an offense if it causes a particular result, the required degree of culpability is required with respect to the result.

(c) Except as otherwise expressly provided, culpability is not required with respect to any fact which is solely a basis for grading.

(d) Except as otherwise expressly provided, culpability is not required with respect to facts which establish that a defense does not exist, if the defense is defined in chapters 12.1–01 through 12.1–06; otherwise the least kind of culpability required for the offense is required with respect to such facts.

(e) A factor as to which it is expressly stated that it must "in fact" exist is a factor for which culpability is not required.

(4) Any lesser degree of required culpability is satisfied if the proven degree of culpability is higher.

(5) Culpability is not required as to the fact that conduct is an offense, except as otherwise expressly provided in a provision outside this title.

§ 12.1–05–03—Self-defense

A person is justified in using force upon another person to defend himself against danger of imminent unlawful bodily injury, sexual assault, or detention by such other person, except that:

(1) A person is not justified in using force for the purpose of resisting arrest, execution of process, or other performance of duty by a public servant under color of law, but excessive force may be resisted.

(2) A person is not justified in using force if:

(a) He intentionally provokes unlawful action by another person to cause bodily injury or death to such other person; or

(b) He has entered into a mutual combat with another person or is the initial aggressor unless he is resisting force which is clearly excessive in the circumstances. A person's use of defensive force after he withdraws from an encounter and indicates to the other person that he has done so is justified if the latter nevertheless continues or menaces unlawful action.

§ 12.1–05–07—Limits on the use of force—Excessive force—Deadly force

(1) A person is not justified in using more force than is necessary and appropriate under the circumstances.

(2) Deadly force is justified in the following instances:

(a) When it is expressly authorized by law or occurs in the lawful conduct of war.

(b) When used in lawful self-defense, or in lawful defense of others, if such force is necessary to protect the actor or anyone else against death, serious bodily injury, or the commission of a felony involving violence. The use of deadly force is not justified if it can be avoided, with safety to the actor and others, by retreat or other conduct involving minimal interference with the freedom of the person menaced. A person seeking to protect someone else must, before using deadly force, try to cause that person to retreat, or otherwise comply with the requirements of this provision, if safety can be obtained thereby. But, (1) a public servant justified in using force in the performance of his duties or a person justified in using force in his assistance need not desist from his efforts because of resistance or threatened resistance by or on behalf of the person against whom his action is directed; and (2) no person is required to retreat from his dwelling, or place of work, unless he was the original aggressor or is assailed by a person who he knows also dwells or works there.

(c) When used by a person in possession or control of a dwelling or place of work, or a person who is licensed or privileged to be there, if such force is necessary to prevent commission of arson, burglary, robbery, or a felony involving violence upon or in the dwelling or place of work, and the use of force other than deadly force for such purposes would expose anyone to substantial danger of serious bodily injury.

*   *   *

§ 12.1–05–08—Excuse

A person's conduct is excused if he believes that the facts are such that his conduct is necessary and appropriate for any of the purposes which would establish a justification or excuse under this chapter, even though his belief is mistaken. However, if his belief is negligently or recklessly held, it is not an excuse in a prosecution for an offense for which negligence or recklessness, as the case may be, suffices to establish culpability. Excuse under this section is a defense or affirmative defense according to which type of defense would be established had the facts been as the person believed them to be.

§ 12.1–05–12—Definitions

In this chapter:

(1) "Deadly force" means force which a person uses with the intent of causing, or which he knows creates a substantial risk of causing, death or serious bodily injury. A threat to cause death or serious bodily injury, by the production of a weapon or otherwise, so long as the actor's intent is limited to creating an apprehension that he will use deadly force if necessary, does not constitute deadly force.

(2) "Dwelling" means any building or structure, though movable or temporary, or a portion thereof, which is for the time being a person's home or place of lodging.

(3) "Force" means physical action, threat, or menace against another, and includes confinement.

(4) "Premises" means all or any part of a building or real property, or any structure, vehicle, or watercraft used for overnight lodging of persons, or used by persons for carrying on business therein.

C.   CURRENT LAW THAT WOULD BE APPLIED WERE THE CASE PROSECUTED TODAY

North Dakota Century Code (2006)

§ 12.1–16–01—Murder

(1) A person is guilty of murder, a class AA felony, if *the person*:

(a) Intentionally or knowingly causes the death of another human being;

(b) Causes the death of another human being under circumstances manifesting extreme indifference to the value of human life; or

(c) Acting either alone or with one or more other persons, commits or attempts to commit treason, robbery, burglary, kidnaping, felonious restraint, arson, gross sexual imposition, *a felony offense against a child under section 12.1–20–03 [Gross sexual imposition], 12.1–27.2–02 [Use of a minor in a sexual performance], 12.1–27.2–03 [Promoting or directing an obscene sexual performance by a minor], 12.1–27.2–04 [Promoting a sexual performance by a minor], or 14–09–22 [Abuse or neglect of child],* or escape and, in the course of and in furtherance of such a crime or of immediate flight therefrom, the person or [another] any other participant *in the crime* [if there be any] causes the death of any person. In any prosecution under this subsection in which the defendant was not the only participant in the underlying crime, it is an affirmative defense that the defendant:

(i) Did not commit the homicidal act or in any way solicit, command, induce, procure, counsel, or aid the commission thereof; and

(ii) Was not armed with a firearm, destructive device, dangerous weapon, or other weapon which under the circumstances indicated a readiness to inflict serious bodily injury; and

(iii) Reasonably believed that no other participant was armed with such a weapon; and

(iv) Reasonably believed that no other participant intended to engage in conduct likely to result in death or serious bodily injury. Subdivisions (a) and (b) are inapplicable in the circumstances covered by subsection (2).

(2) A person is guilty of murder, a class A felony, if the person causes the death of another human being under circumstances which would be class AA felony murder, except that the person causes the death under the influence of extreme emotional disturbance for which there is reasonable excuse. The reasonableness of the excuse must be determined from the viewpoint of a person in that person's situation under the circumstances as that person believes them to be. An extreme emotional disturbance is excusable, within the meaning of this subsection only, if it is occasioned by substantial provocation, or a serious event, or situation for which the offender was not culpably responsible.

§ 12.1–16–02—Manslaughter

A person is guilty of manslaughter, a class B felony, if he recklessly causes the death of another human being.

21. THE CASE OF BARRY KINGSTON (ENGLAND, 1991)

A. THE FACTS

In 1975, Barry Kingston is hired by James Forman and his wife Diedre Forman to run the "Unit One Sauna," their spa in Brighton, England. Three years later, the Formans move to Cyprus, leaving Kingston to run the spa on his own. The Formans' absence allows Kingston a great deal of independence with a pleasant job. He meets and befriends many of the spa's customers. On at least one occasion, one of the customers gives him some sexually explicit material that the customer no longer wants, most of it dealing with young men and teenage boys.

Figure 53. Barry Kingston in the late 1970's, when he was Employed at the Unit One Sauna. (Barry Kingston)

In 1987, the Formans return from Cyprus. Mr. Forman spends most of his time at a house in France, which the couple has just purchased. Mrs. Forman remains in England, becoming active in the running of the spa. She eventually becomes disenchanted with Kingston, and fires him. Kingston files an unfair dismissal claim and is given a substantial award, £12,000, by an industrial tribunal.

The Formans are concerned that Kingston knows a great deal about their business and tax dealings, and fear that he may report this information to authorities. Kevin Penn, a Brighton resident and acquaintance of Kingston, is aware of the situation. Penn has a reputation for money-making schemes, especially of the questionable sort. He offers to allay the Formans' fears of Kingston by providing them with something they can use to blackmail him. After a few false starts, he devises a workable plan and the Formans pay him £1,500.

Penn learns that Kingston has an interest in young men and teens. Kingston has never been charged with any improper involvement with a minor, but Penn plans to drug Kingston and to use Kingston's latent desire to entice him into a compromising situation that he can record for blackmail purposes.

Penn notices a group of local surfers, approximately fifteen years old, who he thinks he may be able to use in his plot. He approaches one of the boys, James Bullock, and asks if James can help him sell a surfboard. They agree that Penn and the boys will meet at the Black Horse Pub, a local tavern. At the tavern, he quickly changes the subject to photography. Penn, who is carrying a high-quality camera, tells the boys they can make a lot of money by posing for photographic sessions. The boys see little reason not to make the easy money. Penn arranges to take a few amateur photos, and encourages the boys to continue posing for him in the future. He is particularly interested in Bullock and Darren Child, who he thinks are the most attractive. In order to set the stage for the blackmail session with Kingston, Penn has the boys pose for him and for a professional photographer, Andrew McLean, several more times during the next month and a half. None of the photos are overtly sexual. During some of the shoots, the boys drink with Penn or smoke cannabis. When McLean is alone with the boys, he warns them to "be careful in your dealings with Penn, as he is always short of money and looking for schemes to get rich quick."

In November 1990, Penn is ready to go ahead with the blackmail session. He calls Kingston and arranges to have him stop by his apartment later that evening. He then meets Darren Child at the Black Horse Pub and invites him to come to his apartment to pick up an old stereo. Child and Penn taxi to Penn's home. Penn offers a glass of lager that Child happily accepts. They go into Penn's bedroom and sit on the bed and smoke cannabis. Penn has laced the lager with triazolam and temazepam. The first is a "sedative-hypnotic primarily used to relieve insomnia;" the second is "used as a sedative and hypnotic." Both can cause drowsiness, impairment of judgment, and loss of memory. The boy soon passes out. Penn removes the boy's clothes and positions him on the bed, lying on his back with his head on the pillow.

Kingston soon arrives, as planned. Penn offers him some coffee laced with sedatives. He adjusts the dosage so that, unlike Child, Kingston will not pass out but will suffer only impaired judgment and loosened inhibitions.

Once the drugs begin to take effect, Kingston says, "I don't know why, am I falling asleep?" Suspicious, Kingston asks Penn, "Have you put something in my coffee?" Kingston is increasingly groggy but still conscious and aware of what is going on. Penn leads him to the bedroom where he presents the boy lying naked on the bed and invites Kingston to have sex with him, which Kingston does. Penn audio-records the episode and takes photographs.

When the boy awakens the next morning he remembers nothing from the night before. Kingston only remembers waking up in his own home the next morning. Soon after, Penn sells the negatives and the audio tape to the Formans. Mrs. Forman arranges a meeting with Kingston and informs him that she possesses the incriminating photos and tape. She explains to him that if he does anything to hurt the Formans' interests, they will give the material to his new employer, the Department of Social Services. For reasons that are unclear (perhaps to discredit an uncooperative Kingston?), Mrs. Forman gives their evidence to the police several months later. Both Penn and Kingston are charged with indecent assault on a minor. Penn is also charged with drugging the boy.

Experts conclude that Kingston would not have committed the sexual offense if he had not been drugged by Penn, but that Kingston was aware of what he was doing, knew it was wrong, and, while his capacity to control his conduct was significantly impaired, he had not completely lost his ability to control his conduct at the time of the offense.

*   *   *

Should Kingston be held criminally liable for sexual assault of the boy? If so, what amount of punishment would you impose?

N	0	1	2	3	4	5	6	7	8	9	10	11
☐	☐	☐	☐	☐	☐	☐	☐	☐	☐	☐	☐	☐
no liability	liability but no punishment	1 day	2 wks.	2 mo.	6 mo.	1 yr.	3 yrs.	7 yrs.	15 yrs.	30 yrs.	life imprison- ment	death

B.   THEN EXISTING LAW

Sexual Offences Act, 1956, 4 & 5 Eliz.2, ch. 69

§ 15—Indecent assault on a man

(1) It is an offence for a person to make an indecent assault on a man.

(2) A boy under the age of sixteen cannot in law give any consent which would prevent an act being an assault for the purposes of this section.

(3) A man who is a defective cannot in law give any consent which would prevent an act being an assault for the purposes of this section, but a person is only to be treated as guilty of an indecent assault on a defective by reason of that incapacity to consent, if that person knew or had reason to suspect him to be a defective.

Cardle v. Mulrainey, SLT 1152 (1992)

Where a man unknowingly consumes amphetamine-laced ale and subsequently attempts to steal a van, involuntary intoxication is not a defense if "the accused knew what he was doing and was aware of the nature and quality of his acts and that what he was doing was wrong, [such that] he cannot be said to be suffering from the total alienation of reason in regard to the crime with which he is charged which the defense requires." [This case was decided after the offense in *Kingston* but before the *Kingston* case came before the House of Lords.]

Regina v. Court, 2 All E.R. 221 (House of Lords, 1988)

The offense of indecent assault requires that the accused "intentionally assaulted the victim and intended to commit not just an assault but an indecent assault, i.e., an assault which right-minded persons would think was indecent."

Regina v. Court, 1 All E.R. 120, 122 (House of Lords, 1987)

The offense of indecent assault includes both a battery, or touching, and psychic assault without touching. If there was touching, it is not necessary to prove that the victim is aware of the assault or of the circumstances of indecency. If there is no touching, then the constitute an indecent assault the victim must be shown to have been aware of the assault and of the circumstances of indecency.

C.   CURRENT LAW THAT WOULD BE APPLIED WERE THE CASE PROSECUTED TODAY

[Statutory changes are not relevant]

22. THE CASE OF ANDREA YATES (TEXAS, 2001)

A. THE FACTS

It is 1989. Twenty-five year old Andrea Kennedy, a champion swimmer and high school valedictorian, swims in the pool of a Houston apartment complex. Rusty Yates, also 25 and a summa cum laude graduate of Auburn University, watches from his apartment. Weeks later, the two talk long into the night, realizing that for some time they have been living in the same building.

On April 17, 1993, they are married in a simple, nondenominational ceremony in Clear Lake Park, Texas. Rusty is employed as an engineer working for NASA; Andrea works at the M.D. Anderson Cancer Center as a post-operative nurse. The couple talk to wedding guests about their plans for the future, including their plan to not use contraceptives. Andrea Yates claims to want as many children as possible.

On February 25, 1994, the Yates' first child, Noah, is born. Andrea Yates leaves her nursing career to become a full-time mother, staying at home to take care of her newborn son. In early 1995, she is pregnant again. Though she tells no one, Yates suffers a recurring vision in which she watches a person get stabbed with a knife. The vision disappears as quickly as it appeared.

As Yates continues her career as a mother, she becomes more withdrawn and secretive, losing touch with many of her oldest friends and alienating others. Soon after the birth of her second son, Yates writes to the wife of a traveling Christian evangelist and longtime advisor to Rusty, complaining of loneliness and depression. The reply urges Yates to read the New Testament, and describes the appropriate role of women as being subservient to their husbands, working at home and raising children. Soon after, Rusty is transferred to Clearwater, Florida for a six-month assignment. The young family sells many of their possessions, including their house, and moves into a 38-foot travel trailer, arriving in Florida and taking up residence at a trailer park in Seminole. While they live in Florida, Andrea gets pregnant twice—miscarrying once but giving birth to a third son after moving back to Texas in June of 1997.

In May of 1998, Rusty and Andrea Yates decide that they would prefer to live a simpler life than the one that they lead in the trailer. Rusty purchases a converted 1978 GMC bus, which they use as a home. The bus has 350 square feet of living space, forcing the two oldest children to sleep in a luggage compartment. The seller of the van, Michael Woroniecki, is the evangelist husband of Andrea's previous confidante. Woroniecki advocates a particularly fundamentalist brand of Christianity, cautioning Rusty against the dangers of organized religion. The Yates family takes his advice to heart, subscribing to many of the religious teachings that Woroniecki preaches.

Figure 54. The Yates family before the birth of their fifth child. (Getty Images)

Figure 55. Andrea Yates. (Getty Images)

Throughout 1998, Andrea becomes more secretive and distant from everyone in her life, including Rusty. She refuses to change her clothes except alone in a closet. She refuses to have guests. Rusty says, "I know a few things about her, but I don't know a lot. I don't probe. I don't want to be nosy." On February 15, 1999, the Yates' fourth child, Luke, is born.

June of 1999 is a particularly difficult month for Andrea. On the 16th, she calls Rusty at work, asking him to come home. He finds her in the back of the bus, shaking uncontrollably and biting her fingers. When he is unable to calm her, he packs the family and drives to Andrea's mother's house.

The next day, Rusty leaves to run errands. Andrea tells her mother that she plans to take a nap, and takes over 40 pills, including Trazodone, an antidepressant prescribed to her mother. Paramedics later take her to a Houston hospital, where she is diagnosed with a major depressive disorder. Andrea tells the hospital staff that she took the pills to "sleep forever."

Over the next week, Yates is treated with a combination of medicines that do not appear to have an effect on her condition. Still, on June 24, doctors conclude that though she is unstable, she is not suicidal. Yates is officially released from the hospital "for insurance reasons."

Though Yates has been prescribed strong antipsychotic medication, she flushes it down the toilet. Her condition progressively worsens. Lying in bed all day, Yates scratches four bald spots into her scalp, cuts her arms and legs, and refuses to feed her children, claiming that they are "eating too much." On July 2, the stabbing vision returns. Voices tell Andrea to get a knife, though she initially refuses.

Yates's mother must tend to the children in addition to her husband, who suffers from Alzheimer's Disease. After learning the full extent of her condition, Andrea's siblings discuss their own difficulties, finding that two of them are being treated for depression, one is bipolar, and that their father more than likely suffered from untreated depression. Yates again attempts to commit suicide on July 20th, holding a knife to her throat in front of a bathroom mirror. She is returned to the psychiatric hospital, where she refuses to cooperate with interviewing nurses. She begins an intensive course of treatment via injections of Haldol, a powerful antipsychotic.

When she is released on August 9, 1999, the family moves out of the bus into a small house in Houston. Andrea leaves outpatient therapy on August 20, and her condition improves markedly over the following months. She begins to home-school the children, begins to swim in the neighborhood pool, and enjoys making costumes for her children and others', in addition to baking cakes from scratch and tending to the household. The family sets aside time three nights a week for Bible study, and their faith becomes deeper. Still, they do not adhere to organized religion, and Andrea remains in contact with Woroniecki, the evangelist. At one point, Woroniecki tells Andrea in a letter that "the role of woman is derived ... from the sin of Eve" and that bad mothers are the cause of bad children.

As Andrea's condition improves, she becomes less conscientious about taking her medication. Despite warnings from her psychotherapist, she becomes pregnant again in March, 2000. The couple's fifth child, Mary, is born on November 30.

In March of 2001, Andrea's father passes away. She is shaken and feels guilty about his death, leading her to stop talking and return to scratching her scalp and extremities. She is admitted to a psychiatric hospital on March 31, but shows little improvement under a new psychiatrist. Soon after she is discharged, she refuses to return for her outpatient appointments and stops taking the newly-prescribed medications. Despite Haldol having worked for her in the past, her new doctor distrusts the medicine and prescribes less powerful treatments. The psychiatrist agrees to her discharge from outpatient treatment, believing that Rusty can take care of her on his own.

On May 3, 2001, Yates's oldest son walks into the bathroom to find his mother filling a bathtub. Yates's mother arrives, and asks why she has filled it. "I might need it," Yates says.

Soon after this episode, Yates is rehospitalized. Again, she is put on Haldol, although this time it appears to be ineffective. Her doctor decides that because she is not suicidal, she should be discharged from the hospital. Rusty is surprised, but takes his wife home on May 14. Soon thereafter, Andrea stops taking the Haldol. On June 19, she plays basketball with Rusty and Noah, her oldest son. Immediately thereafter, she goes to bed, still in her clothing from the day.

Andrea wakes up at 8:10 a.m. on June 20, 2001. Though Rusty had promised his son John that he would take him to work for a day, he decides that because of an important design meeting that day, he cannot take the child. As Rusty leaves the house for work, Andrea is eating handfuls of Sugar Pops straight from the box.

After Rusty leaves for work, Yates fills the bathtub to three inches from the top, moving the bathmat to the side of the room so as to have better traction on the floor. All five children are in the kitchen, having breakfast. Yates has concluded that her children are "doomed to the fires of Hell," and that it is her fault. "My children were not righteous," she says. "I let them stumble." In recent months, Andrea has decided that she is marked by Satan as a bad mother. Woroniecki's rhetoric feeds her feelings of inadequacy. He has told her that parents are responsible for ensuring the salvation of their children. "Hell is right on the doorstep," he says, "waiting to bring you in." Andrea has taken his teaching to heart, deciding that she has been a bad mother and has assured her children's damnation. She has determined that they must die in order to save them from the eternal torment of hell.

Yates walks to the kitchen and picks up infant Mary, the youngest, taking her to the bathroom and putting her on the floor. She then walks Paul, the three year old, to the bathroom. She gives Mary a bottle, then holds Paul's body under the water. Paul dies within a minute, after which she carries him to her bed, tucking him under the sheets. Luke, her two year old, soon follows his older brother, and John, five years old, is next. All are placed on the bed with Paul.

Mary, who is now crying, is then drowned and left face-down in the bathtub while Yates summons Noah, her seven year old. As he comes to the bathroom, he asks "What happened to Mary?" Yates does not respond, but instead puts Noah in the tub with his sister. Noah struggles and attempts to run away, but Yates catches him and forces him under the water. He dies within minutes and is left in the bathtub. Yates takes Mary's body and places it with the others' in her bed, covering all with a sheet.

Figure 56. Houston Police officers stand outside the Yates resident after discovering the drowned children. (CBS News)

Yates picks up the telephone and calls 911, telling the dispatcher that she needs police and an ambulance. She hangs up and calls Rusty at work, telling him "It's time. I finally did it." She asks him to come home. Police arrive within minutes.

* * *

Would you convict Andrea Yates for the deaths of her five children? If so, what amount of punishment would you impose?

N	0	1	2	3	4	5	6	7	8	9	10	11
☐	☐	☐	☐	☐	☐	☐	☐	☐	☐	☐	☐	☐
no liability	liability but no punishment	1 day	2 wks.	2 mo.	6 mo.	1 yr.	3 yrs.	7 yrs.	15 yrs.	30 yrs.	life imprison-ment	no punishment but civil preventive detention for as long as she is dangerous

B. THEN EXISTING LAW

Texas Penal Code (2001)

§ 19.02—Murder

(a) In this section:

(1) "Adequate cause" means cause that would commonly produce a degree of anger, rage, resentment, or terror in a person of ordinary temper, sufficient to render the mind incapable of cool reflection.

(2) "Sudden passion" means passion directly caused by and arising out of provocation by the individual killed or another acting with the person killed which passion arises at the time of the offense and is not solely the result of former provocation.

(b) A person commits an offense if he:

(1) intentionally or knowingly causes the death of an individual;

(2) intends to cause serious bodily injury and commits an act clearly dangerous to human life that causes the death of an individual; or

(3) commits or attempts to commit a felony, other than manslaughter, and in the course of and in furtherance of the commission or attempt, or in immediate flight from the commission or attempt, he commits or attempts to commit an act clearly dangerous to human life that causes the death of an individual.

(c) Except as provided by Subsection (d), an offense under this section is a felony of the first degree.

(d) At the punishment stage of a trial, the defendant may raise the issue as to whether he caused the death under the immediate influence of sudden passion arising from an adequate cause. If the defendant proves the issue in the affirmative by a preponderance of the evidence, the offense is a felony of the second degree.

§ 19.03—Capital Murder

(a) A person commits an offense if he commits murder as defined under Section 19.02(b)(1) and:

(1) the person murders a peace officer or fireman who is acting in the lawful discharge of an official duty and who the person knows is a peace officer or fireman;

(2) the person intentionally commits the murder in the course of committing or attempting to commit kidnapping, burglary, robbery, aggravated sexual assault, arson, or obstruction or retaliation;

(3) the person commits the murder for remuneration or the promise of remuneration or employs another to commit the murder for remuneration or the promise of remuneration;

(4) the person commits the murder while escaping or attempting to escape from a penal institution;

(5) the person, while incarcerated in a penal institution, murders another:

(A) who is employed in the operation of the penal institution; or

(B) with the intent to establish, maintain, or participate in a combination or in the profits of a combination;

(6) the person:

(A) while incarcerated for an offense under this section or Section 19.02, murders another; or

(B) while serving a sentence of life imprisonment or a term of 99 years for an offense under Section 20.04, 22.021, or 29.03, murders another;

(7) the person murders more than one person:

(A) during the same criminal transaction; or

(B) during different criminal transactions but the murders are committed pursuant to the same scheme or course of conduct; or

(8) the person murders an individual under six years of age.

(b) An offense under this section is a capital felony.

(c) If the jury or, when authorized by law, the judge does not find beyond a reasonable doubt that the defendant is guilty of an offense under this section, he may be convicted of murder or of any other lesser included offense.

§ 8.01—Insanity

(a) It is an affirmative defense to prosecution that, at the time of the conduct charged, the actor, as a result of severe mental disease or defect, did not know that his conduct was wrong.

(b) The term "mental disease or defect" does not include an abnormality manifested only by repeated criminal or otherwise antisocial conduct.

§ 9.22—Necessity

Conduct is justified if:

(1) the actor reasonably believes the conduct is immediately necessary to avoid imminent harm;

(2) the desirability and urgency of avoiding the harm clearly outweigh, according to ordinary standards of reasonableness, the harm sought to be prevented by the law proscribing the conduct; and

(3) a legislative purpose to exclude the justification claimed for the conduct does not otherwise plainly appear.

§ 9.33—Defense of Third Person

A person is justified in using force or deadly force against another to protect a third person if:

(1) under the circumstances as the actor reasonably believes them to be, the actor would be justified under Section 9.31 [Self–Defense] or 9.32 [Deadly Force in Defense of Person] in using force or deadly force to protect himself against the unlawful force or unlawful deadly force he reasonably believes to be threatening the third person he seeks to protect; and

(2) the actor reasonably believes that his intervention is immediately necessary to protect the third person.

§ 1.07—Definitions

(a) In this code:

* * *

(42) "Reasonable belief" means a belief that would be held by an ordinary and prudent man in the same circumstances as the actor.

Bigby v. State, 892 S.W.2d 864 (Tex.Crim.App. 1994)

If, at the time of the conduct charged, the defendant understood the nature and quality of his action and knew that the conduct was "illegal" by the standards of society, then for the purpose of the insanity defense that person understood that his conduct was "wrong."

C. Current Law That Would Be Applied Were the Case Prosecuted Today

[Statutory changes are not relevant]

23.   THE CASE OF DAVID KENNEY HAWKINS (NEVADA, 1986)

A.   THE FACTS

In 1986, the Reno Police Department is concerned because of rising crime rates in downtown Reno, Nevada. The department has received a large number of reports of crimes in the area, mainly robbery, grand larceny, and larceny. Many people avoid the downtown area because of their fear of crime. The casino operators, fearing the loss of tourist trade, become increasingly irritated with the police department's ineffectiveness. Some have discussed organizing their own street patrols, a suggestion that the police find to be disturbing.

Reno's small downtown area is dominated by casinos, which have the unfortunate tendency to bring together two groups of people: tourists and panhandlers, who often double as petty thieves. The panhandlers gather downtown for the cheap casino food and drink and the ample opportunities to collect small change from casino patrons. The tourists, of course, come for the gambling and for the drink, which makes both winners and losers more vulnerable as they walk the streets after their spin at the casino. Tourists present a special problem for effective law enforcement because they often are too embarrassed to notify the police of a robbery or too inconvenienced to return from out-of-state for court hearings concerning a $20 or $100 loss.

The police increase uniformed squad car and foot patrols, as well as plainclothes officers in the downtown area. Despite these responses, the downtown Reno crime rate continues to increase. Frustrated by the failures, the police and district attorney's office meet several times to discuss ways to control the crime problem, eventually settling on a decoy operation. An earlier operation decreased crime by 50% while in operation.

Edwin T. Basil, an assistant district attorney, asks the police department to study and report on the specific characteristics of the crime problem. The crime statistics analyzed by Lieutenant David Kieckbusch for the last two months show the bulk of the cases to be "crimes of convenience," where the perpetrators do not plan the crimes in advance, but seize an opportunity for an easy score when it presents itself. The 93 cases of robbery, larceny, and grand larceny reviewed suggest that the perpetrators are typically young men in their late teens or twenties. The victims are generally tourists, most of them female, elderly, or disabled. The analysis also shows the downtown areas where the risk of such crime is greatest. Using Kieckbusch's analysis, the police and District Attorney tailor a decoy operation that will focus on the high-risk areas and the profiled offenders.

The night of May 27, 1986, a few weeks after the operation begins, is a routine example of how the operation works and of the people it snares. Officer Roger Linscott serves as the decoy, playing the part of a defenseless elderly man lying in a building alcove near First and Center Streets. The street corner is downtown, but is a little off the beaten path. Linscott faces away from pedestrian traffic and is unresponsive to passing pedestrians. Sticking out of his right-rear pants pocket is an IRS tax-return envelope inside a blue checkbook. Hanging about a half-inch out from the envelope are the edges of some U.S. currency, a total of $126. The package is not obvious, but is visible and will easily slide out of the decoy's pocket if pulled. The serial numbers of the four bills have been recorded in order to later identify the money.

Linscott is dressed in gray slacks, tennis shoes, a dark multicolored shirt, and a dark brown leisure jacket. His dress and demeanor are intended to give the appearance of a tourist who has had too much to drink and passed out, the type of person commonly the victim in the downtown area. To reduce the chance of having the operation interrupted by "good Samaritan" types who might intervene to help a drunk old man, the officers do not douse Linscott or leave empty bottles of alcohol near him; however, a passerby might nonetheless come to the conclusion that the prostrate man is passed out from drink.

A number of people pass by during the hour and a half that Linscott lies on the sidewalk. It is Officer Linda Peters' job to keep constant visual contact from the third floor of the parking garage across the street. Some of the passersby do not fit the profile of the offender at which the operation is aimed. When these people come by, or obvious good Samaritans or seriously down-and-out bums who might succumb to the temptation simply because of their own difficult situation, Officer Peters notifies Linscott by a radio transmitter to cover the money. The bait is exposed only to those who match the general offender profile.

Among the passersby are David Kenney Hawkins and a friend, who are on their way to the Brass Moose Saloon. Hawkins, 28, is a dealer at a downtown Reno casino. He fits the profile, so Linscott leaves the bait exposed as the pair approach. They appear to notice the "tourist" but do not stop.

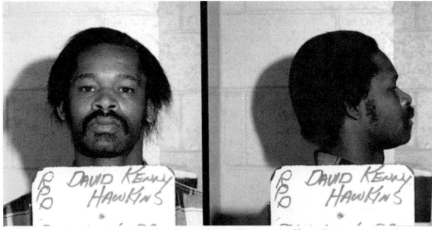

Figure 57. David Kenny Hawkins. (Reno Police Department)

They enter the saloon, stay for about 45 minutes, then leave. As they approach Linscott the second time, they stop and inspect him. Hawkins' friend jumps up and down on the ground and yells, to see if the prone man is passed out. Linscott does not move. Hawkins takes a few more moments to look the man over and then bends down and slowly removes the money from the decoy's right rear pocket.

He moves so carefully that Linscott is unaware the money has been taken. Without searching any other pockets, Hawkins and his friend continue walking and cross the street.

Seeing this, Peters notifies the perimeter officers by radio that the bait has been taken and gives the location of the suspect. Officer David Jenkins approaches Hawkins and observes the bait money protruding from Hawkins' right front pocket. When stopped, Hawkins points to several people on the street and says they told him to do it. Hawkins is immediately arrested and taken to the Reno City Jail. In addition to the bait money, he has $50 in his possession at the time of his arrest, and wears designer-label clothes.

Because of past court cases regarding entrapment, the police only charge persons they catch who have a prior criminal record. A check of police records shows that Hawkins has 25 to 30 arrests in Nevada and California, mostly small-time property crimes or generally lawless behavior. (Hawkins' friend has no criminal record and is released.) Among Hawkins' "highlights" are a 1979 arrest for petty larceny, a 1980 arrest for possession of stolen property, a 1981 arrest for petty larceny, a 1982 arrest for receiving stolen property, and a 1984 arrest for theft. Easy crimes of opportunity are not new to him. On one occasion, he took a helmet off an unattended motorcycle and, on another, he picked up a priest's toolbox as he walked by.

Hawkins is charged with grand larceny, the statutory grand larceny threshold being $100. Hawkins pleads not guilty and claims police entrapment.

The police continue their decoy operation for several more weeks and arrest other similar offenders.

* * *

Would you convict Hawkins? If so, what amount of punishment would you impose?

N	0	1	2	3	4	5	6	7	8	9	10	11
☐	☐	☐	☐	☐	☐	☐	☐	☐	☐	☐	☐	☐
no liability	liability but no punishment	1 day	2 wks.	2 mo.	6 mo.	1 yr.	3 yrs.	7 yrs.	15 yrs.	30 yrs.	life imprison- ment	death

B. THEN EXISTING LAW

Nevada Revised Statutes (1986)

§ 205.220—Grand larceny: Definition; punishment

[E]very person who feloniously steals, takes and carries away, leads or drives away the personal goods or property of another of the value of $100 or more, or the motor vehicle of another regardless of its value, is guilty of grand larceny, and shall be punished by imprisonment in the state prison for not less than 1 year nor more than 10 years and by a fine of not more than $10,000.

Shrader v. State, 706 P.2d 834 (Nevada 1985)

"Entrapment, under the subjective approach applicable in this state, encompasses two elements: (1) an opportunity to commit a crime is presented by the state (2) to a person not predisposed to commit the act. The subjective approach focuses on the origin of the criminal intent. The objective approach, on the other hand, dismisses the defendant's state of mind as irrelevant and focuses on police misconduct." The defendant must prove the first element by presenting "evidence of governmental instigation." The state must prove the second element by demonstrating "the defendant's predisposition."

C. CURRENT LAW THAT WOULD BE APPLIED WERE THE CASE PROSECUTED TODAY

Nevada Revised Statutes (2006)

§ 205.220—Grand Larceny: Definition

[A] person commits grand larceny if the person:

(1) Intentionally steals, takes and carries away, leads away or drives away:

    (a) Personal goods or property, with a value of $250 or more, owned by another person; ...

§ 205.222—Grand Larceny: Penalties

(1) Unless a greater penalty is imposed by a specific statute, a person who commits grand larceny in violation of NRS 205.220 shall be punished pursuant to the provisions of this section.

(2) If the value of the property involved in the grand larceny is less than $2,500, the person who committed the grand larceny is guilty of a category C felony and shall be punished as provided in NRS 193.130 [which provides a minimum term of not less than 1 year and a maximum term of not more than 5 years. The court may impose an additional fine of not more than $10,000.]

(3) If the value of the property involved in the grand larceny is $2,500 or more, the person who committed the grand larceny is guilty of a category B felony and shall be punished by imprisonment in the state prison for a minimum term of not less than 1 year and a maximum term of not more than 10 years, and by a fine of not more than $10,000.

(4) In addition to any other penalty, the court shall order the person who committed the grand larceny to pay restitution.

§ 205.240—Petit larceny: Definition; punishment

(1) Except as otherwise provided in NRS 205.220 ..., a person commits petit larceny if the person:

    (a) Intentionally steals, takes and carries away, leads away or drives away:

        (1) Personal goods or property, with a value of less than $250, owned by another person;

(2) A person who commits petit larceny is guilty of a misdemeanor [which provides a penalty of imprisonment in the county jail for not more than 6 months, or of a fine of not more than $1,000, or by both fine and imprisonment]. In addition to any other penalty, the court shall order the person to pay restitution.

CHAPTER 8.   ARE WE RESPONSIBLE FOR WHO WE ARE?

24.   THE CASE OF RICHARD R. TENNESON (FEDERAL, 1954)

A.   THE FACTS

It is May 18, 1951. 17–year-old Richard Tenneson is on the front line in Korea with the 2nd Army Division, south of the 38th parallel. The Communist Chinese are in the midst of a spring offensive that has pushed the 2nd Division back toward Seoul and has cut it off from the main body of American forces. Communist forces overrun Richard's position and take him prisoner, along with hundreds of others.

During the next five months, Richard and the other prisoners are marched north. At first, they move at night to hide from enemy planes. When out of enemy aircraft range, they are marched all day as well. Prisoners must forage for their own food, often eating insects, raw frogs, and the sides of corn stalks. Dysentery and starvation are common. Prisoners die all around Richard. More than half drop before the march ends 300 miles north of where it began, at a prison camp on the Yalu River near Chungsong.

Figure 58. Richard Tenneson (lower right) in 1955. This photograph was enclosed in a letter he wrote to his mother. (AP/Wide World Photos)

It is an experience like nothing before for Richard. He grew up on a small farm in rural Minnesota, some distance from the nearest hamlet of Alden, which is itself some distance from the nearest town, Albert Lea (population 14,000). He has never before traveled outside of Minnesota.

His upbringing was neither idyllic nor tragic. His father and mother divorced when he was 2, but he was always well cared for. He does not get along with his stepfather but is close to his mother, who is very religious. The family is in the poultry business.

Like most American teenagers of the time, he knows little of politics or international affairs, but he does know easy patriotism. When the Korean War breaks out, Richard quits high school and persuades his mother to sign his enlistment papers. During his visit home after basic training and before being shipped to Korea, Richard tells his mother, "If I should win the Congressional Medal of Honor, I still wouldn't have done enough for my country."

When the prisoners reach the camp, they are given blue cotton-padded uniforms that resemble pajamas. They live in large mud and bamboo huts. Body lice, dysentery, intestinal worms, pneumonia, and other diseases are common. During the winter, temperatures drop below zero.

A few weeks after reaching the camp, Richard is removed from the general population; his captors say he is being hospitalized for pneumonia. When Richard emerges from his "hospital" stay, he has a different view of the world. He is a devoted believer in the Communist Chinese cause.

Richard makes propaganda broadcasts for his captors and works to promote their cause, even among the prisoners. A few months later, in February 1952, Richard, now 18, formally renounces his United States citizenship and his belief in God and defects to Communist China. If anyone doubts the sincerity of his commitment, the doubts are removed the next year. In December 1953, when the Korean hostilities cease, Richard joins twenty other POWs who refuse repatriation to the United States and elect to stay with their former captors.

His stunned mother travels at her own expense to talk him out of his decision. She is not allowed to see him. Instead, she is given a rude and mocking letter, composed by him at a group meeting with his fellow defectors, where each sentence, once composed, is read aloud to be criticized or cheered by the group. At one point in the letter he warns her, "United States authorities ... have probably told you that I was forced, doped, brainwashed or some other horse manure that they use to slander and defile people like myself who will stand up for his own rights and the rights of man." He tells her he will stay with the Communist Chinese because that is how he can best bring peace to mankind.

* * *

What was the path of this sudden transformation from patriotic rural Minnesota farm boy to enthusiastic aid to his country's wartime enemy?

In the aftermath of the revolution in China, the Communists developed considerable expertise in what is now called "coercive indoctrination." Their methods have been studied by Westerners and their effectiveness proven. In fact, after the experience in Korea, the United States military changed its policy to no longer expect POW's to give only name, rank, and serial number, as the Geneva convention provides. The human psyche is too vulnerable, they concluded, to resist indoctrination by an experienced captor. The military services began giving special training to those in danger of capture to help them resist indoctrination. But early forms of the training, which give trainees a brief taste of the Communist Chinese methods, were discontinued when it became apparent they are counterproductive, causing trainees to fear the power and inevitability of the indoctrination process.

The Communist Chinese coercive indoctrination techniques do not rely on physical beatings or torture. Such methods were used crudely by the Viet Cong against some POW's in Vietnam, but are judged counterproductive to effective coercive indoctrination because they trigger undesirable resistance by the subject. Nor does effective coercive indoctrination use drugs or hypnosis, as the popular 1962 American movie *The Manchurian Candidate* suggests. Torture or drugs may be used to obtain a confession or some other single propaganda performance, but creation of a fully indoctrinated true believer requires a more subtle process of several stages.

The indoctrinator first must establish isolation and control of the subject—isolation from other persons and information, and control over the prisoner's body and environment. These conditions then allow implementation of the two-stage program: destruction of the previously existing self, and construction of a new self with new beliefs and values.

The destruction stage follows several avenues: (a) systematic physiological debilitation, commonly by means of inadequate diet, insufficient sleep, and poor sanitation; (b) creation of constant background anxiety, including implied threats of injury or death by a seemingly all-powerful captor (often with occasional periods of leniency, to create expectations that can be dashed, thereby reinforcing the subject's helplessness and the captor's power); (c) degradation of the subject's pre-existing self, including at later stages the use of peer pressure among indoctrinees, often applied through ritual "struggle" sessions; and (d) required performance of symbolic acts of self-betrayal, betrayal of group norms, and public confession. The severe conditions of the five month march to the prison camp were a useful prelude to the destruction process, which formally began upon Richard's isolation from the general population for "hospital" treatment.

The construction stage is more prosaic. Once the subject is psychologically broken, he is built up again in the form that the captor desires through the alleviation of physical stress and deprivation and offerings of emotional support tied to the subject's appreciation of the rightness of the indoctrinator's views. The result is a true believer. While physical or psychological duress may be used during the indoctrination process, once the process is complete, the subject has internalized the captor's values and beliefs. His statements and conduct thereafter are guided by the coercively-induced beliefs and values, but are not themselves coerced. Focusing only on the present, one would say that the "brainwashed" subject's beliefs and values are as much his own as our beliefs and values are our own.

In milder form, the techniques of coercive indoctrination are used in cults, which even in their less coercive form have the power to take over lives and even produce mass suicides. One may have thought it peculiar for a leader to move an entire cult from San Francisco to Guyana, as occurred in the Jonestown case, but shifting members to a faraway jungle is an ingenious means for inexpensively creating complete isolation and dependency.

The psychological dynamics behind the indoctrination power of the captor is sufficiently great that a captor can have an effect almost without effort or intention. "Stockholm Syndrome" is named for a 1973 episode in which four hostages of bank robbers bonded with their captors during six days in captivity, coming to conclude that the captors actually were protecting them from the police. A 1982 study reports that Stockholm Syndrome develops in half of all victims of hostage cases, even though captors rarely plan such an effect.

* * *

After refusing repatriation, Richard, now 20, participates in a propaganda campaign of which his defector group is the centerpiece. The group shuttles around China from one event to another, generating a steady stream of newspaper pictures of cheering locals welcoming the group to one holiday celebration or another. Eventually, the need for such propaganda passes and the defectors become old news. They are given factory or communal farming jobs and left to themselves. As continued reinforcement of indoctrination fades, Richard becomes homesick, especially missing his mother. Late in 1954, he arranges to return to the United States through the Red Cross.

During his trip back to the United States, he explains to reporters that he had a falling out with some of his communist colleagues but does not speak ill of his former captors or of communism. He says he does not regret his earlier decision to refuse repatriation.

After his return to the States, however, his views change quickly. Five days after his return, he is allowed to travel to Alden, Minnesota to see his mother, where he attends church. He becomes increasingly bitter toward his former captors.

It was only four years ago that he left high school and Alden. Much has happened to him since then—his capture, indoctrination, propaganda work, and return. He is now 21 years old and is still confused by what happened.

Richard is charged with several offenses, including aiding the enemy, and is subject to the death penalty or imprisonment for up to life.

* * *

Figures 59 & 60. Richard Tenneson's crossing into British Hong Kong from communist China (above) and the subsequent press conference at the Hong Kong hotel. (AP/World Wide photos)

Would you convict Richard Tenneson? If so, what amount of punishment would you impose?

N	0	1	2	3	4	5	6	7	8	9	10	11
☐	☐	☐	☐	☐	☐	☐	☐	☐	☐	☐	☐	☐

| no liability | liability but no punishment | 1 day | 2 wks. | 2 mo. | 6 mo. | 1 yr. | 3 yrs. | 7 yrs. | 15 yrs. | 30 yrs. | life imprison-ment | death |

B. THEN EXISTING LAW

Uniform Code of Military Justice, 50 U.S.C.A. (1954)

§ 698—Aiding the enemy

Any person who—

(1) aids, or attempts to aid, the enemy with arms, ammunition, supplies, money, or other things; or

(2) without proper authority, knowingly harbors or protects or gives intelligence to, or communicates or corresponds with or holds any intercourse with the enemy, either directly or indirectly;

shall suffer death or such other punishment as a court-martial or military commission may direct

§ 699—Misconduct as prisoner

Any person subject to this chapter who, while in the hands of the enemy in time of war—

(1) for the purpose of securing favorable treatment by his captors acts without proper authority in a manner contrary to law, custom, or regulation, to the detriment of others of whatever nationality held by the enemy as civilian or military prisoners; or

(2) while in a position of authority over such persons maltreats them without justifiable cause;

shall be punished as a court-martial may direct.

§ 728—General Article

Though not specifically mentioned in this chapter, all disorders and neglects to the prejudice of good order and discipline in the armed forces, all conduct of a nature to bring discredit upon the armed forces, and crimes and offenses not capital, of which persons subject to this chapter may be guilty, shall be taken cognizance of by a general, special, or summary court-martial, according to the nature and degree of the offense, and shall be punished at the discretion of that court.

C. CURRENT LAW THAT WOULD BE APPLIED WERE THE CASE PROSECUTED TODAY

[Statutory changes are not relevant]

25. THE CASE OF ALEX CABARGA (CALIFORNIA, 1982)

A. THE FACTS

In 1970, when Alex Cabarga is 5, his parents give up their traditional life in the New Jersey suburbs, sell their large house, and move to a San Francisco "experimental community" named

Figure 61.

Figure 62. *Above right:* Alex Cabarga, age 18. *Below left:* Luis "Tree Frog" Johnson. (San Francisco Chronicle)

Project Two. The group, which at that time includes 25 other members, lives in an old warehouse. Their common bond, a sign of the times, is their rejection of all traditional social values. All members, including children, are encouraged to live outside the bounds of existing social norms, including participation in open sexuality and smoking marijuana. The dominant message to Alex from his parents and the other adults is that right-thinking people reject the old conventions.

Several weeks after the family's arrival, a 33 year old man named Luis "Tree Frog" Johnson joins the group. He is a transient who shares the group's goals of throwing off old taboos. He especially favors complete freedom for children. Tree Frog befriends Alex and his two older brothers, and the boys begin spending their days with him. The parents do not like Tree Frog, but follow their new code to be open to other lifestyles and perspectives.

Two years later, Alex's parents separate. His mother takes legal custody of the boys and moves to a trailer near the warehouse. Tree Frog lives in an old school bus on the same property and continues his relationship with the boys, but now without parental monitoring. Tree Frog courts 7–year-old Alex as he would a girlfriend. As the two other boys grow older, they move out. The parents suspect Tree Frog has been having sex with Alex for some time, but do nothing about it. When Alex is 9, his mother hands over parental custody to Tree Frog and Alex moves in with him. His mother explains later that she was simply tired of being a parent. After he gains custody, Tree Frog's physical and sexual abuse of Alex becomes regular. He hits Alex and denies him food if Alex resists having sex or otherwise disobeys.

Tree Frog and Alex move away from the warehouse community. They live a nomadic life in a dilapidated bread van with cardboard on the windows, moving the van from one seedy San Francisco neighborhood to another. For money, Tree Frog sells pornographic movies of Alex.

Figure 63. The bread van in which Tree Frog and Alex lived. (San Francisco Chronicle)

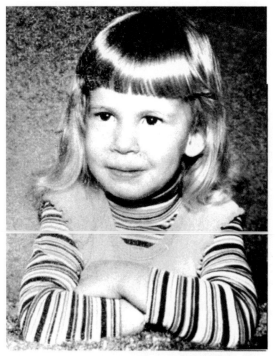

Figure 64. Tara Elizabeth Burke shortly before she was kidnapped from her parents' van. This is the photograph Lieutenant Dick Gordy of the Concord Police Department kept with him during the investigation of the case. (AP/Wide World Photos)

Figure 65. Tara Burke reunited with her mother. December 19, 1982. (AP/Wide World Photos)

Tree Frog believes in a radical dogma that advocates open sexual relations between adults and children and argues that even a very young girl can conceive a child. Tree Frog decides that they will kidnap a little girl and raise her according to his radical tenets, including having her conceive Tree Frog's child, who then also will be so raised.

On February 6, 1982 (Alex is now 17), they kidnap a 2½ year old girl named Tara Burke from her parents' van in an auto supply store parking lot, where she had been left with her 9–year-old brother, Jeremy. Tree Frog treats Tara as he treated Alex after gaining custody. She is denied food unless she obeys directions, which include having sex with Tree Frog and Alex. Tree Frog takes pictures and sometimes movies of Alex and Tara having sex. Tara is not allowed to wash and is kept naked from the waist down. Her once-blond hair becomes dirty brown. Tree Frog soon crops it close to her head.

Two months later, an 11–year-old Vietnamese runaway named Mac Lin Nguyen is befriended by Tree Frog and is offered $200 to babysit Tara. He moves into the van to live with the group. He is treated as Alex was—originally courted, then, once isolated and dependent, increasingly made Tree Frog's subject of abuse. Tree Frog continues his practice of taking pictures and movies as he directs sex between the children.

Figure 66. Alex Cabarga's parents, Ted and Diane Cabarga, wait as the jury deliberates. December 22, 1983. (Gary Fong, San Francisco Chronicle)

For eight months, the four live this way in the bread van. Mac sometimes goes on outings with Tree Frog. He explains later that he did not run away because "I didn't know where to run and I was scared." But on one occasion, Mac escapes through the van's roof ventilator while Tree Frog sleeps and runs to a house and reports the activities at the van. Police return the next day and break down the door of the van. Tree Frog jumps out screaming obscenities. Police find Alex and Tara under blankets, both naked from the waist down. When Tara is reunited with her parents, they do not recognize her. She has an extensive vocabulary, including all of the most vulgar words imaginable. A therapist later concludes that her 10–month ordeal has scarred her for life.

Several months after the police intervention, Alex says, "I can't believe I did those things." When asked about his sex acts, he says, "I feel dirty about them. I feel stupid. I feel like a dog. I don't like to feel about myself that way."

* * *

Tree Frog is convicted of 121 counts of kidnaping, false imprisonment, lewd conduct, sodomy, rape, oral copulation, and assault, and imprisoned for life. Should Alex be held criminally liable? If so, what amount of punishment would you impose?

N	0	1	2	3	4	5	6	7	8	9	10	11
☐	☐	☐	☐	☐	☐	☐	☐	☐	☐	☐	☐	☐
no liability	liability but no punishment	1 day	2 wks.	2 mo.	6 mo.	1 yr.	3 yrs.	7 yrs.	15 yrs.	30 yrs.	life imprison-ment	no punishment but civil preventive detention for as long as he is dangerous

B. Then Existing Law

California Penal Code (1982)

§ 261—Rape defined

Rape is an act of sexual intercourse accomplished with a person not the spouse of the perpetrator, under any of the following circumstances:

* * *

(2) Where it is accomplished against a person's will by means of force or fear of immediate and unlawful bodily injury on the person or another.

* * *

§ 261.5—Unlawful sexual intercourse with female under age 18

Unlawful sexual intercourse is an act of sexual intercourse accomplished with a female not the wife of the perpetrator, where the female is under the age of 18 years.

§ 264—Rape; ... unlawful sexual intercourse; punishment

Rape, as defined in Section 261 ..., is punishable by imprisonment in the state prison for three, six, or eight years.... Unlawful sexual intercourse, as defined in section 261.5, is punishable either by imprisonment in the county jail for not more than one year or in the state prison.

§ 264.1—Punishment for aiding or abetting rape

The provisions of Section 264 notwithstanding [punishment for rape], in any case in which the defendant, voluntarily acting in concert with another person, by force or violence and against the will of the victim, committed an act described in Section 261 ... either personally or by aiding and abetting the other person, that fact shall be charged in the indictment or information and if found to be true by the jury, upon a jury trial, or if found to be true by the court, upon a court trial, or if admitted by the defendant, the defendant shall suffer confinement in the state prison for five, seven, or nine years.

§ 266j—Procurement of child

Any person who intentionally gives, transports, provides, or makes available, or who offers to give, transport, provide, or make available to another person, a child under the age of 14 for the purpose of any lewd or lascivious act as defined in Section 288, or who causes, induces, or persuades a child under the age of 14 to engage in such an act with another person, is guilty of a felony and shall be imprisoned in the state prison for a term of three, six, or eight years.

§ 288—Lewd or lascivious acts involving children

(a) Any person who shall willfully and lewdly commit any lewd or lascivious act including any of the acts constituting other crimes provided for in Part 1 of this code upon or with the body, or any part or member thereof, of a child under the age of 14 years, with the intent of arousing, appealing to, or gratifying the lust or passions or sexual desires of such person or of such child, shall be guilty of a felony and shall be imprisoned in the state prison for a term of three, six, or eight years.

(b) Any person who commits an act described in subdivision (a) by use of force, violence, duress, menace, or threat of great bodily harm, shall be guilty of a felony and shall be imprisoned in the state prison for a term of three, six or eight years.

* * *

§ 207—Abduction [kidnaping], definition

Every person who forcibly steals, takes, or arrests any person in this state, and carries him into another country, state, or county, or into another part of the same county, or ... who hires, persuades, entices, decoys, or seduces by false promises, misrepresentations, or the like, any person to go out of this state, or to be taken or removed therefrom, for the purpose and with the intent to sell such person into slavery or involuntary servitude, or otherwise to employ him for his own use, or to the use of another, without the free will and consent of such persuaded person ... is guilty of kidnaping.

§ 208—[Kidnaping] Punishment; victims under 14 years of age at time of commission of crime

Kidnaping is punishable by imprisonment in the state prison for three, five, or seven years.

§ 26—Persons capable of committing crime; exceptions

All persons are capable of committing crimes except those belonging to the following classes:

(1) Children under the age of 14, in the absence of clear proof that at the time of committing the act charged against them, they knew its wrongfulness;

(2) Idiots;

(3) Persons who committed the act or made the omission charged under an ignorance or mistake of fact, which disproves any criminal intent;

(4) Persons who committed the act charged without being conscious thereof;

(5) Persons who committed the act or made the omission charged through misfortune or by accident, when it appears that there was no evil design, intention, or culpable negligence;

(6) Persons (unless the crime be punishable with death) who committed the act or made the omission charged under threats or menaces sufficient to show that they had reasonable cause to and did believe their lives would be endangered if they refused.

C. CURRENT LAW THAT WOULD BE APPLIED WERE THE CASE PROSECUTED TODAY

[Statutory changes are not relevant, except the following:]

§ 269—Aggravated sexual assault of child

(a) Any person who commits any of the following acts upon a child who is under 14 years of age and 10 or more years younger than the person is guilty of aggravated sexual assault of a child:

(1) A violation of paragraph (2) of subdivision (a) of Section 261 [where rape is accomplished against a person's will by means of force, violence, duress, menace, or fear of immediate and unlawful bodily injury on the person or another]

(2) A violation of Section 264.1.

(3) Sodomy, in violation of Section 286, when committed by force, violence, duress, menace, or fear of immediate and unlawful bodily injury on the victim or another person.

(4) Oral copulation, in violation of Section 288a, when committed by force, violence, duress, menace, or fear of immediate and unlawful bodily injury on the victim or another person.

* * *

(b) Any person who violates this section is guilty of a felony and shall be punished by imprisonment in the state prison for 15 years to life.

§ 207—Kidnapping defined

(a) Every person who forcibly, or by any other means of instilling fear, steals or takes, or holds, detains, or arrests any person in this state, and carries the person into another country, state, or county, or into another part of the same county, is guilty of kidnapping.

(b) Every person, who for the purpose of committing any act defined in Section 288 [lewd or lascivious acts], hires, persuades, entices, decoys, or seduces by false promises, misrepresentations, or the like, any child under the age of 14 years to go out of this country, state, or county, or into another part of the same county, is guilty of kidnapping.

(c) Every person who forcibly, or by any other means of instilling fear, takes or holds, detains, or arrests any person, with a design to take the person out of this state, without having established a claim, according to the laws of the United States, or of this state, or who hires, persuades, entices, decoys, or seduces by false promises, misrepresentations, or the like, any person to go out of this state, or to be taken or removed therefrom, for the purpose and with the intent to sell that person into slavery or involuntary servitude, or otherwise to employ that person for his or her own use, or to the use of another, without the free will and consent of that persuaded person, is guilty of kidnapping.

* * *

(e) For purposes of those types of kidnapping requiring force, the amount of force required to kidnap an unresisting infant or child is the amount of physical force required to take and carry the child away a substantial distance for an illegal purpose or with an illegal intent.

* * *

§ 208—Punishment of kidnapping

(a) Kidnapping is punishable by imprisonment in the state prison for three, five, or eight years.

(b) If the person kidnapped is under 14 years of age at the time of the commission of the crime, the kidnapping is punishable by imprisonment in the state prison for 5, 8, or 11 years....

* * *

§ 209—Kidnapping for gain or to commit robbery or rape; Punishment

(a) Any person who seizes, confines, inveigles, entices, decoys, abducts, conceals, kidnaps or carries away another person by any means whatsoever with intent to hold or detain, or who holds or detains, that person for ransom, reward or to commit extortion or to exact from another person any money or valuable thing, or any person who aids or abets any such act, is guilty of a felony, and upon conviction thereof, shall be punished by imprisonment in the state prison for life without possibility of parole in cases in which any person subjected to any such act suffers death or bodily harm, or is intentionally confined in a manner which exposes that person to a substantial likelihood of death, or shall be punished by imprisonment in the state prison for life with the possibility of parole in cases where no such person suffers death or bodily harm.

(b)(1) Any person who kidnaps or carries away any individual to commit ... rape, ... oral copulation, sodomy, ... shall be punished by imprisonment in the state prison for life with possibility of parole.

*   *   *

26. THE CASE OF ROBERT "YUMMY" SANDIFER (ILLINOIS, 1994)

A. THE FACTS

Robert Sandifer is born the third of eight children to a Chicago woman who is a drug addict and prostitute. Lorina Sandifer's first child was born when she was fifteen. By the time she is 29, she has been arrested 41 times. Robert's father deals drugs and weapons when he is not in prison.

The children are frequently left home alone. When their mother is home, she generally beats the children. (Robert calls his mother "Reen" and his grandmother "Mama.") Before he reaches the age of three, Robert has injuries resulting from regular whippings with an electrical cord, and has burns from cigarette butts. He and his siblings are placed with his grandmother by Family Services, but she is little better than their mother. A psychiatric report finds the grandmother to be suffering a "severe borderline personality disorder." At various times, 40 children live in her three-bedroom house—10 of her own and 30 grandchildren. Neighbors circulate a petition to force her to move out of the neighborhood.

Robert's direction of development shows itself early. During a hospital stay when he is not yet 3, a social worker says something that angers him. He grabs a toy knife and charges the woman, screaming "Fuck you, you bitch." He jabs the rubber knife into the woman's arm, saying "I'm going to cut you."

Figure 67. Robert Sandifer. (Chicago Sun-Times)

Robert misses more of first grade than he attends and, increasingly, lives on the street, where his reputation is bad. "Nobody likes that boy," says 13–year-old Morris Anderson, who often got into fist-fights with the younger and smaller Robert. A local grocer bars Robert from his store for stealing. "He is a crooked son-of-a-bitch. Always in trouble. He stands out there on the corner and strong-arms other kids." Robert often challenges older, bigger kids to fights, sometimes beating them, and earns a reputation as a street fighter and a bully. "I never played with him 'cause he hung out with the older boys," says Donald Hannah, 10, who attended first-grade with Robert. "He would ask you for 50 cents," 11–year-old Steve Nelson explains, "and if he knew you were scared and you gave him the money, he'd ask for another 50 cents." A neighbor says, "You can't really describe how bad he really was. He'd curse you completely out. He broke into school, took money, and burned cars."

Indeed, one of Robert's first vices is cars. He likes big and powerful ones—Lincolns and Cadillacs. Says a 17–year-old who knows him, "He can drive real well. It is like a midget driving a luxury car." Robert sometimes hangs out at a garage and shows interest in learning about cars, but mainly he steals them, throws things at them, or burns them. Because he is too young to be locked up, when Robert is arrested, he is usually just taken back to his grandmother's house. He then heads back out on the street.

Figure 68. Lorina Sandifer, the mother of Robert Sandifer, on her porch with a family friend, Sherman Nelson. (John White, Chicago Sun-Times)

In Robert's world, the strength of the gang speaks loudly. At 8 years old with his father in prison, his mother absent, and his grandmother disconnected, Robert joins the "Black Disciples," one of Chicago's largest street gangs. Young members like Robert are prized because they are immune from detention for more than 30 days.

In the gang Robert finds a family. He picks up the nickname "Yummy" because of his love of cookies and Snickers bars. Although small—4½ feet tall and weighing 86 pounds—Robert is an active and devoted gang member. He has the gang insignia tattooed on his forearm. His first officially recorded offense, at age 9, is an armed robbery. By age 11, he has compiled a rap sheet of 28 crimes, all but five of which are felonies. His short detentions become less frequent when, because of his violence toward other detained children, Family Services refuses to accept even temporary custody.

On August 28, 1994, Robert is assigned by gang higher-ups to shoot a member of a rival gang, the "Gangster Disciples." The attack is part of a larger ongoing conflict between the two groups. At 6:30 p.m., 11–year-old Robert walks up to rival gang member Kianta Britten, 16, who is standing on a street corner with other gang members. Robert draws his gun, and Kianta turns to run away. Robert shoots him twice in the back.

Two hours later, still acting under orders, Robert runs out of a viaduct toward a group of boys playing football and opens fire with his 9 mm semiautomatic handgun. He wounds Sammy Saey, 17, and hits Shavon Dean, a 14–year-old girl, in the head, killing her.

Robert is wanted for murder, attempted murder, and aggravated assault.

Figure 69. One of Robert Sandifer's victims, Shavon Dean. (Family photo)

* * *

If Robert, now 11, is prosecuted in adult court, would you convict? If so, what amount of punishment, would you impose on Robert?

N	0	1	2	3	4	5	6	7	8	9	10	11
☐	☐	☐	☐	☐	☐	☐	☐	☐	☐	☐	☐	☐
no liability	liability but no punishment	1 day	2 wks.	2 mo.	6 mo.	1 yr.	3 yrs.	7 yrs.	15 yrs.	30 yrs.	life imprison-ment	no punishment but civil preventive detention for as long as he is dangerous

B. THEN EXISTING LAW

Illinois Compiled Statutes (1994)

§ 720-5/9-1—First degree Murder—Death penalties—Exceptions—Separate Hearings—Proof—Findings—Appellate procedures—Reversals

(a) A person who kills an individual without lawful justification commits first degree murder if, in performing the acts which cause the death:

(1) he either intends to kill or do great bodily harm to that individual or another, or knows that such acts will cause death to that individual or another; or

(2) he knows that such acts create a strong probability of death or great bodily harm to that individual or another; or

(3) he is attempting or committing a forcible felony other than second degree murder.

(b) Aggravating Factors. A defendant who at the time of the commission of the offense has attained the age of 18 or more and who has been found guilty of first degree murder may be sentenced to death if:

* * *

(7) the murdered individual was under 12 years of age and the death resulted from exceptionally brutal or heinous behavior indicative of wanton cruelty; or

(8) the defendant committed the murder with intent to prevent the murdered individual from testifying in any criminal prosecution or giving material assistance to the State in any investigation or prosecution, either against the defendant or another; or the defendant committed the murder because the murdered individual was a witness in any prosecution or gave material assistance to the State in any investigation or prosecution, either against the defendant or another; or

* * *

(11) the murder was committed in a cold, calculated and premeditated manner pursuant to a preconceived plan, scheme or design to take a human life by unlawful means, and the conduct of the defendant created a reasonable expectation that the death of a human being would result therefrom

* * *

(c) Consideration of Factors in Aggravation and Mitigation. The court shall consider, or shall instruct the jury to consider any aggravating and any mitigating factors which are relevant to the imposition of the death penalty. Aggravating factors may include but need not be limited to those factors set forth in subsection (b). Mitigating factors may include but need not be limited to the following:

(1) the defendant has no significant history of prior criminal activity;

(2) the murder was committed while the defendant was under the influence of extreme mental or emotional disturbance, although not such as to constitute a defense to prosecution;

(3) the murdered individual was a participant in the defendant's homicidal conduct or consented to the homicidal act;

(4) the defendant acted under the compulsion of threat or menace of the imminent infliction of death or great bodily harm;

(5) the defendant was not personally present during commission of the act or acts causing death.

* * *

§ 720–5/6–1—Infancy

No person shall be convicted of any offense unless he had attained his 13th birthday at the time the offence was committed.

§ 720–5/8–4—Attempt

(a) Elements of the offense. A person commits an attempt when, with intent to commit a specific offense, he does any act which constitutes a substantial step toward the commission of that offense.

(b) Impossibility. It shall not be a defense to a charge of attempt that because of a misapprehension of the circumstances it would have been impossible for the accused to commit the offense attempted.

(c) Sentence. A person convicted of an attempt may be fined or imprisoned or both not to exceed the maximum provided for the offense attempted, ...

(1) the sentence for attempt to commit first degree murder is the sentence for a Class X felony, except that an attempt to commit first degree murder when at least one of the aggravating factors specified in paragraphs (1), (2) and (12) of subsection (b) of Section 9–1 [that the murder victim was a peace officer, fireman, correctional employee, or emergency medical person] is present is a Class X felony for which the sentence shall be a term of imprisonment of not less than 15 years and not more than 60 years;

(2) the sentence for attempt to commit a Class X felony is the sentence for a Class 1 felony;

(3) the sentence for attempt to commit a Class 1 felony is the sentence for a Class 2 felony;

(4) the sentence for attempt to commit a Class 2 felony is the sentence for a Class 3 felony; and

(5) the sentence for attempt to commit any felony other than those specified in Subsections (1), (2), (3) and (4) hereof is the sentence for a Class A misdemeanor.

§ 720–5/12–2—Aggravated Assault

(a) A person commits an aggravated assault, when, in committing an assault, he:

(1) Uses a deadly weapon or any device manufactured and designed to be substantially similar in appearance to a firearm, other than by discharging a firearm in the direction of

another person, a peace officer, a person summoned or directed by a peace officer, a correctional officer or a fireman....

* * *

(13) Discharges a firearm.

(b) Sentence. Aggravated assault as defined in paragraphs (1) through (12) of Subsection (a) of this section is a Class A misdemeanor. Aggravated assault as defined in paragraph (13) of Subsection (a) of this section is a Class 4 felony.

C. Current Law That Would Be Applied Were the Case Prosecuted Today

[Statutory changes are not relevant except for the following:]

Illinois Consolidated Statutes (2006)

§ 705–405/5–820—Violent Juvenile Offender

(a) Definition. A minor having been previously adjudicated a delinquent minor for an offense which, had he or she been prosecuted as an adult, would have been a Class 2 or greater felony involving the use or threat of physical force or violence against an individual or a Class 2 or greater felony for which an element of the offense is possession or use of a firearm, and who is thereafter adjudicated a delinquent minor for a second time for any of those offenses shall be adjudicated a Violent Juvenile Offender if:

(1) The second adjudication is for an offense occurring after adjudication on the first; and

(2) The second offense occurred on or after January 1, 1995.

* * *

(d) Trial. Trial on the petition shall be by jury unless the minor demands, in open court and with advice of counsel, a trial by the court without a jury....

(f) Disposition. If the court finds that the prerequisites established in subsection (a) of this Section have been proven, it shall adjudicate the minor a Violent Juvenile Offender and commit the minor to the Department of Juvenile Justice, until his or her 21st birthday, without possibility of parole, furlough, or non-emergency authorized absence. However, the minor shall be entitled to earn one day of good conduct credit for each day served as reductions against the period of his or her confinement. The good conduct credits shall be earned or revoked according to the procedures applicable to the allowance and revocation of good conduct credit for adult prisoners serving determinate sentences for felonies....

§ 730–5/3–10–11—Transfers from Department of Children and Family Services

(a) If (i) a minor 10 years of age or older is adjudicated a delinquent under the Juvenile Court Act or the Juvenile Court Act of 1987 and placed with the Department of Children and Family Services, (ii) it is determined by an interagency review committee that the Department of Children and Family Services lacks adequate facilities to care for and rehabilitate such minor and that placement of such minor with the Department of Corrections, subject to certification by the Department of Corrections, is appropriate, and (iii) the Department of Corrections certifies that it has suitable facilities and personnel available for the confinement of the minor, the Department of Children and Family Services may transfer custody of the minor to the Juvenile Division of the Department of Corrections provided that:

(1) the juvenile court that adjudicated the minor a delinquent orders the transfer after a hearing with opportunity to the minor to be heard and defend; and

(2) the Assistant Director of the Department of Corrections, Juvenile Division, is made a party to the action; and

(3) notice of such transfer is given to the minor's parent, guardian or nearest relative; and

(4) a term of incarceration is permitted by law for adults found guilty of the offense for which the minor was adjudicated delinquent....

*   *   *

(e) In no event shall a minor transferred under this Section remain in the custody of the Department of Corrections for a period of time in excess of that period for which an adult could be committed for the same act.

(Note the Juvenile Court Act of 1987 has been repealed.)

Note on American Law Concerning Minimum Age for Criminal (Adult Court) Prosecution

In 25 states—Alaska, Arizona, Delaware, District of Columbia, Florida, Georgia, Hawaii, Idaho, Indiana, Kansas, Maine, Maryland, Nebraska, Nevada, Oklahoma, Oregon, Pennsylvania, Rhode Island, South Carolina, South Dakota, Tennessee, Vermont, Washington, West Virginia, and Wyoming—Robert Sandifer could have been prosecuted for murder as an adult. See Department of Justice, Juvenile Offenders and Victims: A National Report 114 (2006).

APPENDIX A: SELECTED PROVISIONS OF THE MODEL PENAL CODE

TABLE OF CONTENTS

PART I. GENERAL PROVISIONS

ARTICLE 1. PRELIMINARY

Section
1.02	Purposes; Principles of Construction
1.03	Territorial Applicability
1.04	Classes of Crimes; Violations
1.05	All Offenses Defined by Statute; Application of General Provisions of the Code
1.06	Time Limitations
1.07	Method of Prosecution When Conduct Constitutes More Than One Offense
1.12	Proof Beyond a Reasonable Doubt; Affirmative Defenses; Burden of Proving Fact When Not an Element of an Offense; Presumptions
1.13	General Definitions

ARTICLE 2. GENERAL PRINCIPLES OF LIABILITY

Section
2.01	Requirement of Voluntary Act; Omission as Basis of Liability; Possession as an Act
2.02	General Requirements of Culpability
2.03	Causal Relationship Between Conduct and Result; Divergence Between Result Designed or Contemplated and Actual Result or Between Probable and Actual Result
2.04	Ignorance or Mistake
2.05	When Culpability Requirements Are Inapplicable to Violations and to Offenses Defined by Other Statutes; Effect of Absolute Liability in Reducing Grade of Offense to Violation
2.06	Liability for Conduct of Another; Complicity
2.07	Liability of Corporations, Unincorporated Associations and Persons Acting, or Under a Duty to Act, in Their Behalf
2.08	Intoxication
2.09	Duress
2.10	Military Orders
2.11	Consent
2.12	De Minimis Infractions
2.13	Entrapment

ARTICLE 3. GENERAL PRINCIPLES OF JUSTIFICATION

Section
3.01	Justification an Affirmative Defense; Civil Remedies Unaffected
3.02	Justification Generally: Choice of Evils
3.03	Execution of Public Duty
3.04	Use of Force in Self–Protection
3.05	Use of Force for the Protection of Other Persons
3.06	Use of Force for Protection of Property
3.07	Use of Force in Law Enforcement
3.08	Use of Force by Persons with Special Responsibility for Care, Discipline or Safety of Others
3.09	Mistake of Law as to Unlawfulness of Force of Legality of Arrest; Reckless or Negligent Use of Otherwise Justifiable Force; Reckless or Negligent Injury or Risk of Injury to Innocent Persons
3.10	Justification in Property Crimes
3.11	Definitions

ARTICLE 4. RESPONSIBILITY

Section

4.01   Mental Disease or Defect Excluding Responsibility

4.02   Evidence of Mental Disease or Defect Admissible When Relevant to Element of the Offense; [Mental Disease or Defect Impairing Capacity as Ground for Mitigation of Punishment in Capital Cases]

4.04   Mental Disease or Defect Excluding Fitness to Proceed

4.10   Immaturity Excluding Criminal Convictions; Transfer of Proceedings to Juvenile Court

ARTICLE 5. INCHOATE CRIMES

Section

5.01   Criminal Attempt

5.02   Criminal Solicitation

5.03   Criminal Conspiracy

5.04   Incapacity, Irresponsibility or Immunity of Party to Solicitation or Conspiracy

5.05   Grading of Criminal Attempt, Solicitation and Conspiracy; Mitigation in Cases of Lesser Danger; Multiple Convictions Barred

5.06   Possessing Instruments of Crime; Weapons

5.07   Prohibited Offensive Weapons

ARTICLE 6. AUTHORIZED DISPOSITION OF OFFENDERS

Section

6.01   Degrees of Felonies

6.02   Sentence in Accordance with Code; Authorized Dispositions

6.03   Fines

6.06   Sentence of Imprisonment for Felony; Ordinary Terms

6.07   Sentence of Imprisonment for Felony; Extended Terms

6.08   Sentence of Imprisonment for Misdemeanors and Petty Misdemeanors; Ordinary Terms

6.09   Sentence of Imprisonment for Misdemeanors and Petty Misdemeanors; Extended Terms

6.13   Civil Commitment in Lieu of Prosecution or of Sentence

ARTICLE 7. AUTHORITY OF COURT IN SENTENCING

Section

7.03   Criteria for Sentence of Extended Term of Imprisonment; Felonies

7.04   Criteria for Sentence of Extended Term of Imprisonment; Misdemeanors and Petty Misdemeanors

7.06   Multiple Sentences; Concurrent and Consecutive Terms

PART II. DEFINITION OF SPECIFIC CRIMES

OFFENSES INVOLVING DANGER TO THE PERSON

ARTICLE 210. CRIMINAL HOMICIDE

Section

210.0   Definitions

210.1   Criminal Homicide

210.2   Murder

210.3   Manslaughter

210.4   Negligent Homicide

210.5   Causing or Aiding Suicide

210.6   Sentence of Death for Murder; Further Proceedings to Determine Sentence

ARTICLE 211. ASSAULT; RECKLESS ENDANGERING; THREATS

Section

211.0   Definitions

211.1   Assault

211.2   Recklessly Endangering Another Person

211.3   Terroristic Threats

ARTICLE 212. KIDNAPPING AND RELATED OFFENSES; COERCION

Section

212.0 Definitions

212.1 Kidnapping

212.2 Felonious Restraint

212.3 False Imprisonment

212.4 Interference with Custody

212.5 Criminal Coercion

ARTICLE 213. SEXUAL OFFENSES

Section

213.0 Definitions

213.1 Rape and Related Offenses

213.2 Deviate Sexual Intercourse by Force or Imposition

213.3 Corruption of Minors and Seduction

213.4 Sexual Assault

213.5 Indecent Exposure

213.6 Provisions Generally Applicable to Article 213

OFFENSES AGAINST PROPERTY

ARTICLES 220. ARSON, CRIMINAL MISCHIEF, AND OTHER PROPERTY DESTRUCTION

Section

220.1 Arson and Related Offenses

220.2 Causing or Risking Catastrophe

220.3 Criminal Mischief

ARTICLE 221. BURGLARY AND OTHER CRIMINAL INTRUSION

Section

221.0 Definitions

221.1 Burglary

221.2 Criminal Trespass

ARTICLE 222. ROBBERY

Section

222.1 Robbery

ARTICLE 223. THEFT AND RELATED OFFENSES

Section

223.0 Definitions

223.1 Consolidation of Theft Offenses; Grading; Provisions Applicable to Theft Generally

223.2 Theft by Unlawful Taking or Disposition

223.3 Theft by Deception

223.4 Theft by Extortion

223.5 Theft of Property Lost, Mislaid, or Delivered by Mistake

223.6 Receiving Stolen Property

223.7 Theft of Services

223.8 Theft by Failure to Make Required Disposition of Funds Received

223.9 Unauthorized Use of Automobiles and Other Vehicles

ARTICLE 224. FORGERY AND FRAUDULENT PRACTICES

Section

224.0 Definitions

224.1 Forgery

224.3 Fraudulent Destruction, Removal or Concealment of Recordable Instruments

224.4 Tampering with Records

224.6 Credit Cards

OFFENSES AGAINST THE FAMILY

ARTICLE 230.   OFFENSES AGAINST THE FAMILY

Section
230.3   Abortion
230.4   Endangering Welfare of Children
230.5   Persistent Non–Support

OFFENSES AGAINST PUBLIC ADMINISTRATION

ARTICLE 242.   OBSTRUCTING GOVERNMENTAL OPERATIONS; ESCAPES

Section
242.0   Definitions
242.1   Obstructing Administration of Law or Other Governmental Function
242.2   Resisting Arrest or Other Law Enforcement
242.5   Compounding
242.6   Escape

OFFENSES AGAINST PUBLIC ORDER AND DECENCY

ARTICLE 250.   RIOT, DISORDERLY CONDUCT, AND RELATED OFFENSES

Section
250.1   Riot; Failure to Disperse
250.2   Disorderly Conduct
250.4   Harassment
250.5   Public Drunkenness; Drug Incapacitation
250.9   Desecration of Venerated Objects
250.10   Abuse of Corpse

ARTICLE 251.   PUBLIC INDECENCY

Section
251.3   Loitering to Solicit Deviate Sexual Relations

PART I.   GENERAL PROVISIONS

ARTICLE 1.   PRELIMINARY

Section 1.02.   Purposes; Principles of Construction.

(1) The general purposes of the provisions governing the definition of offenses are:

(a) to forbid and prevent conduct that unjustifiably and inexcusably inflicts or threatens substantial harm to individual or public interests;

(b) to subject to public control persons whose conduct indicates that they are disposed to commit crimes;

(c) to safeguard conduct that is without fault from condemnation as criminal;

(d) to give fair warning of the nature of the conduct declared to constitute an offense;

(e) to differentiate on reasonable grounds between serious and minor offenses.

(2) The general purposes of the provisions governing the sentencing and treatment of offenders are:

(a) to prevent the commission of offenses;

(b) to promote the correction and rehabilitation of offenders;

(c) to safeguard offenders against excessive, disproportionate or arbitrary punishment;

(d) to give fair warning of the nature of the sentences that may be imposed on conviction of an offense;

(e) to differentiate among offenders with a view to a just individualization in their treatment;

(f) to define, coordinate and harmonize the powers, duties and functions of the courts and of administrative officers and agencies responsible for dealing with offenders;

(g) to advance the use of generally accepted scientific methods and knowledge in the sentencing and treatment of offenders;

(h) to integrate responsibility for the administration of the correctional system in a State Department of Correction [or other single department or agency].

(3) The provisions of the Code shall be construed according to the fair import of their terms but when the language is susceptible of differing constructions it shall be interpreted to further the general purposes stated in this Section and the special purposes of the particular provision involved. The discretionary powers conferred by the Code shall be exercised in accordance with the criteria stated in the Code and, insofar as such criteria are not decisive, to further the general purposes stated in this Section.

Section 1.03. Territorial Applicability.

(1) Except as otherwise provided in this Section, a person may be convicted under the law of this State of an offense committed by his own conduct or the conduct of another for which he is legally accountable if:

(a) either the conduct which is an element of the offense or the result which is such an element occurs within this State; or

(b) conduct occurring outside the State is sufficient under the law of this State to constitute an attempt to commit an offense within the State; or

(c) conduct occurring outside the State is sufficient under the law of this State to constitute a conspiracy to commit an offense within the State and an overt act in furtherance of such conspiracy occurs within the State; or

(d) conduct occurring within the State establishes complicity in the commission of, or an attempt, solicitation or conspiracy to commit, an offense in another jurisdiction which also is an offense under the law of this State; or

(e) the offense consists of the omission to perform a legal duty imposed by the law of the State with respect to domicile, residence or a relationship to a person, thing or transaction in the State; or

(f) the offense is based on a statute of this State which expressly prohibits conduct outside the State, when the conduct bears a reasonable relation to a legitimate interest of this State and the actor knows or should know that his conduct is likely to affect that interest.

(2) Subsection (1)(a) does not apply when either causing a specified result or a purpose to cause or danger of causing such a result is an element of an offense and the result occurs or is designed or likely to occur only in another jurisdiction where the conduct charged would not constitute an offense, unless a legislative purpose plainly appears to declare the conduct criminal regardless of the place of the result.

(3) Subsection (1)(a) does not apply when causing a particular result is an element of an offense and the result is caused by conduct occurring outside the State which would not constitute an offense if the result had occurred there, unless the actor purposely or knowingly caused the result within the State.

(4) When the offense is homicide, either the death of the victim or the bodily impact causing death constitutes a "result," within the meaning of Subsection (1)(a) and if the body of a homicide victim is found within the State, it is presumed that such result occurred within the State.

(5) This State includes the land and water and the air space above such land and water with respect to which the State has legislative jurisdiction.

Section 1.04. Classes of Crimes; Violations.

(1) An offense defined by this Code or by any other statute of this State, for which a sentence of [death or of] imprisonment is authorized, constitutes a crime. Crimes are classified as felonies, misdemeanors or petty misdemeanors.

(2) A crime is a felony if it is so designated in this Code or if persons convicted thereof may be sentenced [to death or] to imprisonment for a term which, apart from an extended term, is in excess of one year.

(3) A crime s a misdemeanor if it is so designated in this Code or in a statute other than this Code enacted subsequent thereto.

(4) A crime is a petty misdemeanor if it is so designated in this Code or in a statute other than this Code enacted subsequent thereto or if it is defined by a statute other than this Code which now provides that persons convicted thereof may be sentenced to imprisonment for a term of which the maximum is less than one year.

(5) An offense defined by this Code or by any other statute of this State constitutes a violation if it is so designated in this Code or in the law defining the offense or if no other sentence than a fine, or fine and forfeiture or other civil penalty is authorized upon conviction or if it is defined by a statute other than this Code which now provides that the offense shall not constitute a crime. A violation does not constitute a crime and conviction of a violation shall not give rise to any disability or legal disadvantage based on conviction of a criminal offense.

(6) Any offense declared by law to constitute a crime, without specification of the grade thereof or of the sentence authorized upon conviction, is a misdemeanor.

(7) An offense defined by any statute of this State other than this Code shall be classified as provided in this Section and the sentence that may be imposed upon conviction thereof shall hereafter be governed by this Code.

Section 1.05. All Offenses Defined by Statute; Application of General Provisions of the Code.

(1) No conduct constitutes an offense unless it is a crime or violation under this Code or another statute of this State.

(2) The provisions of Part I of the Code are applicable to offenses defined by other statutes, unless the Code otherwise provides.

(3) This Section does not affect the power of a court to punish for contempt or to employ any sanction authorized by law for the enforcement of an order or a civil judgment or decree.

Section 1.06. Time Limitations.

(1) A prosecution for murder may be commenced at any time.

(2) Except as otherwise provided in this Section, prosecutions for other offenses are subject to the following periods of limitation:

(a) a prosecution for a felony of the first degree must be commenced within six years after it is committed;

(b) a prosecution for any other felony must be commenced within three years after it is committed;

(c) a prosecution for a misdemeanor must be commenced within two years after it is committed;

(d) a prosecution for a petty misdemeanor or a violation must be commenced within six months after it is committed.

(3) If the period prescribed in Subsection (2) has expired, a prosecution may nevertheless be commenced for:

(a) any offense a material element of which is either fraud or a breach of fiduciary obligation within one year after discovery of the offense by an aggrieved party or by a person who has legal duty to represent an aggrieved party and who is himself not a party to the offense, but in no case shall this provision extend the period of limitation otherwise applicable by more than three years; and

(b) any offense based upon misconduct in office by a public officer or employee at any time when the defendant is in public office or employment or within two years thereafter, but in no case shall this provision extend the period of limitation otherwise applicable by more than three years.

(4) An offense is committed either when every element occurs, or, if a legislative purpose to prohibit a continuing course of conduct plainly appears, at the time when the course of conduct or the defendant's complicity therein is terminated. Time starts to run on the day after the offense is committed.

(5) A prosecution is commenced either when an indictment is found [or an information filed] or when a warrant or other process is issued, provided that such warrant or process is executed without unreasonable delay.

(6) The period of limitation does not run:

(a) during any time when the accused is continuously absent from the State or has no reasonably ascertainable place of abode or work within the State, but in no case shall this provision extend the period of limitation otherwise applicable by more than three years; or

(b) during any time when a prosecution against the accused for the same conduct is pending in this State.

Section 1.07. Method of Prosecution When Conduct Constitutes More Than One Offense.

(1) Prosecution for Multiple Offenses; Limitation on Convictions. When the same conduct of a defendant may establish the commission of more than one offense, the defendant may be prosecuted for each such offense. He may not, however, be convicted of more than one offense if:

(a) one offense is included in the other, as defined in Subsection (4) of this Section; or

(b) one offense consists only of a conspiracy or other form of preparation to commit the other; or

(c) inconsistent findings of fact are required to establish the commission of the offenses; or

(d) the offenses differ only in that one is defined to prohibit a designated kind of conduct generally and the other to prohibit a specific instance of such conduct; or

(e) the offense is defined as a continuing course of conduct and the defendant's course of conduct was uninterrupted, unless the law provides that specific periods of such conduct constitute separate offenses.

(2) Limitation on Separate Trials for Multiple Offenses. Except as provided in Subsection (3) of this Section, a defendant shall not be subject to separate trials for multiple offenses based on the same conduct or arising from the same criminal episode, if such offenses are known to the appropriate prosecuting officer at the time of the commencement of the first trial and are within the jurisdiction of a single court.

(3) Authority of Court to Order Separate Trials. When a defendant is charged with two or more offenses based on the same conduct or arising from the same criminal episode, the Court, on application of the prosecuting attorney or of the defendant, may order any such charge to be tried separately, if it is satisfied that justice so requires.

(4) Conviction of Included Offense Permitted. A defendant may be convicted of an offense included in an offense charged in the indictment [or the information]. An offense is so included when:

(a) it is established by proof of the same or less than all the facts required to establish the commission of the offense charged; or

(b) it consists of an attempt or solicitation to commit the offense charged or to commit an offense otherwise included therein; or

(c) it differs from the offense charged only in the respect that a less serious injury or risk of injury to the same person, property or public interest or a lesser kind of culpability suffices to establish its commission.

(5) Submission of Included Offense to Jury. The Court shall not be obligated to charge the jury with respect to an included offense unless there is a rational basis for a verdict acquitting the defendant of the offense charged and convicting him of the included offense.

Section 1.12. Proof Beyond a Reasonable Doubt; Affirmative Defenses; Burden of Proving Fact When Not an Element of an Offense; Presumptions.

(1) No person may be convicted of an offense unless each element of such offense is proved beyond a reasonable doubt. In the absence of such proof, the innocence of the defendant is assumed.

(2) Subsection (1) of this Section does not:

(a) require the disproof of an affirmative defense unless and until there is evidence supporting such defense; or

(b) apply to any defense which the Code or another statute plainly requires the defendant to prove by a preponderance of evidence.

(3) A ground of defense is affirmative, within the meaning of Subsection (2)(a) of this Section, when:

(a) it arises under a section of the Code which so provides; or

(b) it relates to an offense defined by a statute other than the Code and such statute so provides; or

(c) it involves a matter of excuse or justification peculiarly within the knowledge of the defendant on which he can fairly be required to adduce supporting evidence.

(4) When the application of the Code depends upon the finding of a fact which is not an element of an offense, unless the Code otherwise provides:

(a) the burden of proving the fact is on the prosecution or defendant, depending on whose interest or contention will be furthered if the finding should be made; and

(b) the fact must be proved to the satisfaction of the Court or jury, as the case may be.

(5) When the Code establishes a presumption with respect to any fact which is an element of an offense, it has the following consequences:

(a) when there is evidence of the facts which give rise to the presumption, the issue of the existence of the presumed fact must be submitted to the jury, unless the Court is satisfied that the evidence as a whole clearly negatives the presumed fact; and

(b) when the issue of the existence of the presumed fact is submitted to the jury, the Court shall charge that while the presumed fact must, on all the evidence, be proved beyond a reasonable doubt, the law declares that the jury may regard the facts giving rise to the presumption as sufficient evidence of the presumed fact.

(6) A presumption not established by the Code or inconsistent with it has the consequences otherwise accorded it by law.

Section 1.13. General Definitions.

In this Code, unless a different meaning plainly is required:

(1) "statute" includes the Constitution and a local law or ordinance of a political subdivision of the State;

(2) "act" or "action" means a bodily movement whether voluntary or involuntary;

(3) "voluntary" has the meaning specified in Section 2.01;

(4) "omission" means a failure to act;

(5) "conduct" means an action or omission and its accompanying state of mind, or, where relevant, a series of acts and omissions;

(6) "actor" includes, where relevant, a person guilty of an omission;

(7) "acted" includes, where relevant, "omitted to act";

(8) "person," "he" and "actor" include any natural person and, where relevant, a corporation or an unincorporated association;

(9) "element of an offense" means (i) such conduct or (ii) such attendant circumstances or (iii) such a result of conduct as

(a) is included in the description of the forbidden conduct in the definition of the offense; or

(b) establishes the required kind of culpability; or

(c) negatives an excuse or justification for such conduct; or

(d) negatives a defense under the statute of limitations; or

(e) establishes jurisdiction or venue;

(10) "material element of an offense" means an element that does not relate exclusively to the statute of limitations, jurisdiction, venue or to any other matter similarly unconnected with (i) the harm or evil, incident to conduct, sought to be prevented by the law defining the offense, or (ii) the existence of a justification or excuse for such conduct;

(11) "purposely" has the meaning specified in Section 2.02 and equivalent terms such as "with purpose," "designed" or "with design" have the same meaning;

(12) "intentionally" or "with intent" means purposely;

(13) "knowingly" has the meaning specified in Section 2.02 and equivalent terms such as "knowing" or "with knowledge" have the same meaning;

(14) "recklessly" has the meaning specified in Section 2.02 and equivalent terms such as "recklessness" or "with recklessness" have the same meaning;

(15) "negligently" has the meaning specified in Section 2.02 and equivalent terms such as "negligence' " or "with negligence" have the same meaning;

(16) "reasonably believes" or "reasonable belief" designates a belief which the actor is not reckless or negligent in holding.

ARTICLE 2.   GENERAL PRINCIPLES OF LIABILITY.

Section 2.01.   Requirement of Voluntary Act; Omission as Basis of Liability; Possession as an Act.

(1) A person is not guilty of an offense unless his liability is based on conduct which includes a voluntary act or the omission to perform an act of which he is physically capable.

(2) The following are not voluntary acts within the meaning of this Section:

(a) a reflex or convulsion;

(b) a bodily movement during unconsciousness or sleep;

(c) conduct during hypnosis or resulting from hypnotic suggestion;

(d) a bodily movement that otherwise is not a product of the effort or determination of the actor, either conscious or habitual.

(3) Liability for the commission of an offense may not be based on an omission unaccompanied by action unless:

(a) the omission is expressly made sufficient by the law defining the offense; or

(b) a duty to perform the omitted act is otherwise imposed by law.

(4) Possession is an act, within the meaning of this Section, if the possessor knowingly procured or received the thing possessed or was aware of his control thereof for a sufficient period to have been able to terminate his possession.

Section 2.02.   General Requirements of Culpability.

(1) Minimum Requirements of Culpability. Except as provided in Section 2.05, a person is not guilty of an offense unless he acted purposely, knowingly, recklessly or negligently, as the law may require, with respect to each material element of the offense.

(2) Kinds of Culpability Defined.

(a) Purposely. A person acts purposely with respect to a material element of an offense when:

(i) if the element involves the nature of his conduct or a result thereof, it is his conscious object to engage in conduct of that nature or to cause such a result; and

(ii) if the element involves the attendant circumstances, he is aware of the existence of such circumstances or he believes or hopes that they exist.

(b) Knowingly. A person acts knowingly with respect to a material element of an offense when:

(i) if the element involves the nature of his conduct or the attendant circumstances, he is aware that his conduct is of that nature or that such circumstances exist; and

(ii) if the element involves a result of his conduct, he is aware that it is practically certain that his conduct will cause such a result.

(c) Recklessly. A person acts recklessly with respect to a material element of an offense when he consciously disregards a substantial and unjustifiable risk that the material element exists or will result from his conduct. The risk must be of such a nature and degree that, considering the nature and purpose of the actor's conduct and the circumstances known to him, its disregard involves a gross deviation from the standard of conduct that a law-abiding person would observe in the actor's situation.

(d) Negligently. A person acts negligently with respect to a material element of an offense when he should be aware of a substantial and unjustifiable risk that the material element exists or will result from his conduct. The risk must be of such a nature and degree that the actor's failure to perceive it, considering the nature and purpose of his conduct and the circumstances known to him, involves a gross deviation from the standard of care that a reasonable person would observe in the actor's situation.

(3) Culpability Required Unless Otherwise Provided. When the culpability sufficient to establish a material element of an offense is not prescribed by law, such element is established if a person acts purposely, knowingly or recklessly with respect thereto.

(4) Prescribed Culpability Requirement Applies to All Material Elements. When the law defining an offense prescribes the kind of culpability that is sufficient for the commission of an offense, without distinguishing among the material elements thereof, such provision shall apply to all the material elements of the offense, unless a contrary purpose plainly appears.

(5) Substitutes for Negligence, Recklessness and Knowledge. When the law provides that negligence suffices to establish an element of an offense, such element also is established if a person acts purposely, knowingly or recklessly. When recklessness suffices to establish an element, such element also is established if a person acts purposely or knowingly. When acting knowingly suffices to establish an element, such element also is established if a person acts purposely.

(6) Requirement of Purpose Satisfied if Purpose Is Conditional. When a particular purpose is an element of an offense, the element is established although such purpose is conditional, unless the condition negatives the harm or evil sought to be prevented by the law defining the offense.

(7) Requirement of Knowledge Satisfied by Knowledge of High Probability. When knowledge of the existence of a particular fact is an element of an offense, such knowledge is established if a person is aware of a high probability of its existence, unless he actually believes that it does not exist.

(8) Requirement of Wilfulness Satisfied by Acting Knowingly. A requirement that an offense be committed wilfully is satisfied if a person acts knowingly with respect to the material elements of the offense, unless a purpose to impose further requirements appears.

(9) Culpability as to Illegality of Conduct. Neither knowledge nor recklessness or negligence as to whether conduct constitutes an offense or as to the existence, meaning or application of the law determining the elements of an offense is an element of such offense, unless the definition of the offense or the Code so provides.

(10) Culpability as Determinant of Grade of Offense. When the grade or degree of an offense depends on whether the offense is committed purposely, knowingly, recklessly or negligently, its grade or degree shall be the lowest for which the determinative kind of culpability is established with respect to any material element of the offense.

Section 2.03. Causal Relationship Between Conduct and Result; Divergence Between Result Designed or Contemplated and Actual Result or Between Probable and Actual Result.

(1) Conduct is the cause of a result when:

(a) it is an antecedent but for which the result in question would not have occurred; and

(b) the relationship between the conduct and result satisfies any additional causal requirements imposed by the Code or by the law defining the offense.

(2) When purposely or knowingly causing a particular result is an element of an offense, the element is not established if the actual result is not within the purpose or the contemplation of the actor unless:

(a) the actual result differs from that designed or contemplated, as the case may be, only in the respect that a different person or different property is injured or affected or that the injury or harm designed or contemplated would have been more serious or more extensive than that caused; or

(b) the actual result involves the same kind of injury or harm as that designed or contemplated and is not too remote or accidental in its occurrence to have a [just] bearing on the actor's liability or on the gravity of his offense.

(3) When recklessly or negligently causing a particular result is an element of an offense, the element is not established if the actual result is not within the risk of which the actor is aware or, in the case of negligence, of which he should be aware unless:

(a) the actual result differs from the probable result only in the respect that a different person or different property is injured or affected or that the probable injury or harm would have been more serious or more extensive than that caused; or

(b) the actual result involves the same kind of injury or harm as the probable result and is not too remote or accidental in its occurrence to have a [just] bearing on the actor's liability or on the gravity of his offense.

(4) When causing a particular result is a material element of an offense for which absolute liability is imposed by law, the element is not established unless the actual result is a probable consequence of the actor's conduct.

Section 2.04. Ignorance or Mistake.

(1) Ignorance or mistake as to a matter of fact or law is a defense if:

(a) the ignorance or mistake negatives the purpose, knowledge, belief, recklessness or negligence required to establish a material element of the offense; or

(b) the law provides that the state of mind established by such ignorance or mistake constitutes a defense.

(2) Although ignorance or mistake would otherwise afford a defense to the offense charged, the defense is not available if the defendant would be guilty of another offense had the situation been as he supposed. In such case, however, the ignorance or mistake of the defendant shall reduce the grade and degree of the offense of which he may be convicted to those of the offense of which he would be guilty had the situation been as he supposed.

(3) A belief that conduct does not legally constitute an offense is a defense to a prosecution for that offense based upon such conduct when:

(a) the statute or other enactment defining the offense is not known to the actor and has not been published or otherwise reasonably made available prior to the conduct alleged; or

(b) he acts in reasonable reliance upon an official statement of the law, afterward determined to be invalid or erroneous, contained in (i) a statute or other enactment; (ii) a judicial decision, opinion or judgment; (iii) an administrative order or grant of permission; or (iv) an official interpretation of the public officer or body charged by law with responsibility for the interpretation, administration or enforcement of the law defining the offense.

(4) The defendant must prove a defense arising under Subsection (3) of this Section by a preponderance of evidence.

Section 2.05. When Culpability Requirements Are Inapplicable to Violations and to Offenses Defined by Other Statutes; Effect of Absolute Liability in Reducing Grade of Offense to Violation.

(1) The requirements of culpability prescribed by Sections 2.01 and 2.02 do not apply to:

(a) offenses which constitute violations, unless the requirement involved is included in the definition of the offense or the Court determines that its application is consistent with effective enforcement of the law defining the offense; or

(b) offenses defined by statutes other than the Code, insofar as a legislative purpose to impose absolute liability for such offenses or with respect to any material element thereof plainly appears.

(2) Notwithstanding any other provision of existing law and unless a subsequent statute otherwise provides:

(a) when absolute liability is imposed with respect to any material element of an offense defined by a statute other than the Code and a conviction is based upon such liability, the offense constitutes a violation; and

(b) although absolute liability is imposed by law with respect to one or more of the material elements of an offense defined by a statute other than the Code, the culpable commission of the offense may be charged and proved, in which event negligence with respect to such elements constitutes sufficient culpability and the classification of the offense and the sentence that may be imposed therefor upon conviction are determined by Section 1.04 and Article 6 of the Code.

Section 2.06. Liability for Conduct of Another; Complicity.

(1) A person is guilty of an offense if it is committed by his own conduct or by the conduct of another person for which he is legally accountable, or both.

(2) A person is legally accountable for the conduct of another person when:

(a) acting with the kind of culpability that is sufficient for the commission of the offense, he causes an innocent or irresponsible person to engage in such conduct; or

(b) he is made accountable for the conduct of such other person by the Code or by the law defining the offense; or

(c) he is an accomplice of such other person in the commission of the offense.

(3) A person is an accomplice of another person in the commission of an offense if:

(a) with the purpose of promoting or facilitating the commission of the offense, he

(i) solicits such other person to commit it; or

(ii) aids or agrees or attempts to aid such other person in planning or committing it; or

(iii) having a legal duty to prevent the commission of the offense, fails to make proper effort so to do; or

(b) his conduct is expressly declared by law to establish his complicity.

(4) When causing a particular result is an element of an offense, an accomplice in the conduct causing such result is an accomplice in the commission of that offense, if he acts with the kind of culpability, if any, with respect to that result that is sufficient for the commission of the offense.

(5) A person who is legally incapable of committing a particular offense himself may be guilty thereof if it is committed by the conduct of another person for which he is legally accountable, unless such liability is inconsistent with the purpose of the provision establishing his incapacity.

(6) Unless otherwise provided by the Code or by the law defining the offense, a person is not an accomplice in an offense committed by another person if:

(a) he is a victim of that offense; or

(b) the offense is so defined that his conduct is inevitably incident to its commission; or

(c) he terminates his complicity prior to the commission of the offense and

(i) wholly deprives it of effectiveness in the commission of the offense; or

(ii) gives timely warning to the law enforcement authorities or otherwise makes proper effort to prevent the commission of the offense.

(7) An accomplice may be convicted on proof of the commission of the offense and of his complicity therein, though the person claimed to have committed the offense has not been prosecuted or convicted or has been convicted of a different

offense or degree of offense or has an immunity to prosecution or conviction or has been acquitted.

Section 2.07. Liability of Corporations, Unincorporated Associations and Persons Acting, or Under a Duty to Act, in Their Behalf.

(1) A corporation may be convicted of the commission of an offense if:

(a) the offense is a violation or the offense is defined by a statute other than the Code in which a legislative purpose to impose liability on corporations plainly appears and the conduct is performed by an agent of the corporation acting in behalf of the corporation within the scope of his office or employment, except that if the law defining the offense designates the agents for whose conduct the corporation is accountable or the circumstances under which it is accountable, such provisions shall apply; or

(b) the offense consists of an omission to discharge a specific duty of affirmative performance imposed on corporations by law; or

(c) the commission of the offense was authorized, requested, commanded, performed or recklessly tolerated by the board of directors or by a high managerial agent acting in behalf of the corporation within the scope of his office or employment.

(2) When absolute liability is imposed for the commission of an offense, a legislative purpose to impose liability on a corporation shall be assumed, unless the contrary plainly appears.

(3) An unincorporated association may be convicted of the commission of an offense if:

(a) the offense is defined by a statute other than the Code which expressly provides for the liability of such an association and the conduct is performed by an agent of the association acting in behalf of the association within the scope of his office or employment, except that if the law defining the offense designates the agents for whose conduct the association is accountable or the circumstances under which it is accountable, such provisions shall apply; or

(b) the offense consists of an omission to discharge a specific duty of affirmative performance imposed on associations by law.

(4) As used in this Section:

(a) "corporation" does not include an entity organized as or by a governmental agency for the execution of a governmental program;

(b) "agent" means any director, officer, servant, employee or other person authorized to act in behalf of the corporation or association and, in the case of an unincorporated association, a member of such association;

(c) "high managerial agent" means an officer of a corporation or an unincorporated association, or, in the case of a partnership, a partner, or any other agent of a corporation or association having duties of such responsibility that his conduct may fairly be assumed to represent the policy of the corporation or association.

(5) In any prosecution of a corporation or an unincorporated association for the commission of an offense included within the terms of Subsection (1)(a) or Subsection (3)(a) of this Section, other than an offense for which absolute liability has been imposed, it shall be a defense if the defendant proves by a preponderance of evidence that the high managerial agent having supervisory responsibility over the subject matter of the offense employed due diligence to prevent its commission. This paragraph shall not apply if it is plainly inconsistent with the legislative purpose in defining the particular offense.

(6) (a) A person is legally accountable for any conduct he performs or causes to be performed in the name of the corporation or an unincorporated association or in its behalf to the same extent as if it were performed in his own name or behalf.

(b) Whenever a duty to act is imposed by law upon a corporation or an unincorporated association, any agent of the corporation or association having primary responsibility for the discharge of the duty is legally accountable for a reckless omission to perform the required act to the same extent as if the duty were imposed by law directly upon himself.

(c) When a person is convicted of an offense by reason of his legal accountability for the conduct of a corporation or an unincorporated association, he is subject to the sentence authorized by law when a natural person is convicted of an offense of the grade and the degree involved.

Section 2.08. Intoxication.

(1) Except as provided in Subsection (4) of this Section, intoxication of the actor is not a defense unless it negatives an element of the offense.

(2) When recklessness establishes an element of the offense, if the actor, due to self-induced intoxication, is unaware of a risk of which he would have been aware had he been sober, such unawareness is immaterial.

(3) Intoxication does not, in itself, constitute mental disease within the meaning of Section 4.01.

(4) Intoxication which (a) is not self-induced or (b) is pathological is an affirmative defense if by reason of such intoxication the actor at the time of his conduct lacks substantial capacity either to appreciate its criminality [wrongfulness] or to conform his conduct to the requirements of law.

(5) Definitions. In this Section unless a different meaning plainly is required:

(a) "intoxication" means a disturbance of mental or physical capacities resulting from the introduction of substances into the body;

(b) "self-induced intoxication" means intoxication caused by substances which the actor knowingly introduces into his body, the tendency of which to cause intoxication he knows or ought to know, unless he introduces them pursuant to medical advice or under such circumstances as would afford a defense to a charge of crime;

(c) "pathological intoxication" means intoxication grossly excessive in degree, given the amount of the intoxicant, to which the actor does not know he is susceptible.

Section 2.09. Duress.

(1) It is an affirmative defense that the actor engaged in the conduct charged to constitute an offense because he was coerced to do so by the use of, or a threat to use, unlawful force against his person or the person of another, which a person of reasonable firmness in his situation would have been unable to resist.

(2) The defense provided by this Section is unavailable if the actor recklessly placed himself in a situation in which it was probable that he would be subjected to duress. The defense is also unavailable if he was negligent in placing himself in such a situation, whenever negligence suffices to establish culpability for the offense charged.

(3) It is not a defense that a woman acted on the command of her husband, unless she acted under such coercion as would establish a defense under this Section. [The presumption that a woman, acting in the presence of her husband, is coerced is abolished.]

(4) When the conduct of the actor would otherwise be justifiable under Section 3.02, this Section does not preclude such defense.

Section 2.10. Military Orders.

It is an affirmative defense that the actor, in engaging in the conduct charged to constitute an offense, does no more than execute an order of his superior in the armed services which he does not know to be unlawful.

Section 2.11. Consent.

(1) In General. The consent of the victim to conduct charged to constitute an offense or to the result thereof is a defense if such consent negatives an element of the offense or precludes the infliction of the harm or evil sought to be prevented by the law defining the offense.

(2) Consent to Bodily Injury. When conduct is charged to constitute an offense because it causes or threatens bodily injury, consent to such conduct or to the infliction of such injury is a defense if:

(a) the bodily injury consented to or threatened by the conduct consented to is not serious; or

(b) the conduct and the injury are reasonably foreseeable hazards of joint participation in a lawful athletic contest or competitive sport or other concerted activity not forbidden by law; or

(c) the consent establishes a justification for the conduct under Article 3 of the Code.

(3) Ineffective Consent. Unless otherwise provided by the Code or by the law defining the offense, assent does not constitute consent if:

(a) it is given by a person who is legally incompetent to authorize the conduct charged to constitute the offense; or

(b) it is given by a person who by reason of youth, mental disease or defect or intoxication is manifestly unable or known by the actor to be unable to make a reasonable judgment as to the nature or harmfulness of the conduct charged to constitute the offense; or

(c) it is given by a person whose improvident consent is sought to be prevented by the law defining the offense; or

(d) it is induced by force, duress or deception of a kind sought to be prevented by the law defining the offense.

Section 2.12. De Minimis Infractions.

The Court shall dismiss a prosecution if, having regard to the nature of the conduct charged to constitute an offense and the nature of the attendant circumstances, it finds that the defendant's conduct:

(1) was within a customary license or tolerance, neither expressly negatived by the person whose interest was infringed nor inconsistent with the purpose of the law defining the offense; or

(2) did not actually cause or threaten the harm or evil sought to be prevented by the law defining the offense or did so only to an extent too trivial to warrant the condemnation of conviction; or

(3) presents such other extenuations that it cannot reasonably be regarded as envisaged by the legislature in forbidding the offense. The Court shall not dismiss a prosecution under Subsection (3) of this Section without filing a written statement of its reasons.

Section 2.13. Entrapment.

(1) A public law enforcement official or a person acting in cooperation with such an official perpetrates an entrapment if for the purpose of obtaining evidence of the commission of an offense, he induces or encourages another person to engage in conduct constituting such offense by either:

(a) making knowingly false representations designed to induce the belief that such conduct is not prohibited; or

(b) employing methods of persuasion or inducement which create a substantial risk that such an offense will be committed by persons other than those who are ready to commit it.

(2) Except as provided in Subsection (3) of this Section, a person prosecuted for an offense shall be acquitted if he proves by a preponderance of evidence that his conduct occurred in response to an entrapment. The issue of entrapment shall be tried by the Court in the absence of the jury.

(3) The defense afforded by this Section is unavailable when causing or threatening bodily injury is an element of the offense charged and the prosecution is based on conduct causing or threatening such injury to a person other than the person perpetrating the entrapment.

ARTICLE 3. GENERAL PRINCIPLES OF JUSTIFICATION.

Section 3.01. Justification an Affirmative Defense; Civil Remedies Unaffected.

(1) In any prosecution based on conduct which is justifiable under this Article, justification is an affirmative defense.

(2) The fact that conduct is justifiable under this Article does not abolish or impair any remedy for such conduct which is available in any civil action.

Section 3.02. Justification Generally: Choice of Evils.

(1) Conduct which the actor believes to be necessary to avoid a harm or evil to himself or to another is justifiable, provided that:

(a) the harm or evil sought to be avoided by such conduct is greater than that sought to be prevented by the law defining the offense charged; and

(b) neither the Code nor other law defining the offense provides exceptions or defenses dealing with the specific situation involved; and

(c) a legislative purpose to exclude the justification claimed does not otherwise plainly appear.

(2) When the actor was reckless or negligent in bringing about the situation requiring a choice of harms or evils or in appraising the necessity for his conduct, the justification afforded by this Section is unavailable in a prosecution for any offense for which recklessness or negligence, as the case may be, suffices to establish culpability.

Section 3.03. Execution of Public Duty.

(1) Except as provided in Subsection (2) of this Section, conduct is justifiable when it is required or authorized by:

(a) the law defining the duties or functions of a public officer or the assistance to be rendered to such officer in the performance of his duties; or

(b) the law governing the execution of legal process; or

(c) the judgment or order of a competent court or tribunal; or

(d) the law governing the armed services or the lawful conduct of war; or

(e) any other provision of law imposing a public duty.

(2) The other sections of this Article apply to:

(a) the use of force upon or toward the person of another for any of the purposes dealt with in such sections; and

(b) the use of deadly force for any purpose, unless the use of such force is otherwise expressly authorized by law or occurs in the lawful conduct of war.

(3) The justification afforded by Subsection (1) of this Section applies:

(a) when the actor believes his conduct to be required or authorized by the judgment or direction of a competent court or tribunal or in the lawful execution of legal process, notwithstanding lack of jurisdiction of the court or defect in the legal process; and

(b) when the actor believes his conduct to be required or authorized to assist a public officer in the performance of his duties, notwithstanding that the officer exceeded his legal authority.

Section 3.04. Use of Force in Self–Protection.

(1) Use of Force Justifiable for Protection of the Person. Subject to the provisions of this Section and of Section 3.09, the use of force upon or toward another person is justifiable when the actor believes that such force is immediately necessary for the purpose of protecting himself against the use of unlawful force by such other person on the present occasion.

(2) Limitations on Justifying Necessity for Use of Force.

(a) The use of force is not justifiable under this Section:

(i) to resist an arrest which the actor knows is being made by a peace officer, although the arrest is unlawful; or

(ii) to resist force used by the occupier or possessor of property or by another person on his behalf, where the actor knows that the person using the force is doing so under a claim of right to protect the property, except that this limitation shall not apply if:

(1) the actor is a public officer acting in the performance of his duties or a person lawfully assisting him therein or a person making or assisting in a lawful arrest; or

(2) the actor has been unlawfully dispossessed of the property and is making a re-entry or recaption justified by Section 3.06; or

(3) the actor believes that such force is necessary to protect himself against death or serious bodily harm.

(b) The use of deadly force is not justifiable under this Section unless the actor believes that such force is necessary to protect himself against death, serious bodily harm, kidnapping or sexual intercourse compelled by force or threat; nor is it justifiable if:

(i) the actor, with the purpose of causing death or serious bodily harm, provoked the use of force against himself in the same encounter; or

(ii) the actor knows that he can avoid the necessity of using such force with complete safety by retreating or by surrendering possession of a thing to a person asserting a claim of right thereto or by complying with a demand that he abstain from any action which he has no duty to take, except that:

(1) the actor is not obliged to retreat from his dwelling or place of work, unless he was the initial aggressor or is assailed in his place of work by another person whose place of work the actor knows it to be; and

(2) a public officer justified in using force in the performance of his duties or a person justified in using force in his assistance or a person justified in using force in making an arrest or preventing an escape is not obliged to desist from efforts to perform such duty, effect such arrest or prevent such escape because of resistance or threatened resistance by or on behalf of the person against whom such action is directed.

(c) Except as required by paragraphs (a) and (b) of this Subsection, a person employing protective force may estimate the necessity thereof under the circumstances as he believes them to be when the force is used, without retreating, surrendering possession, doing any other act which he has no legal duty to do or abstaining from any lawful action.

(3) Use of Confinement as Protective Force. The justification afforded by this Section extends to the use of confinement as protective force only if the actor takes all reasonable measures to terminate the confinement as soon as he knows that he safely can, unless the person confined has been arrested on a charge of crime.

Section 3.05. Use of Force for the Protection of Other Persons.

(1) Subject to the provisions of this Section and of Section 3.09, the use of force upon or toward the person of another is justifiable to protect a third person when:

(a) the actor would be justified under Section 3.04 in using such force to protect himself against the injury he believes to be threatened to the person whom he seeks to protect; and

(b) under the circumstances as the actor believes them to be, the person whom he seeks to protect would be justified in using such protective force; and

(c) the actor believes that his intervention is necessary for the protection of such other person.

(2) Notwithstanding Subsection (1) of this Section:

(a) when the actor would be obliged under Section 3.04 to retreat, to surrender the possession of a thing or to comply with a demand before using force in self-protection, he is not obliged to do so before using force for the protection of another person, unless he knows that he can thereby secure the complete safety of such other person; and

(b) when the person whom the actor seeks to protect would be obliged under Section 3.04 to retreat, to surrender the possession of a thing or to comply with a demand if he knew that he could obtain complete safety by so doing, the actor is obliged to try to cause him to do so before using force in his protection if the actor knows that he can obtain complete safety in that way; and

(c) neither the actor nor the person whom he seeks to protect is obliged to retreat when in the other's dwelling or place of work to any greater extent than in his own.

Section 3.06. Use of Force for the Protection of Property.

(1) Use of Force Justifiable for Protection of Property. Subject to the provisions of this Section and of Section 3.09, the use of force upon or toward the person of another is justifiable when the actor believes that such force is immediately necessary:

(a) to prevent or terminate an unlawful entry or other trespass upon land or a trespass against or the unlawful carrying away of tangible, movable property, provided that such land or movable property is, or is believed by the actor to be, in his possession or in the possession of another person for whose protection he acts; or

(b) to effect an entry or re-entry upon land or to retake tangible movable property, provided that the actor believes that he or the person by whose authority he acts or a person from whom he or such other person derives title was unlawfully dispossessed of such land or movable property and is entitled to possession, and provided, further, that:

(i) the force is used immediately or on fresh pursuit after such dispossession; or

(ii) the actor believes that the person against whom he uses force has no claim of right to the possession of the property and, in the case of land, the circumstances, as the actor believes them to be, are of such urgency that it would be an exceptional hardship to postpone the entry or re-entry until a court order is obtained.

(2) Meaning of Possession. For the purposes of Subsection (1) of this Section:

(a) a person who has parted with the custody of property to another who refuses to restore it to him is no longer in possession, unless the property is movable and was and still is located on land in his possession;

(b) a person who has been dispossessed of land does not regain possession thereof merely by setting foot thereon;

(c) a person who has a license to use or occupy real property is deemed to be in possession thereof except against the licensor acting under claim of right.

(3) Limitations on Justifiable Use of Force.

(a) Request to Desist. The use of force is justifiable under this Section only if the actor first requests the person against whom such force is used to desist from his interference with the property, unless the actor believes that:

(i) such request would be useless; or

(ii) it would be dangerous to himself or another person to make the request; or

(iii) substantial harm will be done to the physical condition of the property which is sought to be protected before the request can effectively be made.

(b) Exclusion of Trespasser. The use of force to prevent or terminate a trespass is not justifiable under this Section if the actor knows that the exclusion of the trespasser will expose him to substantial danger of serious bodily harm.

(c) Resistance of Lawful Re-entry or Recaption. The use of force to prevent an entry or re-entry upon land or the recaption of movable property is not justifiable under this Section, although the actor believes that such re-entry or recaption is unlawful, if:

(i) the re-entry or recaption is made by or on behalf of a person who was actually dispossessed of the property; and

(ii) it is otherwise justifiable under paragraph (1)(b) of this Section.

(d) Use of Deadly Force. The use of deadly force is not justifiable under this Section unless the actor believes that:

(i) the person against whom the force is used is attempting to dispossess him of his dwelling otherwise than under a claim of right to its possession; or

(ii) the person against whom the force is used is attempting to commit or consummate arson, burglary, robbery or other felonious theft or property destruction and either:

(1) has employed or threatened deadly force against or in the presence of the actor; or

(2) the use of force other than deadly force to prevent the commission or the consummation of the crime would expose the actor or another in his presence to substantial danger of serious bodily harm.

(4) Use of Confinement as Protective Force. The justification afforded by this Section extends to the use of confinement as protective force only if the actor takes all reasonable measures to terminate the confinement as soon as he knows that he can do so with safety to the property, unless the person confined has been arrested on a charge of crime.

(5) Use of Device to Protect Property. The justification afforded by this Section extends to the use of a device for the purpose of protecting property only if:

(a) the device is not designed to cause or known to create a substantial risk of causing death or serious bodily harm; and

(b) the use of the particular device to protect the property from entry or trespass is reasonable under the circumstances, as the actor believes them to be; and

(c) the device is one customarily used for such a purpose or reasonable care is taken to make known to probable intruders the fact that it is used.

(6) Use of Force to Pass Wrongful Obstructor. The use of force to pass a person whom the actor believe to be purposely or knowingly and unjustifiably obstructing the actor from going to a place to which he may lawfully go is justifiable, provided that:

(a) the actor believes that the person against whom he uses force has no claim of right to obstruct the actor; and

(b) the actor is not being obstructed from entry or movement on land which he knows to be in the possession or custody of the person obstructing him, or in the possession or custody of another person by whose authority the obstructor acts, unless the circumstances, as the actor believes them to be, are of such urgency that it would not be reasonable to postpone the entry or movement on such land until a court order is obtained; and

(c) the force used is not greater than would be justifiable if the person obstructing the actor were using force against him to prevent his passage.

Section 3.07. Use of Force in Law Enforcement.

(1) Use of Force Justifiable to Effect an Arrest. Subject to the provisions of this Section and of Section 3.09, the use of force upon or toward the person of another is justifiable when the actor is making or assisting in making an arrest and the actor believes that such force is immediately necessary to effect a lawful arrest.

(2) Limitations on the Use of Force.

(a) The use of force is not justifiable under this Section unless:

(i) the actor makes known the purpose of the arrest or believes that it is otherwise known by or cannot reasonably be made known to the person to be arrested; and

(ii) when the arrest is made under a warrant, the warrant is valid or believed by the actor to be valid.

(b) The use of deadly force is not justifiable under this Section unless:

(i) the arrest is for a felony; and

(ii) the person effecting the arrest is authorized to act as a peace officer or is assisting a person whom he believes to be authorized to act as a peace officer; and

(iii) the actor believes that the force employed creates no substantial risk of injury to innocent persons; and

(iv) the actor believes that:

(1) the crime for which the arrest is made involved conduct including the use or threatened use of deadly force; or

(2) there is a substantial risk that the person to be arrested will cause death or serious bodily harm if his apprehension is delayed.

(3) Use of Force to Prevent Escape from Custody. The use of force to prevent the escape of an arrested person from custody is justifiable when the force could justifiably have been employed to effect the arrest under which the person is in custody, except that a guard or other person authorized to act as a peace officer is justified in using any force, including deadly force, which he believes to be immediately necessary to prevent the escape of a person from a jail, prison, or other institution for the detention of persons charged with or convicted of a crime.

(4) Use of Force by Private Person Assisting an Unlawful Arrest.

(a) A private person who is summoned by a peace officer to assist in effecting an unlawful arrest, is justified in using any force which he would be justified in using if the arrest were lawful, provided that he does not believe the arrest is unlawful.

(b) A private person who assists another private person in effecting an unlawful arrest, or who, not being summoned, assists a peace officer in effecting an unlawful arrest, is justified in using any force which he would be justified in using if the arrest were lawful, provided that (i) he believes the arrest is lawful, and (ii) the arrest would be lawful if the facts were as he believes them to be.

(5) Use of Force to Prevent Suicide or the Commission of a Crime.

(a) The use of force upon or toward the person of another is justifiable when the actor believes that such force is immediately necessary to prevent such other person from committing suicide, inflicting serious bodily harm upon himself, committing or consummating the commission of a crime involving or threatening bodily harm, damage to or loss of property or a breach of the peace, except that:

(i) any limitations imposed by the other provisions of this Article on the justifiable use of force in self-protection, for the protection of others, the protection of property, the effectuation of an arrest or the prevention of an escape from custody shall apply notwithstanding the criminality of the conduct against which such force is used; and

(ii) the use of deadly force is not in any event justifiable under this Subsection unless:

(1) the actor believes that there is a substantial risk that the person whom he seeks to prevent from committing a crime will cause death or serious bodily harm to another unless the commission or the consummation of the crime is prevented and that the use of such force presents no substantial risk of injury to innocent persons; or

(2) the actor believes that the use of such force is necessary to suppress a riot or mutiny after the rioters or mutineers have been ordered to disperse and warned, in any particular manner that the law may require, that such force will be used if they do not obey.

(b) The justification afforded by this Subsection extends to the use of confinement as preventive force only if the actor takes all reasonable measures to terminate the confinement as soon as he knows that he safely can, unless the person confined has been arrested on a charge of crime.

Section 3.08. Use of Force by Persons with Special Responsibility for Care, Discipline or Safety of Others.

The use of force upon or toward the person of another is justifiable if:

(1) the actor is the parent or guardian or other person similarly responsible for the general care and supervision of a minor or a person acting at the request of such parent, guardian or other responsible person and:

(a) the force is used for the purpose of safeguarding or promoting the welfare of the minor, including the prevention or punishment of his misconduct; and

(b) the force used is not designed to cause or known to create a substantial risk of causing death, serious bodily harm, disfigurement, extreme pain or mental distress or gross degradation; or

(2) the actor is a teacher or a person otherwise entrusted with the care or supervision for a special purpose of a minor and:

    (a) the actor believes that the force used is necessary to further such special purpose, including the maintenance of reasonable discipline in a school, class or other group, and that the use of such force is consistent with the welfare of the minor; and

    (b) the degree of force, if it had been used by the parent or guardian of the minor, would not be unjustifiable under Subsection (1)(b) of this Section; or

(3) the actor is the guardian or other person similarly responsible for the general care and supervision of an incompetent person; and:

    (a) the force is used for the purpose of safeguarding or promoting the welfare of the incompetent person, including the prevention of his misconduct, or, when such incompetent person is in a hospital or other institution for his care and custody, for the maintenance of reasonable discipline in such institution; and

    (b) the force used is not designed to cause or known to create a substantial risk of causing death, serious bodily harm, disfigurement, extreme or unnecessary pain, mental distress, or humiliation; or

(4) the actor is a doctor or other therapist or a person assisting him at his direction, and:

    (a) the force is used for the purpose of administering a recognized form of treatment which the actor believes to be adapted to promoting the physical or mental health of the patient; and

    (b) the treatment is administered with the consent of the patient or, if the patient is a minor or an incompetent person, with the consent of his parent or guardian or other person legally competent to consent in his behalf, or the treatment is administered in an emergency when the actor believes that no one competent to consent can be consulted and that a reasonable person, wishing to safeguard the welfare of the patient, would consent; or

(5) the actor is a warden or other authorized official of a correctional institution, and:

    (a) he believes that the force used is necessary for the purpose of enforcing the lawful rules or procedures of the institution, unless his belief in the lawfulness of the rule or procedure sought to be enforced is erroneous and his error is due to ignorance or mistake as to the provisions of the Code, any other provision of the criminal law or the law governing the administration of the institution; and

    (b) the nature or degree of force used is not forbidden by Article 303 or 304 of the Code; and

    (c) if deadly force is used, its use is otherwise justifiable under this Article; or

(6) the actor is a person responsible for the safety of a vessel or an aircraft or a person acting at his direction, and:

    (a) he believes that the force used is necessary to prevent interference with the operation of the vessel or aircraft or obstruction of the execution of a lawful order, unless his belief in the lawfulness of the order is erroneous and his error is due to ignorance or mistake as to the law defining his authority; and

    (b) if deadly force is used, its use is otherwise justifiable under this Article; or

(7) the actor is a person who is authorized or required by law to maintain order or decorum in a vehicle, train or other carrier or in a place where others are assembled, and:

    (a) he believes that the force used is necessary for such purpose; and

    (b) the force used is not designed to cause or known to create a substantial risk of causing death, bodily harm, or extreme mental distress.

Section 3.09. Mistake of Law as to Unlawfulness of Force or Legality of Arrest; Reckless or Negligent Use of Otherwise Justifiable Force; Reckless or Negligent Injury or Risk of Injury to Innocent Persons.

(1) The justification afforded by Sections 3.04 to 3.07, inclusive, is unavailable when:

    (a) the actor's belief in the unlawfulness of the force or conduct against which he employs protective force or his belief in the lawfulness of an arrest which he endeavors to effect by force is erroneous; and

    (b) his error is due to ignorance or mistake as to the provisions of the Code, any other provision of the criminal law or the law governing the legality of an arrest or search.

(2) When the actor believes that the use of force upon or toward the person of another is necessary for any of the purposes for which such belief would establish a justification under Sections 3.03 to 3.08 but the actor is reckless or negligent in having such belief or in acquiring or failing to acquire any knowledge or belief which is material to the justiciability of his use of force, the justification afforded by those Sections is unavailable in a prosecution for an offense for which recklessness or negligence, as the case may be, suffices to establish culpability.

(3) When the actor is justified under Sections 3.03 to 3.08 in using force upon or toward the person of another but he recklessly or negligently injures or creates a risk of injury to innocent persons, the justification afforded by those Sections is unavailable in a prosecution for such recklessness or negligence towards innocent persons.

Section 3.10. Justification in Property Crimes.

Conduct involving the appropriation, seizure or destruction of, damage to, intrusion on or interference with property is justifiable under circumstances which would establish a defense of privilege in a civil action based thereon, unless:

(1) the Code or the law defining the offense deals with the specific situation involved; or

(2) a legislative purpose to exclude the justification claimed otherwise plainly appears.

Section 3.11. Definitions.

In this Article, unless a different meaning plainly is required:

(1) "unlawful force" means force, including confinement, which is employed without the consent of the person against whom it is directed and the employment of which constitutes an offense or actionable tort or would constitute such offense or tort except for a defense (such as the absence of intent, negligence, or mental capacity; duress; youth; or diplomatic status) not amounting to a privilege to use the force. Assent constitutes consent, within the meaning of this Section, whether or not it otherwise is legally effective, except assent to the infliction of death or serious bodily harm.

(2) "deadly force" means force which the actor uses with the purpose of causing or which he knows to create a substantial risk of causing death or serious bodily harm. Purposely firing a firearm in the direction of another person or at a vehicle in which another person is believed to be constitutes deadly force. A threat to cause death or serious bodily harm, by the production of a weapon or otherwise, so long as the actor's purpose is limited to creating an apprehension that he will use deadly force if necessary, does not constitute deadly force;

(3) "dwelling" means any building or structure, though movable or temporary, or a portion thereof, which is for the time being the actor's home or place of lodging.

ARTICLE 4. RESPONSIBILITY.

Section 4.01. Mental Disease or Defect Excluding Responsibility.

(1) A person is not responsible for criminal conduct if at the time of such conduct as a result of mental disease or defect he lacks substantial capacity either to appreciate the criminality [wrongfulness] of his conduct or to conform his conduct to the requirements of law.

(2) As used in this Article, the terms "mental disease or defect" do not include an abnormality manifested only by repeated criminal or otherwise anti-social conduct.

Section 4.02. Evidence of Mental Disease or Defect Admissible When Relevant to Element of the Offense; [Mental Disease or Defect Impairing Capacity as Ground for Mitigation of Punishment in Capital Cases].

(1) Evidence that the defendant suffered from a mental disease or defect is admissible whenever it is relevant to prove that the defendant did or did not have a state of mind which is an element of the offense.

[(2) Whenever the jury or the Court is authorized to determine or to recommend whether or not the defendant shall be sentenced to death or imprisonment upon conviction, evidence that the capacity of the defendant to appreciate the criminality [wrongfulness] of his conduct or to conform his conduct to the requirements of law was impaired as a result of mental disease or defect is admissible in favor of sentence of imprisonment.]

Section 4.04. Mental Disease or Defect Excluding Fitness to Proceed.

No person who as a result of mental disease or defect lacks capacity to understand the proceedings against him or to assist in his own defense shall be tried, convicted or sentenced for the commission of an offense so long as such incapacity endures.

Section 4.10. Immaturity Excluding Criminal Convictions; Transfer of Proceedings to Juvenile Court.

(1) A person shall not be tried for or convicted of an offense if:

(a) at the time of the conduct charged to constitute the offense he was less than sixteen years of age [, in which case the Juvenile Court shall have exclusive jurisdiction**]; or

(b) at the time of the conduct charged to constitute the offense he was sixteen or seventeen years of age, unless:

(i) the Juvenile Court has no jurisdiction over him, or,

(ii) the Juvenile Court has entered an order waiving jurisdiction and consenting to the institution of criminal proceedings against him.

(2) No court shall have jurisdiction to try or convict a person of an offense if criminal proceedings against him are barred by Subsection (1) of this Section. When it appears that a person charged with the commission of an offense may be of such an age that criminal proceedings may be barred under Subsection (1) of this Section, the Court shall hold a hearing thereon, and the burden shall be on the prosecution to establish to the satisfaction of the Court that the criminal proceeding is not barred upon such grounds. If the Court determines that the proceeding is barred, custody of the person charged shall be surrendered to the Juvenile Court, and the case, including all papers and processes relating thereto, shall be transferred.

ARTICLE 5. INCHOATE CRIMES.

Section 5.01. Criminal Attempt.

(1) Definition of Attempt. A person is guilty of an attempt to commit a crime if, acting with the kind of culpability otherwise required for commission of the crime, he:

** The bracketed words are unnecessary if the Juvenile Court Act so provides or is amended accordingly.

(a) purposely engages in conduct which would constitute the crime if the attendant circumstances were as he believes them to be; or

(b) when causing a particular result is an element of the crime, does or omits to do anything with the purpose of causing or with the belief that it will cause such result without further conduct on his part; or

(c) purposely does or omits to do anything which, under the circumstances as he believes them to be, is an act or omission constituting a substantial step in a course of conduct planned to culminate in his commission of the crime.

(2) Conduct Which May Be Held Substantial Step Under Subsection (1)(c). Conduct shall not be held to constitute a substantial step under Subsection (1)(c) of this Section unless it is strongly corroborative of the actor's criminal purpose. Without negativing the sufficiency of other conduct, the following, if strongly corroborative of the actor's criminal purpose, shall not be held insufficient as a matter of law:

(a) lying in wait, searching for or following the contemplated victim of the crime;

(b) enticing or seeking to entice the contemplated victim of the crime to go to the place contemplated for its commission;

(c) reconnoitering the place contemplated for the commission of the crime;

(d) unlawful entry of a structure, vehicle or enclosure in which it is contemplated that the crime will be committed;

(e) possession of materials to be employed in the commission of the crime, which are specially designed for such unlawful use or which can serve no lawful purpose of the actor under the circumstances;

(f) possession, collection or fabrication of materials to be employed in the commission of the crime, at or near the place contemplated for its commission, where such possession, collection or fabrication serves no lawful purpose of the actor under the circumstances;

(g) soliciting an innocent agent to engage in conduct constituting an element of the crime.

(3) Conduct Designed to Aid Another in Commission of a Crime. A person who engages in conduct designed to aid another t commit a crime which would establish his complicity under Section 2.06 if the crime were committed by such other person, is guilty of an attempt to commit the crime, although the crime is not committed or attempted by such other person.

(4) Renunciation of Criminal Purpose. When the actor's conduct would otherwise constitute an attempt under Subsection (1)(b) or (1)(c) of this Section, it is an affirmative defense that he abandoned his effort to commit the crime or otherwise prevented its commission, under circumstances manifesting a complete and voluntary renunciation of his criminal purpose. The establishment of such defense does not, however, affect the liability of an accomplice who did not join in such abandonment or prevention. Within the meaning of this Article, renunciation of criminal purpose is not voluntary if it is motivated, in whole or in part, by circumstances, not present or apparent at the inception of the actor's course of conduct, which increase the probability of detection or apprehension or which make more difficult the accomplishment of the criminal purpose. Renunciation is not complete if it is motivated by a decision to postpone the criminal conduct until a more advantageous time or to transfer the criminal effort to another but similar objective or victim.

Section 5.02. Criminal Solicitation.

(1) Definition of Solicitation. A person is guilty of solicitation to commit a crime if with the purpose of promoting or facilitating its commission he commands, encourages or requests another person to engage in specific conduct which would constitute such crime or an attempt to commit such crime or which would establish his complicity in its commission or attempted commission.

(2) Uncommunicated Solicitation. It is immaterial under Subsection (1) of this Section that the actor fails to communicate with the person he solicits to commit a crime if his conduct was designed to effect such communication.

(3) Renunciation of Criminal Purpose. It is an affirmative defense that the actor, after soliciting another person to commit a crime, persuaded him not to do so or otherwise prevented the commission of the crime, under circumstances manifesting a complete and voluntary renunciation of his criminal purpose.

Section 5.03. Criminal Conspiracy.

(1) Definition of Conspiracy. A person is guilty of conspiracy with another person or persons to commit a crime if with the purpose of promoting or facilitating its commission he:

(a) agrees with such other person or persons that they or one or more of them will engage in conduct which constitutes such crime or an attempt or solicitation to commit such crime; or

(b) agrees to aid such other person or persons in the planning or commission of such crime or of an attempt or solicitation to commit such crime.

(2) Scope of Conspiratorial Relationship. If a person guilty of conspiracy, as defined by Subsection (1) of this Section, knows that a person with whom he conspires to commit a crime has conspired with another person or persons to commit the same crime, he is guilty of conspiring with such other person or persons, whether or not he knows their identity, to commit such crime.

(3) Conspiracy With Multiple Criminal Objectives. If a person conspires to commit a number of crimes, he is guilty of only one conspiracy so long as such multiple crimes are the object of the same agreement or continuous conspiratorial relationship.

(4) Joinder and Venue in Conspiracy Prosecutions.

(a) Subject to the provisions of paragraph (b) of this Subsection, two or more persons charged with criminal conspiracy may be prosecuted jointly if:

(i) they are charged with conspiring with one another; or

(ii) the conspiracies alleged, whether they have the same or different parties, are so related that they constitute different aspects of a scheme of organized criminal conduct.

(b) In any joint prosecution under paragraph (a) of this Subsection:

(i) no defendant shall be charged with a conspiracy in any county [parish or district] other than one in which he entered into such conspiracy or in which an overt act pursuant to such conspiracy was done by him or by a person with whom he conspired; and

(ii) neither the liability of any defendant nor the admissibility against him of evidence of acts or declarations of another shall be enlarged by such joinder; and

(iii) the Court shall order a severance or take a special verdict as to any defendant who so requests, if it deems it necessary or appropriate to promote the fair determination of his guilt or innocence, and shall take any other proper measures to protect the fairness of the trial.

(5) Overt Act. No person may be convicted of conspiracy to commit a crime, other than a felony of the first or second degree, unless an overt act in pursuance of such conspiracy is alleged and proved to have been done by him or by a person with whom he conspired.

(6) Renunciation of Criminal Purpose. It is an affirmative defense that the actor, after conspiring to commit a crime, thwarted the success of the conspiracy, under circumstances manifesting a complete and voluntary renunciation of his criminal purpose.

(7) Duration of Conspiracy. For purposes of Section 1.06(4):

(a) conspiracy is a continuing course of conduct which terminates when the crime or crimes which are its object are committed or the agreement that they be committed is abandoned by the defendant and by those with whom he conspired; and

(b) such abandonment is presumed if neither the defendant nor anyone with whom he conspired does any overt act in pursuance of the conspiracy during the applicable period of limitation; and

(c) if an individual abandons the agreement, the conspiracy is terminated as to him only if and when he advises those with whom he conspired of his abandonment or he informs the law enforcement authorities of the existence of the conspiracy and of his participation therein.

Section 5.04. Incapacity, Irresponsibility or Immunity of Party to Solicitation or Conspiracy.

(1) Except as provided in Subsection (2) of this Section, it is immaterial to the liability of a person who solicits or conspires with another to commit a crime that:

(a) he or the person who he solicits or with whom he conspires does not occupy a particular position or have a particular characteristic which is an element of such crime, if he believes that one of them does; or

(b) the person whom he solicits or with whom he conspires is irresponsible or has an immunity to prosecution or conviction for the commission of the crime.

(2) It is a defense to a charge of solicitation or conspiracy to commit a crime that if the criminal object were achieved, the actor would not be guilty of a crime under the law defining the offense or as an accomplice under Section 2.06(5) or 2.06(6)(a) or (b).

Section 5.05. Grading of Criminal Attempt, Solicitation and Conspiracy; Mitigation in Cases of Lesser Danger; Multiple Convictions Barred.

(1) Grading. Except as otherwise provided in this Section, attempt, solicitation and conspiracy are crimes of the same grade and degree as the most serious offense which is attempted or solicited or is an object of the conspiracy. An attempt, solicitation or conspiracy to commit a [capital crime or a] felony of the first degree is a felony of the second degree.

(2) Mitigation. If the particular conduct charged to constitute a criminal attempt, solicitation or conspiracy is so inherently unlikely to result or culminate in the commission of a crime that neither such conduct nor the actor presents a public danger warranting the grading of such offense under this Section, the Court shall exercise its power under Section 6.12 to enter judgment and impose sentence for a crime of lower grade or degree or, in extreme cases, may dismiss the prosecution.

(3) Multiple Convictions. A person may not be convicted of more than one offense defined by this Article for conduct designed to commit or to culminate in the commission of the same crime.

Section 5.06. Possessing Instruments of Crime; Weapons.

(1) Criminal Instruments Generally. A person commits a misdemeanor if he possesses any instrument of crime with purpose to employ it criminally. "Instrument of crime" means:

(a) anything specially made or specially adapted for criminal use; or

(b) anything commonly used for criminal purposes and possessed by the actor under circumstances which do not negative unlawful purpose.

(2) Presumption of Criminal Purpose from Possession of Weapon. If a person possesses a firearm or other weapon on or about his person, in a vehicle occupied by him, or otherwise readily available for use, it is presumed that he had the purpose to employ it criminally, unless:

(a) the weapon is possessed in the actor's home or place of business;

(b) the actor is licensed or otherwise authorized by law to possess such weapon; or

(c) the weapon is of a type commonly used in lawful sport.

"Weapon" means anything readily capable of lethal use and possessed under circumstances not manifestly appropriate for lawful uses which it may have; the term includes a firearm which is not loaded or lacks a clip or other component to render it immediately operable, and components which can readily be assembled into a weapon.

(3) Presumptions as to Possession of Criminal Instruments in Automobiles. Where a weapon or other instrument of crime is found in an automobile, it shall be presumed to be in the possession of the occupant if there is but one. If there is more than one occupant, it shall be presumed to be in the possession of all, except under the following circumstances:

(a) where it is found upon the person of one of the occupants;

(b) where the automobile is not a stolen one and the weapon or instrument is found out of view in a glove compartment, car trunk, or other enclosed customary depository, in which case it shall be presumed to be in the possession of the occupant or occupants who own or have authority to operate the automobile;

(c) in the case of a taxicab, a weapon or instrument found in the passengers' portion of the vehicle shall be presumed to be in the possession of all the passengers, if there are any, and, if not, in the possession of the driver.

Section 5.07. Prohibited Offensive Weapons.

A person commits a misdemeanor if, except as authorized by law, he makes, repairs, sells, or otherwise deals in, uses, or possesses any offensive weapon. "Offensive weapon" means any bomb, machine gun, sawed-off shotgun, firearm specially made or specially adapted for concealment or silent discharge, any blackjack, sandbag, metal knuckles, dagger, or other implement for the infliction of serious bodily injury which serves no common lawful purpose. It is a defense under this Section for the defendant to prove by a preponderance of evidence that he possessed or dealt with the weapon solely as a curio or in a dramatic performance, or that he possessed it briefly in consequence of having found it or taken it from an aggressor, or under circumstances similarly negativing any purpose or likelihood that the weapon would be used unlawfully. The presumptions provided in Section 5.06(3) are applicable to prosecutions under this Section.

ARTICLE 6. AUTHORIZED DISPOSITION OF OFFENDERS.

Section 6.01. Degrees of Felonies.

(1) Felonies defined by this Code are classified, for the purpose of sentence, into three degrees, as follows:

(a) felonies of the first degree;

(b) felonies of the second degree;

(c) felonies of the third degree. A felony is of the first or second degree when it is so designated by the Code. A crime declared to be a felony, without specification of degree, is of the third degree.

(2) Notwithstanding any other provision of law, a felony defined by any statute of this State other than this Code shall constitute for the purpose of sentence a felony of the third degree.

Section 6.02. Sentence in Accordance with Code; Authorized Dispositions.

(1) No person convicted of an offense shall be sentenced otherwise than in accordance with this Article.

[(2) The Court shall sentence a person who has been convicted of murder to death or imprisonment, in accordance with Section 210.6.]

(3) Except as provided in Subsection (2) of this Section and subject to the applicable provisions of the Code, the Court may suspend the imposition of sentence on a person who has been convicted of a crime, may order him to be committed in lieu of sentence, in accordance with Section 6.13, or may sentence him as follows:

(a) to pay a fine authorized by Section 6.03; or

(b) to be placed on probation [, and, in the case of a person convicted of a felony or misdemeanor to imprisonment for a term fixed by the Court not exceeding thirty days to be served as a condition of probation]; or

(c) to imprisonment for a term authorized by Sections 6.05, 6.06, 6.07, 6.08, 6.09, or 7.06; or

(d) to fine and probation or fine and imprisonment, but not to probation and imprisonment [, except as authorized in paragraph (b) of this Subsection].

(4) The Court may suspend the imposition of sentence on a person who has been convicted of a violation or may sentence him to pay a fine authorized by Section 6.03.

(5) This Article does not deprive the Court of any authority conferred by law to decree a forfeiture of property, suspend or cancel a license, remove a person from office, or impose any other civil penalty. Such a judgment or order may be included in the sentence.

Section 6.03. Fines.

A person who has been convicted of an offense may be sentenced to pay a fine not exceeding:

(1) $10,000, when the conviction is of a felony of the first or second degree;

(2) $5,000, when the conviction is of a felony of the third degree;

(3) $1,000, when the conviction is of a misdemeanor;

(4) $500, when the conviction is of a petty misdemeanor or a violation;

(5) any higher amount equal to double the pecuniary gain derived from the offense by the offender;

(6) any higher amount specifically authorized by statute.

Section 6.06. Sentence of Imprisonment for Felony; Ordinary Terms.

A person who has been convicted of a felony may be sentenced to imprisonment, as follows:

(1) in the case of a felony of the first degree, for a term the minimum of which shall be fixed by the Court at not less than one year nor more than ten years, and the maximum of which shall be life imprisonment;

(2) in the case of a felony of the second degree, for a term the minimum of which shall be fixed by the Court at not less than one year nor more than three years, and the maximum of which shall be ten years;

(3) in the case of a felony of the third degree, for a term the minimum of which shall be fixed by the Court at not less than one year nor more than two years, and the maximum of which shall be five years.

Alternate Section 6.06. Sentence of Imprisonment for Felony; Ordinary Terms.

A person who has been convicted of a felony may be sentenced to imprisonment, as follows:

(1) in the case of a felony of the first degree, for a term the minimum of which shall be fixed by the Court at not less than one year nor more than ten years, and the maximum at not more than twenty years or at life imprisonment;

(2) in the case of a felony of the second degree, for a term the minimum of which shall be fixed by the Court at not less than one year nor more than three years, and the maximum at not more than ten years;

(3) in the case of a felony of the third degree, for a term the minimum of which shall be fixed by the Court at not less than one year nor more than two years, and the maximum at not more than five years. No sentence shall be imposed under this Section of which the minimum is longer than one-half the maximum, or, when the maximum is life imprisonment, longer than ten years.

Section 6.07. Sentence of Imprisonment for Felony; Extended Terms.

In the cases designated in Section 7.03, a person who has been convicted of a felony may be sentenced to an extended term of imprisonment, as follows:

(1) in the case of a felony of the first degree, for a term the minimum of which shall be fixed by the Court at not less than five years nor more than ten years, and the maximum of which shall be life imprisonment;

(2) in the case of a felony of the second degree, for a term the minimum of which shall be fixed by the Court at not less than one year nor more than five years, and the maximum of which shall be fixed by the Court at not less than ten years nor more than twenty years;

(3) in the case of a felony of the third degree, for a term the minimum of which shall be fixed by the Court at not less than one year nor more than three years, and the maximum of which shall be fixed by the Court at not less than five years nor more than ten years.

Section 6.08. Sentence of Imprisonment for Misdemeanors and Petty Misdemeanors; Ordinary Terms.

A person who has been convicted of a misdemeanor or a petty misdemeanor may be sentenced to imprisonment for a definite term which shall be fixed by the Court and shall not exceed one year in the case of a misdemeanor or thirty days in the case of a petty misdemeanor.

Section 6.09. Sentence of Imprisonment for Misdemeanors and Petty Misdemeanors; Extended Terms.

(1) In the cases designated in Section 7.04, a person who has been convicted of a misdemeanor or a petty misdemeanor may be sentenced to an extended term of imprisonment, as follows:

(a) in the case of a misdemeanor, for a term the minimum of which shall be fixed by the Court at not more than one year and the maximum of which shall be three years;

(b) in the case of a petty misdemeanor, for a term the minimum of which shall be fixed by the Court at not more than six months and the maximum of which shall be two years.

(2) No such sentence for an extended term shall be imposed unless:

(a) the Director of Correction has certified that there is an institution in the Department of Correction, or in a county, city [or other appropriate political subdivision of the State] which is appropriate for the detention and correctional treatment of such misdemeanants or petty misdemeanants, and that such institution is available to receive such commitments; and

(b) the [Board of Parole] [Parole Administrator] has certified that the Board of Parole is able to visit such institution and to assume responsibility for the release of such prisoners on parole and for their parole supervision.

Section 6.13. Civil Commitment in Lieu of Prosecution or of Sentence.

(1) When a person prosecuted for a [felony of the third degree,] misdemeanor or petty misdemeanor is a chronic alcoholic, narcotic addict [or prostitute] or person suffering from mental abnormality and the Court is authorized by law to order the civil commitment of such person to a hospital or other institution for medical, psychiatric or other rehabilitative treatment, the Court may order such commitment and dismiss the prosecution.

The order of commitment may be made after conviction, in which event the Court may set aside the verdict or judgment of conviction and dismiss the prosecution.

(2) The Court shall not make an order under Subsection (1) of this Section unless it is of the view that it will substantially further the rehabilitation of the defendant and will not jeopardize the protection of the public.

ARTICLE 7. AUTHORITY OF COURT IN SENTENCING.

Section 7.03. Criteria for Sentence of Extended Term of Imprisonment; Felonies.

The Court may sentence a person who has been convicted of a felony to an extended term of imprisonment if it finds one or more of the grounds specified in this Section. The finding of the Court shall be incorporated in the record.

(1) The defendant is a persistent offender whose commitment for an extended term is necessary for protection of the public.

The Court shall not make such a finding unless the defendant is over twenty-one years of age and has previously been convicted of two felonies or of one felony and two misdemeanors, committed at different times when he was over [insert Juvenile Court age] years of age.

(2) The defendant is a professional criminal whose commitment for an extended term is necessary for protection of the public.

The Court shall not make such a finding unless the defendant is over twenty-one years of age and:

(a) the circumstances of the crime show that the defendant has knowingly devoted himself to criminal activity as a major source of livelihood; or

(b) the defendant has substantial income or resources not explained to be derived from a source other than criminal activity.

(3) The defendant is dangerous, mentally abnormal person whose commitment for an extended term is necessary for protection of the public.

The Court shall not make such a finding unless the defendant has been subjected to a psychiatric examination resulting in the conclusions that his mental condition is gravely abnormal; that his criminal conduct has been characterized by a pattern of repetitive or compulsive behavior or by persistent aggressive behavior with heedless indifference to consequences; and that such condition makes him a serious danger to others.

(4) The defendant is a multiple offender whose criminality was so extensive that a sentence of imprisonment for an extended term is warranted.

The Court shall not make such a finding unless:

(a) the defendant is being sentenced for two or more felonies, or is already under sentence of imprisonment for felony, and the sentences of imprisonment involved will run concurrently under Section 7.06; or

(b) the defendant admits in open court the commission of one or more other felonies and asks that they be taken into account when he is sentenced; and

(c) the longest sentences of imprisonment authorized for each of the defendant's crimes, including admitted crimes taken into account, if made to run consecutively would exceed in length the minimum and maximum of the extended term imposed.

Section 7.04. Criteria for Sentence of Extended Term of Imprisonment; Misdemeanors and Petty Misdemeanors.

The Court may sentence a person who has been convicted of a misdemeanor or petty misdemeanor to an extended term of imprisonment if it finds one or more of the grounds specified in the Section. The finding of the Court shall be incorporated in the record.

(1) The defendant is a persistent offender whose commitment for an extended term is necessary for protection of the public.

The Court shall not make such a finding unless the defendant has previously been convicted of two crimes, committed at different times when he was over [insert Juvenile Court age] years of age.

(2) The defendant is a professional criminal whose commitment for an extended term is necessary for protection of the public.

The Court shall not make such a finding unless:

(a) the circumstances of the crime show that the defendant has knowingly devoted himself to criminal activity as a major source of livelihood; or

(b) the defendant has substantial income or resources not explained to be derived from a source other than criminal activity.

(3) The defendant is a chronic alcoholic, narcotic addict, prostitute or person of abnormal mental condition who requires rehabilitative treatment for a substantial period of time.

The Court shall not make such a finding unless, with respect to the particular category to which the defendant belongs, the Director of Correction has certified that there is a specialized institution or facility which is satisfactory for the rehabilitative treatment of such persons and which otherwise meets the requirements of Section 6.09, Subsection (2).

(4) The defendant is a multiple offender whose criminality was so extensive that a sentence of imprisonment for an extended term is warranted.

The Court shall not make such a finding unless:

(a) the defendant is being sentenced for a number of misdemeanors or petty misdemeanors or is already under sentence of imprisonment for crimes of such grades, or admits in open court that commission of one or more such crimes and asks that they be taken into account when he is sentenced; and

(b) maximum fixed sentences of imprisonment for each of the defendant's crimes, including admitted crimes taken into account, if made to run consecutively, would exceed in length the maximum period of the extended term imposed.

Section 7.06. Multiple Sentences; Concurrent and Consecutive Terms.

(1) Sentence of Imprisonment for More Than One Crime. When multiple sentences of imprisonment are imposed on a defendant for more than one crime, including a crime for which a previous suspended sentence of sentence of probation has been revoked, such multiple sentences shall run concurrently or consecutively as the Court determines at the time of sentence, except that:

(a) a definite and an indefinite term shall run concurrently and both sentences shall be satisfied by service of the indefinite term; and

(b) the aggregate of consecutive definite terms shall not exceed one year; and

(c) the aggregate of consecutive indefinite terms shall not exceed in minimum or maximum length the longest extended term authorized for the highest grade and degree of crime for which any of the sentences was imposed; and

(d) not more than one sentence for an extended term shall be imposed.

(2) Sentences of Imprisonment Imposed at Different Times. When a defendant who has previously been sentenced to imprisonment is subsequently sentenced to another term for a crime committed prior to the former sentence, other than a crime committed while in custody:

(a) the multiple sentences imposed shall so far as possible conform to Subsection (1) of this Section; and

(b) whether the Court determines that the terms shall run concurrently or consecutively, the defendant shall be credited with the time served in imprisonment on the prior sentence in determining the permissible aggregate length of the term or terms remaining to be served; and

(c) when a new sentence is imposed on a prisoner who is on parole, the balance of the parole term on the former sentence shall be deemed to run during the period of the new imprisonment.

(3) Sentence of Imprisonment for Crime Committed While on Parole. When a defendant is sentenced to imprisonment for a crime committed while on parole in the State, such term of imprisonment and any period of reimprisonment that the Board of Parole may require the defendant to serve upon the revocation of his parole shall run concurrently, unless the Court orders them to run consecutively.

(4) Multiple Sentences of Imprisonment in Other Cases. Except as otherwise provided in this Section, multiple terms of imprisonment shall run concurrently or consecutively as the Court determines when the second or subsequent sentence is imposed.

(5) Calculation of Concurrent and Consecutive Terms in Imprisonment

(a) When indefinite terms run concurrently, the shorter minimum terms merge in and are satisfied by serving the longest minimum term and the shorter maximum terms merge in and are satisfied by discharge of the longest maximum term.

(b) When indefinite terms run consecutively, the minimum terms are added to arrive at an aggregate minimum to be served equal to the sum of all minimum terms and the maximum terms are added to arrive at an aggregate maximum equal to the sum of all maximum terms.

(c) When a definite and indefinite term run consecutively, the period of the definite term is added to both the minimum and the maximum of the indefinite term and both sentences are satisfied by serving the indefinite term.

(6) Suspension of Sentence or Probation and Imprisonment; Multiple Terms of Suspension and Probation. When a defendant in sentenced for more than one offense or a defendant already under sentence is sentenced for another offense committed prior to the former sentence:

(a) the Court shall not sentence to probation a defendant who is under sentence of imprisonment [with more than thirty days to run] or impose a sentence of probation and a sentence of imprisonment [, except as authorized by Section 6.02(3) (b)]; and

(b) multiple periods of suspension or probation shall run concurrently from the date of the first such disposition; and

(c) when a sentence of imprisonment is imposed for an indefinite term, the service of such sentence shall satisfy a suspended sentence on another count or a prior suspended sentence r sentence to probation; and

(d) when a sentence of imprisonment is imposed for a definite term, the period of a suspended sentence on another count or a prior suspended sentence or sentence to probation shall run during the period of such imprisonment.

(7) Offense Committed While Under Suspension of Sentence or Probation. When a defendant is convicted of an offense committed while under suspension of sentence or on probation and such suspension or probation is not revoked:

(a) if the defendant is sentenced to imprisonment for an indefinite term, the service of such sentence shall satisfy the prior suspended sentence or sentence to probation; and

(b) if the defendant is sentenced to imprisonment for a definite term, the period of the suspension or probation shall not run during the period of such imprisonment; and

(c) if sentence is suspended or the defendant is sentenced to probation, the period of such suspension or probation shall run concurrently with or consecutively to the remainder of the prior periods, as the Court determines at the time of sentence.

PART II.   DEFINITION OF SPECIFIC CRIMES

OFFENSES INVOLVING DANGER TO THE PERSON

ARTICLE 210.   CRIMINAL HOMICIDE.

Section 210.0.   Definitions.

In Articles 210–213, unless a different meaning plainly is required:

(1) "human being" means a person who has been born and is alive;

(2) "bodily injury" means physical pain, illness or any impairment of physical condition;

(3) "serious bodily injury" means bodily injury which creates a substantial risk of death or which causes serious, permanent disfigurement, or protracted loss or impairment of the function of any bodily member or organ;

(4) "deadly weapon" means any firearm, or other weapon, device, instrument, material or substance, whether animate or inanimate, which in the manner it is used or is intended to be used is known to be capable of producing death or serious bodily injury.

Section 210.1.   Criminal Homicide.

(1) A person is guilty of criminal homicide if he purposely, knowingly, recklessly or negligently causes the death of another human being.

(2) Criminal homicide is murder, manslaughter or negligent homicide.

Section 210.2.   Murder.

(1) Except as provided in Section 210.3(1)(b), criminal homicide constitutes murder when:

(a) it is committed purposely or knowingly; or

(b) it is committed recklessly under circumstances manifesting extreme indifference to the value of human life. Such recklessness and indifference are presumed if the actor is engaged or is an accomplice in the commission of, or an attempt to commit, or flight after committing or attempting to commit robbery, rape or deviate sexual intercourse by force or threat of force, arson, burglary, kidnapping or felonious escape.

(2) Murder is a felony of the first degree [but a person convicted of murder may be sentenced to death, as provided in Section 210.6].

Section 210.3.   Manslaughter.

(1) Criminal homicide constitutes manslaughter when:

(a) it is committed recklessly; or

(b) a homicide which would otherwise be murder is committed under the influence of extreme mental or emotional disturbance for which there is reasonable explanation or excuse. The reasonableness of such explanation or excuse shall be determined from the viewpoint of a person in the actor's situation under the circumstances as he believes them to be.

(2) Manslaughter is a felony of the second degree.

Section 210.4.   Negligent Homicide.

(1) Criminal homicide constitutes negligent homicide when it is committed negligently.

(2) Negligent homicide is a felony of the third degree.

Section 210.5. Causing or Aiding Suicide.

(1) Causing Suicide as Criminal Homicide. A person may be convicted of criminal homicide for causing another to commit suicide only if he purposely causes such suicide by force, duress or deception.

(2) Aiding or Soliciting Suicide as an Independent Offense. A person who purposely aids or solicits another to commit suicide is guilty of a felony of the second degree if his conduct causes such suicide or an attempted suicide, and otherwise of a misdemeanor.

[Section 210.6. Sentence of Death for Murder; Further Proceedings to Determine Sentence].

(1) Death Sentence Excluded. When a defendant is found guilty of murder, the Court shall impose sentence for a felony of the first degree if it is satisfied that:

(a) none of the aggravating circumstances enumerated in Subsection (3) of this Section was established by the evidence at the trial or will be established if further proceedings are initiated under Subsection (2) of this Section; or

(b) substantial mitigating circumstances, established by the evidence at the trial, call for leniency; or

(c) the defendant, with the consent of the prosecuting attorney and the approval of the Court, pleaded guilty to murder as a felony of the first degree; or

(d) the defendant was under 18 years of age at the time of the commission of the crime; or

(e) the defendant's physical or mental condition calls for leniency; or

(f) although the evidence suffices to sustain the verdict, it does not foreclose all doubt respecting the defendant's guilt.

(2) Determination by Court or by Court and Jury. Unless the Court imposes sentence under Subsection (1) of this Section, it shall conduct a separate proceeding to determine whether the defendant should be sentenced for a felony of the first degree or sentenced to death. The proceeding shall be conducted before the Court alone if the defendant was convicted by a Court sitting without a jury or upon his plea of guilty or if the prosecuting attorney and the defendant waive a jury with respect to sentence. In other cases it shall be conducted before the Court sitting with the jury which determined the defendant's guilt or, if the Court for good cause shown discharges that jury, with a new jury empaneled for the purpose.

In the proceeding, evidence may be presented as to any matter that the Court deems relevant to sentence, including but not limited to the nature and circumstances of the crime, the defendant's character, background, history, mental and physical condition and any of the aggravating or mitigating circumstances enumerated in Subsections (3) and (4) of this Section. Any such evidence, not legally privileged, which the Court deems to have probative force, may be received, regardless of its admissibility under the exclusionary rules of evidence, provided that the defendant's counsel is accorded a fair opportunity to rebut such evidence. The prosecuting attorney and the defendant or his counsel shall be permitted to present argument for or against sentence of death.

The determination whether sentence of death shall be imposed shall be in the discretion of the Court, except that when the proceeding is conducted before the Court sitting with a jury, the Court shall not impose sentence of death unless it submits to the jury the issue whether the defendant should be sentenced to death or to imprisonment and the jury returns a verdict that the sentence should be death. If the jury is unable to reach a unanimous verdict, the Court shall dismiss the jury and impose sentence for a felony of the first degree.

The Court, in exercising its discretion as to sentence, and the jury, in determining upon its verdict, shall take into account the aggravating and mitigating circumstances enumerated in Subsections (3) and (4) and any other facts that it deems relevant, but it shall not impose or recommend sentence of death unless it finds one of the aggravating circumstances enumerated in Subsection (3) and further finds that there are no mitigating circumstances sufficiently substantial to call for leniency. When the issue is submitted to the jury, the Court shall so instruct and also shall inform the jury of the nature of the sentence of imprisonment that may be imposed, including its implication with respect to possible release upon parole, if the jury verdict is against sentence of death.

Alternative formulation of Subsection (2):

(2) Determination by Court. Unless the Court imposes sentence under Subsection (1) of this Section, it shall conduct a separate proceeding to determine whether the defendant should be sentenced for a felony of the first degree or sentenced to death. In the proceeding, the Court, in accordance with Section 7.07, shall consider the report of the pre-sentence investigation and, if a psychiatric examination has been ordered, the report of such examination. In addition, evidence may be presented as to any matter that the Court deems relevant to sentence, including but not limited to the nature and circumstances of the crime, the defendant's character, background, history, mental and physical condition and any of the aggravating or mitigating circumstances enumerated in Subsections (3) and (4) of this Section. Any such evidence, not legally privileged, which the Court deems to have probative force, may be received, regardless of its admissibility under the exclusionary rules of evidence, provided that the defendant's counsel is accorded a fair opportunity to rebut such evidence. The prosecuting attorney and the defendant or his counsel shall be permitted to present argument for or against sentence of death.

The determination whether sentence of death shall be imposed shall be in the discretion of the Court. In exercising such discretion, the Court shall take into account the aggravating and mitigating circumstances enumerated in Subsections (3) and (4) and any other facts that it deems relevant but shall not impose sentence of death unless it finds one of the aggravating circumstances enumerated in Subsection (3) and further finds that there are no mitigating circumstances sufficiently substantial to call for leniency.

(3) Aggravating Circumstances.

(a) The murder was committed by a convict under sentence of imprisonment.

(b) The defendant was previously convicted of another murder or of a felony involving the use or threat of violence to the person.

(c) At the time the murder was committed the defendant also committed another murder.

(d) The defendant knowingly created a great risk of death to many persons.

(e) The murder was committed while the defendant was engaged or was an accomplice in the commission of, or an attempt to commit, or flight after committing or attempting to commit robbery, rape or deviate sexual intercourse by force or threat of force, arson, burglary or kidnapping.

(f) The murder was committed for the purpose of avoiding or preventing a lawful arrest or effecting an escape from lawful custody.

(g) The murder was committed for pecuniary gain.

(h) The murder was especially heinous, atrocious or cruel, manifesting exceptional depravity.

(4) Mitigating Circumstances.

(a) The defendant has no significant history of prior criminal activity.

(b) The murder was committed while the defendant was under the influence of extreme mental or emotional disturbance.

(c) The victim was a participant in the defendant's homicidal conduct or consented to the homicidal act.

(d) The murder was committed under circumstances which the defendant believed to provide a moral justification or extenuation for his conduct.

(e) The defendant was an accomplice in a murder committed by another person and his participation in the homicidal act was relatively minor.

(f) The defendant acted under duress or under the domination of another person.

(g) At the time of the murder, the capacity of the defendant to appreciate the criminality [wrongfulness] of his conduct or to conform his conduct to the requirements of law was impaired as a result of mental disease or defect or intoxication.

(h) The youth of the defendant at the time of the crime.]

ARTICLE 211. ASSAULT; RECKLESS ENDANGERING; THREATS.

Section 211.0. Definitions.

In this Article, the definitions given in Section 210.0 apply unless a different meaning plainly is required.

Section 211.1. Assault.

(1) Simple Assault. A person is guilty of assault if he:

(a) attempts to cause or purposely, knowingly or recklessly causes bodily injury to another; or

(b) negligently causes bodily injury to another with a deadly weapon; or

(c) attempts by physical menace to put another in fear of imminent serious bodily injury. Simple assault is a misdemeanor unless committed in a fight or scuffle entered into by mutual consent, in which case it is a petty misdemeanor.

(2) Aggravated Assault. A person is guilty of aggravated assault if he:

(a) attempts to cause serious bodily injury to another, or causes such injury purposely, knowingly or recklessly under circumstances manifesting extreme indifference to the value of human life; or

(b) attempts to cause or purposely or knowingly causes bodily injury to another with a deadly weapon. Aggravated assault under paragraph (a) is a felony of the second degree; aggravated assault under paragraph (b) is a felony of the third degree.

Section 211.2. Recklessly Endangering Another Person.

A person commits a misdemeanor if he recklessly engages in conduct which places or may place another person in danger of death or serious bodily injury. Recklessness and danger shall be presumed where a person knowingly points a firearm at or in the direction of another, whether or not the actor believed the firearm to be loaded.

Section 211.3. Terroristic Threats.

A person is guilty of a felony of the third degree if he threatens to commit any crime of violence with purpose to terrorize another or to cause evacuation of a building, place of assembly, or facility of public transportation, or otherwise to cause serious public inconvenience, or in reckless disregard of the risk of causing such terror or inconvenience.

ARTICLE 212.   KIDNAPPING AND RELATED OFFENSES; COERCION.

Section 212.0.   Definitions.

In this Article, the definitions given in Section 210.0 apply unless a different meaning plainly is required.

Section 212.1.   Kidnapping.

A person is guilty of kidnapping if he unlawfully removes another from his place of residence or business, or a substantial distance from the vicinity where he is found, or if he unlawfully confines another for a substantial period in a place of isolation, with any of the following purposes:

(a) to hold for ransom or reward, or as a shield or hostage; or

(b) to facilitate commission of any felony or flight thereafter; or

(c) to inflict bodily injury on or to terrorize the victim or another; or

(d) to interfere with the performance of any governmental or political function. Kidnapping is a felony of the first degree unless the actor voluntarily releases the victim alive and in a safe place prior to trial, in which case it is a felony of the second degree. A removal or confinement is unlawful within the meaning of this Section if it is accomplished by force, threat or deception, or, in the case of a person who is under the age of 14 or incompetent, if it is accomplished without the consent of a parent, guardian or other person responsible for general supervision of his welfare.

Section 212.2.   Felonious Restraint.

A person commits a felony of the third degree if he knowingly:

(a) restrains another unlawfully in circumstances exposing him to risk of serious bodily injury; or

(b) holds another in a condition of involuntary servitude.

Section 212.3.   False Imprisonment.

A person commits a misdemeanor if he knowingly restrains another unlawfully so as to interfere substantially with his liberty.

Section 212.4.   Interference with Custody.

(1) Custody of Children. A person commits an offense if he knowingly or recklessly takes or entices any child under the age of 18 from the custody of its parent, guardian or other lawful custodian, when he has no privilege to do so. It is an affirmative defense that:

(a) the actor believed that his action was necessary to preserve the child from danger to its welfare; or

(b) the child, being at the time not less than 14 years old, as taken away at its own instigation without enticement and without purpose to commit a criminal offense with or against the child. Proof that the child was below the critical age gives rise to a presumption that the actor knew the child's age or acted in reckless disregard thereof. The offense is a misdemeanor unless the actor, not being a parent or person in equivalent relation to the child, acted with knowledge that his conduct would cause serious alarm for the child's safety, or in reckless disregard of a likelihood of causing such alarm, in which case the offense is a felony of the third degree.

(2) Custody of Committed Persons. A person is guilty of a misdemeanor if he knowingly or recklessly takes or entices any committed person away from lawful custody when he is not privileged to do so. "Committed person" means, in addition to anyone committed under judicial warrant, any orphan, neglected or delinquent child, mentally defective or insane person, or other dependent or incompetent person entrusted to another's custody by or through a recognized social agency or otherwise by authority of law.

Section 212.5.   Criminal Coercion.

(1) Offense Defined. A person is guilty of criminal coercion if, with purpose unlawfully to restrict another's freedom of action to his detriment, he threatens to:

(a) commit any criminal offense; or

(b) accuse anyone of a criminal offense; or

(c) expose any secret tending to subject any person to hatred, contempt or ridicule, or to impair his credit or business repute; or

(d) take or withhold action as an official, or cause an official to take or withhold action. It is an affirmative defense to prosecution based on paragraphs (b), (c) or (d) that the actor believed the accusation or secret to be true or the proposed official action justified and that his purpose was limited to compelling the other to behave in a way reasonably related to the circumstances which were the subject of the accusation, exposure or proposed official action, as by desisting from further misbehavior, making good a wrong done, refraining from taking any action or responsibility for which the actor believes the other disqualified.

(2) Grading. Criminal coercion is a misdemeanor unless the threat is to commit a felony or the actor's purpose is felonious, in which cases the offense is a felony of the third degree.

ARTICLE 213.   SEXUAL OFFENSES.

Section 213.0   Definitions.

In this Article, unless a different meaning plainly is required:

(1) the definitions given in Section 210.0 apply;

(2) "Sexual intercourse" includes intercourse per os or per anum, with some penetration however slight; emission is not required;

(3) "Deviate sexual intercourse" means sexual intercourse per os or per anum between human beings who are not husband and wife, and any form of sexual intercourse with an animal.

Section 213.1.   Rape and Related Offenses.

(1) Rape. A male who has sexual intercourse with a female not his wife is guilty of rape if:

(a) he compels her to submit by force or by threat of imminent death, serious bodily injury, extreme pain or kidnapping, to be inflicted on anyone; or

(b) he has substantially impaired her power to appraise or control her conduct by administering or employing without her knowledge drugs, intoxicants or other means for the purpose of preventing resistance; or

(c) the female is unconscious; or

(d) the female is less than 10 years old. Rape is a felony of the second degree unless (i) in the course thereof the actor inflicts serious bodily injury upon anyone, or (ii) the victim was not a voluntary social companion of the actor upon the occasion of the crime and had not previously permitted him sexual liberties, in which cases the offense is a felony of the first degree.

(2) Gross Sexual Imposition. A male who has sexual intercourse with a female not his wife commits a felony of the third degree if:

(a) he compels her to submit by any threat that would prevent resistance by a woman of ordinary resolution; or

(b) he knows that she suffers from a mental disease or defect which renders her incapable of appraising the nature of her conduct; or

(c) he knows that she is unaware that a sexual act is being committed upon her or that she submits because she mistakenly supposes that he is her husband.

Section 213.2.   Deviate Sexual Intercourse by Force or Imposition.

(1) By Force or Its Equivalent. A person who engages in deviate sexual intercourse with another person, or who causes another to engage in deviate sexual intercourse, commits a felony of the second degree if:

(a) he compels the other person to participate by force or by threat of imminent death, serious bodily injury, extreme pain or kidnapping, to be inflicted on anyone; or

(b) he has substantially impaired the other person's power to appraise or control his conduct, by administering or employing without the knowledge of the other person drugs, intoxicants or other means for the purpose of preventing resistance; or

(c) the other person is unconscious; or

(d) the other person is less than 10 years old.

(2) By Other Imposition. A person who engages in deviate sexual intercourse with another person, or who causes another to engage in deviate sexual intercourse, commits a felony of the third degree if:

(a) he compels the other person to participate by any threat that would prevent resistance by a person of ordinary resolution; or

(b) he knows that the other person suffers from a mental disease or defect which renders him incapable of appraising the nature of his conduct; or

(c) he knows that the other person submits because he is unaware that a sexual act is being committed upon him.

Section 213.3.   Corruption of Minors and Seduction.

(1) Offense Defined. A male who has sexual intercourse with a female not his wife, or any person who engages in deviate sexual intercourse or causes another to engage in deviate sexual intercourse, is guilty of an offense if:

(a) the other person is less than [16] years old and the actor is at least [4] years older than the other person; or

(b) the other person is less than 21 years old and the actor is his guardian or otherwise responsible for general supervision of his welfare; or

(c) the other person is in custody of law or detained in a hospital or other institution and the actor has supervisory or disciplinary authority over him; or

(d) the other person is a female who is induced to participate by a promise of marriage which the actor does not mean to perform.

(2) Grading. An offense under paragraph (a) of Subsection () is a felony of the third degree. Otherwise an offense under this section is a misdemeanor.

Section 213.4. Sexual Assault.

A person who has sexual contact with another not his spouse, or causes such other to have sexual contact with him, is guilty of sexual assault, a misdemeanor, if:

(1) he knows that the contact is offensive to the other person; or

(2) he knows that the other person suffers from a mental disease or defect which renders him or her incapable of appraising the nature of his or her conduct; or

(3) he knows that the other person is unaware that a sexual act is being committed; or

(4) the other person is less than 10 years old; or

(5) he has substantially impaired the other person's power to appraise or control his or her conduct, by administering or employing without the other's knowledge drugs, intoxicants or other means for the purpose of preventing resistance; or

(6) the other person is less than [16] years old and the actor is at least [4] years older than the other person; or

(7) the other person is less than 21 years old and the actor is his guardian or otherwise responsible for general supervision of his welfare; or

(8) the other person is in custody of law or detained in a hospital or other institution and the actor has supervisory or disciplinary authority over him. Sexual contact is any touching of the sexual or other intimate parts of the person for the purpose of arousing or gratifying sexual desire.

Section 213.5. Indecent Exposure.

A person commits a misdemeanor if, for the purpose of arousing or gratifying sexual desire of himself or of any person other than his spouse, he exposes his genitals under circumstances in which he knows his conduct is likely to cause affront or alarm.

Section 213.6. Provisions Generally Applicable to Article 213.

(1) Mistake as to Age. Whenever in this Article the criminality of conduct depends on a child's being below the age of 10, it is no defense that the actor did not know the child's age, or reasonably believed the child to be older than 10. When criminality depends on the child's being below a critical age other than 10, it is a defense for the actor to prove by a preponderance of the evidence that he reasonably believed the child to be above the critical age.

(2) Spouse Relationships. Whenever in this Article the definition of an offense excludes conduct with a spouse, the exclusion shall be deemed to extend to persons living as man and wife, regardless of the legal status of their relationship. The exclusion shall be inoperative as respects spouses living apart under a decree of judicial separation. Where the definition of an offense excludes conduct with a spouse or conduct by a woman, this shall not preclude conviction of a spouse or woman as accomplice in a sexual act which he or she causes another person, not within the exclusion, to perform.

(3) Sexually Promiscuous Complainants. It is a defense to prosecution under Section 213.3 and paragraphs (6), (7) and (8) of Section 213.4 for the actor to prove by a preponderance of the evidence that the alleged victim had, prior to the time of the offense charged, engaged promiscuously in sexual relations with others.

(4) Prompt Complaint. No prosecution may be instituted or maintained under this Article unless the alleged offense was brought to the notice of public authority within [3] months of its occurrence or, where the alleged victim was less than [16] years old or otherwise incompetent to make complaint, within [3] months after a parent, guardian or other competent person specially interested in the victim learns of the offense.

(5) Testimony of Complainants. No person shall be convicted of any felony under this Article upon the uncorroborated testimony of the alleged victim. Corroboration may be circumstantial. In any prosecution before a jury for an offense under this Article, the jury shall be instructed to evaluate the testimony of a victim or complaining witness with special care in view of the emotional involvement of the witness and the difficulty of determining the truth with respect to alleged sexual activities carried out in private.

OFFENSES AGAINST PROPERTY

ARTICLE 220. ARSON, CRIMINAL MISCHIEF, AND OTHER PROPERTY DESTRUCTION.

Section 220.1. Arson and Related Offenses.

(1) Arson. A person is guilty of arson, a felony of the second degree, if he starts a fire or causes an explosion with the purpose of:

(a) destroying a building or occupied structure of another; or

(b) destroying or damaging any property, whether his own or another's, to collect insurance for such loss. It shall be an affirmative defense to prosecution under this paragraph that the actor's conduct did not recklessly endanger any building or occupied structure of another or place any other person in danger of death or bodily injury.

(2) Reckless Burning or Exploding. A person commits a felony of the third degree if he purposely starts a fire or causes an explosion, whether on his own property or another's, and thereby recklessly:

(a) places another person in danger of death or bodily injury; or

(b) places a building or occupied structure of another in danger of damage or destruction.

(3) Failure to Control or Report Dangerous Fire. A person who knows that a fire is endangering life or a substantial amount of property of another and fails to take reasonable measures to put out or control the fire, when he can do so without substantial risk to himself, or to give a prompt fire alarm, commits a misdemeanor if:

(a) he knows that he is under an official, contractual, or other legal duty to prevent or combat the fire; or

(b) the fire was started, albeit lawfully, by him or with his assent, or on property in his custody or control.

(4) Definitions. "Occupied structure" means any structure, vehicle or place adapted for overnight accommodation of persons, or for carrying on business therein, whether or not a person is actually present. Property is that of another, for the purposes of this section, if anyone other than the actor has a possessory or proprietary interest therein. If a building or structure is divided into separately occupied units, any unit not occupied by the actor is an occupied structure of another.

Section 220.2. Causing or Risking Catastrophe.

(1) Causing Catastrophe. A person who causes a catastrophe by explosion, fire, flood, avalanche, collapse of building, release of poison gas, radioactive material or other harmful or destructive force or substance, or by any other means of causing potentially widespread injury or damage, commits a felony of the second degree if he does so purposely or knowingly, or a felony of the third degree if he does so recklessly.

(2) Risking Catastrophe. A person is guilty of a misdemeanor if he recklessly creates a risk of catastrophe in the employment of fire, explosives or other dangerous means listed in Subsection (1).

(3) Failure to Prevent Catastrophe. A person who knowingly or recklessly fails to take reasonable measures to prevent or mitigate a catastrophe commits a misdemeanor if:

(a) he knows that he is under an official, contractual or other legal duty to take such measures; or

(b) he did or assented to the act causing or threatening the catastrophe.

Section 220.3. Criminal Mischief.

(1) Offense Defined. A person is guilty of criminal mischief if he:

(a) damages tangible property of another purposely, recklessly, or by negligence in the employment of fire, explosives, or other dangerous means listed in Section 220.2(1); or

(b) purposely or recklessly tampers with tangible property of another so as to endanger person or property; or

(c) purposely or recklessly causes another to suffer pecuniary loss by deception or threat.

(2) Grading. Criminal mischief is a felony of the third degree if the actor purposely causes pecuniary loss in excess of $5,000, or a substantial interruption or impairment of public communication, transportation, supply of water, gas or power, or other public service. It is a misdemeanor if the actor purposely causes pecuniary loss in excess of $100, or a petty misdemeanor if he purposely or recklessly causes pecuniary loss in excess of $25. Otherwise criminal mischief is a violation.

ARTICLE 221. BURGLARY AND OTHER CRIMINAL INTRUSION.

Section 221.0. Definitions.

In this Article, unless a different meaning plainly is required:

(1) "occupied structure" means any structure, vehicle or place adapted for overnight accommodation of persons, or for carrying on business therein, whether or not a person is actually present.

(2) "night" means the period between thirty minutes past sunset and thirty minutes before sunrise.

Section 221.1. Burglary.

(1) Burglary Defined. A person is guilty of burglary if he enters a building or occupied structure, or separately secured or occupied portion thereof, with purpose to commit a crime therein, unless the premises are at the time open to the public or the actor is licensed or privileged to enter. It is an affirmative defense to prosecution for burglary that the building or structure was abandoned.

(2) Grading. Burglary is a felony of the second degree if it is perpetrated in the dwelling of another at night, or if, in the course of committing the offense, the actor:

(a) purposely, knowingly or recklessly inflicts or attempts to inflict bodily injury on anyone; or

(b) is armed with explosives or a deadly weapon. Otherwise, burglary is a felony of the third degree. An act shall be deemed "in the course of committing" an offense if it occurs in an attempt to commit the offense or in flight after the attempt or commission.

(3) Multiple Convictions. A person may not be convicted both for burglary and for the offense which it was his purpose to commit after the burglarious entry or for an attempt to commit that offense, unless the additional offense constitutes a felony of the first or second degree.

Section 221.2. Criminal Trespass.

(1) Buildings and Occupied Structures. A person commits an offense if, knowing that he is not licensed or privileged to do so, he enters or surreptitiously remains in any building or occupied structure, or separately secured or occupied por-

tion thereof. An offense under this Subsection is a misdemeanor if it is committed in a dwelling at night. Otherwise it is a petty misdemeanor.

(2) Defiant Trespasser. A person commits an offense if, knowing that he is not licensed or privileged to do so, he enters or remains in any place as to which notice against trespass is given by:

(a) actual communication to the actor; or

(b) posting in a manner prescribed by law or reasonably likely to come to the attention of intruders; or

(c) fencing or other enclosure manifestly designed to exclude intruders. An offense under this Subsection constitutes a petty misdemeanor if the offender defies an order to leave personally communicated to him by the owner of the premises or other authorized person. Otherwise it is a violation.

(3) Defenses. It is an affirmative defense to prosecution under this Section that:

(a) a building or occupied structure involved in an offense under Subsection (1) was abandoned; or

(b) the premises were at the time open to members of the public and the actor complied with all lawful conditions imposed on access to or remaining in the premises; or

(c) the actor reasonably believed that the owner of the premises, or other person empowered to license access thereto, would have licensed him to enter or remain.

ARTICLE 222. ROBBERY.

Section 222.1. Robbery.

(1) Robbery Defined. A person is guilty of robbery if, in the course of committing a theft, he:

(a) inflicts serious bodily injury upon another; or

(b) threatens another with or purposely puts him in fear of immediate serious bodily injury; or

(c) commits or threatens immediately to commit any felony of the first or second degree. An act shall be deemed "in the course of committing a theft" if it occurs in an attempt to commit theft or in flight after the attempt or commission.

(2) Grading. Robbery is a felony of the second degree, except that it is a felony of the first degree if in the course of committing the theft the actor attempts to kill anyone, or purposely inflicts or attempts to inflict serious bodily injury.

ARTICLE 223. THEFT AND RELATED OFFENSES.

Section 223.0. Definitions.

In this Article, unless a different meaning plainly is required:

(1) "deprive" means:

(a) to withhold property of another permanently or for so extended a period as to appropriate a major portion of its economic value, or with intent to restore only upon payment of reward or other compensation; or (b) to dispose of the property so as to make it unlikely that the owner will recover it.

(2) "financial institution" means a bank, insurance company, credit union, building and loan association, investment trust or other organization held out to the public as a place of deposit of funds or medium of savings or collective investment.

(3) "government" means the United States, any State, county, municipality, or other political unit, or any department, agency or subdivision of any of the foregoing, or any corporation or other association carrying out the functions of government.

(4) "movable property" means property the location of which can be changed, including things growing on, affixed to, or found in land, and documents although the rights represented thereby have no physical location. "Immovable property" is all other property.

(5) "obtain" means:

(a) in relation to property, to bring about a transfer or purported transfer of a legal interest in the property, whether to the obtainer or another; or (b) in relation to labor or service, to secure performance thereof.

(6) "property" means anything of value, including real estate, tangible and intangible personal property, contract rights, chooses-in-action and other interests in or claims to wealth, admission or transportation tickets, captured or domestic animals, food and drink, electric or other power.

(7) "property of another" includes property in which any person other than the actor has an interest which the actor is not privileged to infringe, regardless of the fact that the actor also has an interest in the property and regardless of the fact that the other person might be precluded from civil recovery because the property was used in an unlawful transaction or was subject to forfeiture as contraband. Property in possession of the actor shall not be deemed property of another who has only a security interest therein, even if legal title is in the creditor pursuant to a conditional sales contract or other security agreement.

Section 223.1.   Consolidation of Theft Offenses; Grading; Provisions Applicable to Theft Generally.

(1) Consolidation of Theft Offenses. Conduct denominated theft in this Article constitutes a single offense. An accusation of theft may be supported by evidence that it was committed in any manner that would be theft under this Article, notwithstanding the specification of a different manner in the indictment or information, subject only to the power of the Court to ensure fair trial by granting a continuance or other appropriate relief where the conduct of the defense would be prejudiced by lack of fair notice or by surprise.

(2) Grading of Theft Offenses.

(a) Theft constitutes a felony of the third degree if the amount involved exceeds $500, or if the property stolen is a firearm, automobile, airplane, motorcycle, motorboat, or other motor-propelled vehicle, or in the case of theft by receiving stolen property, if the receiver is in the business of buying or selling stolen property.

(b) Theft not within the preceding paragraph constitutes a misdemeanor, except that if the property was not taken from the person or by threat, or in breach of a fiduciary obligation, and the actor proves by a preponderance of the evidence that the amount involved was less than $50, the offense constitutes a petty misdemeanor.

(c) The amount involved in a theft shall be deemed to be the highest value, by any reasonable standard, of the property or services which the actor stole or attempted to steal. Amounts involved in thefts committed pursuant to one scheme or course of conduct, whether from the same person or several persons, may be aggregated in determining the grade of the offense.

(3) Claim of Right. It is an affirmative defense to prosecution for theft that the actor:

(a) was unaware that the property or service was that of another; or

(b) acted under an honest claim of right to the property or service involved o that he had a right to acquire or dispose of it as he did; or

(c) took property exposed for sale, intending to purchase and pay for it promptly, or reasonably believing that the owner, if present, would have consented.

(4) Theft from Spouse. It is no defense that theft was from the actor's spouse, except that misappropriation of household and personal effects, or other property normally accessible to both spouses, is theft only if it occurs after the parties have ceased living together.

Section 223.2.   Theft by Unlawful Taking or Disposition.

(1) Movable Property. A person is guilty of theft if he unlawfully takes, or exercises unlawful control over, movable property of another with purpose to deprive him thereof.

(2) Immovable Property. A person is guilty of theft if he unlawfully transfers immovable property of another or any interest therein with purpose to benefit himself or another not entitled thereto.

Section 223.3.   Theft by Deception.

A person is guilty of theft if he purposely obtains property of another by deception. A person deceives if he purposely:

(1) creates or reinforces a false impression, including false impressions as to law, vale, intention or other state of mind; but deception as to a person's intention to perform a promise shall not be inferred from the fact alone that he did not subsequently perform the promise; or

(2) prevents another from acquiring information which would affect his judgment of a transaction; or

(3) fails to correct a false impression which the deceiver previously created or reinforced, or which the deceiver knows to be influencing another to whom he stands in a fiduciary or confidential relationship; or

(4) fails to disclose a known lien, adverse claim or other legal impediment to the enjoyment of property which he transfers or encumbers in consideration for the property obtained, whether such impediment is or is not valid, or is or is not a matter of official record.

The term "deceive" does not, however, include falsity as to matters having no pecuniary significance, or puffing by statements unlikely to deceive ordinary persons in the group addressed.

Section 223.4.   Theft by Extortion.

A person is guilty of theft if he purposely obtains property of another by threatening to:

(1) inflict bodily injury on anyone or commit any other criminal offense; or

(2) accuse anyone of a criminal offense; or

(3) expose any secret tending to subject any person to hatred, contempt or ridicule, or to impair his credit or business repute; or

(4) take or withhold action as an official, or cause an official to take or withhold action; or

(5) bring about or continue a strike, boycott or other collective unofficial action, if the property is not demanded or received for the benefit of the group in whose interest the actor purports to act; or

(6) testify or provide information or withhold testimony or information with respect to another's legal claim or defense; or

(7) inflict any other harm which would not benefit the actor. It is an affirmative defense to prosecution based on paragraphs (2), (3) or (4) that the property obtained by threat of accusation, exposure, lawsuit or other invocation of official action was honestly claimed as restitution or indemnification for harm done in the circumstances to which such accusation, exposure, lawsuit or other official action relates, or as compensation for property or lawful services.

Section 223.5.   Theft of Property Lost, Mislaid, or Delivered by Mistake.

A person who comes into control of property of another that he knows to have been lost, mislaid, or delivered under a mistake as to the nature or amount of the property or the identity of the recipient is guilty of theft if, with purpose to deprive the owner thereof, he fails to take reasonable measures to restore the property to a person entitled to have it.

Section 223.6.   Receiving Stolen Property.

(1) Receiving. A person is guilty of theft if he purposely receives, retains, or disposes of movable property of another knowing that it has been stolen, or believing that it has probably been stolen, unless the property is received, retained, or disposed with purpose to restore it to the owner. "Receiving" means acquiring possession, control or title, or lending on the security of the property.

(2) Presumption of Knowledge. The requisite knowledge or belief is presumed in the case of a dealer who:

(a) is found in possession or control of property stolen from two or more persons on separate occasions; or

(b) has received stolen property in another transaction within the year preceding the transaction charged; or

(c) being a dealer in property of the sort received, acquires it for a consideration which he knows is far below its reasonable value.

"Dealer" means a person in the business of buying or selling goods including a pawnbroker.

Section 223.7.   Theft of Services.

(1) A person is guilty of theft is he purposely obtains services which he knows are available only for compensation, by deception or threat, or by false token or other means to avoid payment for the service. "Services" includes labor, professional service, transportation, telephone or other public service, accommodation in hotels, restaurants or elsewhere, admission to exhibitions, use of vehicles or other movable property. Where compensation for service is ordinarily paid immediately upon the rendering of such service, as in the case of hotels and restaurants, refusal to pay or absconding without payment or offer to pay gives rise to a presumption that the service was obtained by deception as to intention to pay. (2) A person commits theft if, having control over the disposition of services of others, to which he is not entitled, he knowingly diverts such services to his own benefit or to the benefit of another not entitled thereto.

Section 223.8.   Theft by Failure to Make Required Disposition of Funds Received.

A person who purposely obtains property upon agreement, or subject to a known legal obligation, to make specified payment or other disposition, whether from such property or its proceeds or from his own property to be reserved in equivalent amount, is guilty of theft if he deals with the property obtained as his own and fails to make the required payment or disposition. The foregoing applies notwithstanding that it may be impossible to identify particular property as belonging to the victim at the time of the actor's failure to make the required payment or disposition. An officer or employee of the government or of a financial institution is presumed: (i) to know any legal obligation relevant to his criminal liability under this Section, and (ii) to have dealt with the property as his own if he fails to pay or account upon lawful demand, or if an audit reveals a shortage or falsification of accounts.

Section 223.9.   Unauthorized Use of Automobiles and Other Vehicles.

A person commits a misdemeanor if he operates another's automobile, airplane, motorcycle, motorboat, or other motor-propelled vehicle without consent of the owner. It is an affirmative defense to prosecution under this Section that the actor reasonably believed that the owner would have consented to the operation had he known of it.

ARTICLE 224.   FORGERY AND FRAUDULENT PRACTICES.

Section 224.0.   Definitions.

In this Article, the definitions given in Section 223.0 apply unless a different meaning plainly is required.

Section 224.1.   Forgery.

(1) Definition. A person is guilty of forgery if, with purpose to defraud or injure anyone, or with knowledge that he is facilitating a fraud or injury to be perpetrated by anyone, the actor:

(a) alters any writing of another without his authority; or

(b) makes, completes, executes, authenticates, issues or transfers any writing so that it purports to be the act of another who did not authorize that act, or to have been executed at a time or place or in a numbered sequence other than was in fact the case, or to be a copy of an original when no such original existed; or

(c) utters any writing which he knows to be forged in a manner specified in paragraphs (a) or (b). "Writing" includes printing or any other method of recording information, money, coins, tokens, stamps, seals, credit cards, badges, trade-marks, and other symbols of value, right, privilege, or identification.

(2) Grading. Forgery is a felony of the second degree if the writing is or purports to be part of an issue of money, securities, postage or revenue stamps, or other instruments issued by the government, or part of an issue of stock, bonds or other instruments representing interests in or claims against any property or enterprise. Forgery is a felony of the third

degree if the writing is or purports to be a will, deed, contract, release, commercial instrument, or other document evidencing, creating, transferring, altering, terminating, or otherwise affecting legal relations. Otherwise forgery is a misdemeanor.

Section 224.3. Fraudulent Destruction, Removal or Concealment of Recordable Instruments.

A person commits a felony of the third degree if, with purpose to deceive or injure anyone, he destroys, removes or conceals any will, deed, mortgage, security instrument or other writing for which the law provides public recording.

Section 224.4. Tampering with Records.

A person commits a misdemeanor if, knowing that he has no privilege to do so, he falsifies, destroys, removes or conceals any writing or record, with purpose to deceive or injure anyone or to conceal any wrongdoing.

Section 224.6. Credit Cards.

A person commits an offense if he uses a credit card for the purpose of obtaining property or services with knowledge that:

(1) the card is stolen or forged; or

(2) the card has been revoked or cancelled; or

(3) for any other reason his use of the card is unauthorized by the issuer.

It is an affirmative defense to prosecution under paragraph (3) if the actor proves by a preponderance of the evidence that he had the purpose and ability to meet all obligations to the issuer arising out of his use of the card. "Credit card" means a writing or other evidence of an undertaking to pay for property or services delivered or rendered to or upon the order of a designated person or bearer. An offense under this Section is a felony of the third degree if the value of the property or services secured or sought to be secured by means of the credit card exceeds $500; otherwise it is a misdemeanor.

OFFENSES AGAINST THE FAMILY

ARTICLE 230. OFFENSES AGAINST THE FAMILY.

Section 230.3. Abortion.

(1) Unjustified Abortion. A person who purposely and unjustifiably terminates the pregnancy of another otherwise than by a live birth commits a felony of the third degree or, where the pregnancy has continued beyond the twenty-sixth week, a felony of the second degree.

(2) Justifiable Abortion. A licensed physician is justified in terminating a pregnancy if he believes there is substantial risk that continuance of the pregnancy would gravely impair the physical or mental health of the mother or that the child would be born with grave physical or mental defect, or that the pregnancy resulted from rape,incest, or other felonious intercourse. All illicit intercourse with a girl below the age of 16 shall be deemed felonious for purposes of this subsection. Justifiable abortions shall be performed only in a licensed hospital except in case of emergency when hospital facilities are unavailable. [Additional exceptions from the requirement of hospitalization may be incorporated here to take account of situations in sparsely settled areas where hospitals are not generally accessible.]

(3) Physicians' Certificates; Presumption from Non–Compliance. No abortion shall be performed unless two physicians, one of whom may be the person performing the abortion, shall have certified in writing the circumstances which they believe to justify the abortion. Such certificate shall be submitted before the abortion to the hospital where it is to be performed and, in the case of abortion following felonious intercourse, to the prosecuting attorney or the police. Failure to comply with any of the requirements of this Subsection gives rise to a presumption that the abortion was unjustified.

(4) Self–Abortion. A woman whose pregnancy has continued beyond the twenty-sixth week commits a felony of the third degree if she purposely terminates her own pregnancy otherwise than by a live birth, or if she uses instruments, drugs or violence upon herself for that purpose. Except as justified under Subsection (2), a person who induces or knowingly aids a woman to use instruments, drugs or violence upon herself for the purpose of terminating her pregnancy otherwise than by a live birth commits a felony of the third degree whether or not the pregnancy has continued beyond the twenty-sixth week.

(5) Pretended Abortion. A person commits a felony of the third degree if, representing that it is his purpose to perform an abortion, he does an act adapted to cause abortion in a pregnant woman although the woman is in fact not pregnant, or the actor does not believe she is. A person charged with unjustified abortion under Subsection (1) or an attempt to commit that offense may be convicted thereof upon proof of conduct prohibited by this Subsection.

(6) Distribution of Abortifacients. A person who sells, offers to sell, possesses with intent to sell, advertises, or displays for sale anything specially designed to terminate a pregnancy, or held out by the actor as useful for that purpose, commits a misdemeanor, unless:

(a) the sale, offer or display is to a physician or druggist or to an intermediary in a chain of distribution to physicians or druggists; or

(b) the sale is made upon prescription or order of a physician; or

(c) the possession is with intent to sell as authorized in paragraphs (a) and (b); or

(d) the advertising is addressed to persons named in paragraph (a) and confined to trade or professional channels not likely to reach the general public.

(7) Section Inapplicable to Prevention of Pregnancy. Nothing in this Section shall be deemed applicable to the prescription, administration or distribution of drugs or other substances for avoiding pregnancy, whether by preventing implantation of a fertilized ovum or by any other method that operates before, at or immediately after fertilization.

Section 230.4. Endangering Welfare of Children.

A parent, guardian, or other person supervising the welfare of a child under 18 commits a misdemeanor if he knowingly endangers the child's welfare by violating a duty of care, protection or support.

Section 230.5. Persistent Non–Support.

A person commits a misdemeanor if he persistently fails to provide support which he can provide and which he knows he is legally obliged to provide to a spouse, child or other dependent.

ARTICLE 242. OBSTRUCTING GOVERNMENTAL OPERATIONS; ESCAPES.

Section 242.0. Definitions.

In this Article, unless another meaning plainly is required, the definitions given in Section 240.0 apply.

Section 242.1. Obstructing Administration of Law or Other Governmental Function.

A person commits a misdemeanor if he purposely obstructs, impairs or perverts the administration of law or other governmental function by force, violence, physical interference or obstacle, breach of official duty, or any other unlawful act, except that this Section does not apply to flight by a person charged with crime, refusal to submit to arrest, failure to perform a legal duty other than an official duty, or any other means of avoiding compliance with law without affirmative interference with governmental functions.

Section 242.2. Resisting Arrest or Other Law Enforcement.

A person commits a misdemeanor if, for the purpose of preventing a public servant from effecting a lawful arrest or discharging any other duty, the person creates a substantial risk of bodily injury to the public servant or anyone else, or employs means justifying or requiring substantial force to overcome the resistance.

Section 242.5. Compounding.

A person commits a misdemeanor if he accepts or agrees to accept any pecuniary benefit in consideration of refraining from reporting to law enforcement authorities the commission or suspected commission of any offense or information relating to an offense. It is an affirmative defense to prosecution under this Section that the pecuniary benefit did not exceed an amount which the actor believed to be due as restitution or indemnification for harm caused by the offense.

Section 242.6. Escape.

(1) Escape. A person commits an offense if he unlawfully removes himself from official detention or fails to return to official detention following temporary leave granted for a specific purpose or limited period. "Official detention" means arrest, detention in any facility for custody of persons under charge or conviction of crime or alleged or found to be delinquent, detention for extradition or deportation, or any other detention for law enforcement purposes; but "official detention" does not include supervision of probation or parole, or constraint incidental to release on bail.

(2) Permitting or Facilitating Escape. A public servant concerned in detention commits an offense if he knowingly or recklessly permits an escape. Any person who knowingly causes or facilitates an escape commits an offense.

(3) Effect of Legal Irregularity in Detention. Irregularity in bringing about or maintaining detention, or lack of jurisdiction of the committing or detaining authority, shall not be a defense to prosecution under this Section if the escape is from a prison or other custodial facility or from detention pursuant to commitment by official proceedings. In the case of other detentions, irregularity or lack of jurisdiction shall be a defense only if:

(a) the escape involved no substantial risk of harm to the person or property of anyone other than the detainee; or

(b) the detaining authority did not act in good faith under color of law.

(4) Grading of Offenses. An offense under this Section is a felony of the third degree where:

(a) the actor was under arrest for or detained on a charge of felony or following conviction of crime; or

(b) the actor employs force, threat, deadly weapon or other dangerous instrumentality to effect the escape; or

(c) a public servant concerned in detention of persons convicted of crime purposely facilitates or permits an escape from a detention facility. Otherwise an offense under this section is a misdemeanor.

OFFENSES AGAINST PUBLIC ORDER AND DECENCY

ARTICLE 250. RIOT, DISORDERLY CONDUCT, AND RELATED OFFENSES.

Section 250.1. Riot; Failure to Disperse.

(1) Riot. A person is guilty of riot, a felony of the third degree, if he participates with [two] or more others in a course of disorderly conduct:

(a) with purpose to commit or facilitate the commission of a felony or misdemeanor;

(b) with purpose to prevent or coerce official action; or

(c) when the actor or any other participant to the knowledge of the actor uses or plans to use a firearm or other deadly weapon.

(2) Failure of Disorderly Persons to Disperse Upon Official Order. Where [three] or more persons are participating in a course of disorderly conduct likely to cause substantial harm or serious inconvenience, annoyance or alarm, a peace officer or other public servant engaged in executing or enforcing the law may order the participants and others in the immediate vicinity to disperse. A person who refuses or knowingly fails to obey such an order commits a misdemeanor.

Section 250.2. Disorderly Conduct.

(1) Offense Defined. A person is guilty of disorderly conduct if, with purpose to cause public inconvenience, annoyance or alarm, or recklessly creating a risk thereof, he:

(a) engages in fighting or threatening, or in violent or tumultuous behavior; or

(b) makes unreasonable noise or offensively coarse utterance, gesture or display, or addresses abusive language to any person present; or

(c) creates a hazardous or physically offensive condition by any act which serves no legitimate purpose of the actor.

"Public" means affecting or likely to affect persons in a place to which the public or a substantial group has access; among the places included are highways, transport facilities, schools, prisons, apartment houses, places of business or amusement, or any neighborhood.

(2) Grading. An offense under this section is a petty misdemeanor if the actor's purpose is to cause substantial harm or serious inconvenience, or if he persists in disorderly conduct after reasonable warning or request to desist. Otherwise disorderly conduct is a violation.

Section 250.4. Harassment.

A person commits a petty misdemeanor if, with purpose to harass another, he:

(1) makes a telephone call without purpose of legitimate communication; or

(2) insults, taunts or challenges another in a manner likely to provoke violent or disorderly response; or

(3) makes repeated communications anonymously or at extremely inconvenient hours, or in offensively coarse language; or

(4) subjects another to an offensive touching; or

(5) engages in any other course of alarming conduct serving no legitimate purpose of the actor.

Section 250.5. Public Drunkenness; Drug Incapacitation.

A person is guilty of an offense if he appears in any public place manifestly under the influence of alcohol, narcotics or other drug, not therapeutically administered, to the degree that he may endanger himself or other persons or property, or annoy persons in his vicinity. An offense under this Section constitutes a petty misdemeanor if the actor has been convicted hereunder twice before within a period of one year. Otherwise the offense constitutes a violation.

Section 250.9. Desecration of Venerated Objects.

A person commits a misdemeanor if he purposely desecrates any public monument or structure, or place of worship or burial, or if he purposely desecrates the national flag or any other object of veneration by the public or a substantial segment thereof in any public place. "Desecrate" means defacing, damaging, polluting or otherwise physically mistreating in a way that the actor knows will outrage the sensibilities of persons likely to observe or discover his action.

Section 250.10. Abuse of Corpse.

Except as authorized by law, a person who treats a corpse in a way that he knows would outrage ordinary family sensibilities commits a misdemeanor.

ARTICLE 251. PUBLIC INDECENCY.

Section 251.3. Loitering to Solicit Deviate Sexual Relations.

A person is guilty of a petty misdemeanor if he loiters in or near any public place for the purpose of soliciting or being solicited to engage in deviate sexual relations.

Student Identifier: _____

ANSWER SHEET FOR LIABILITY JUDGMENTS

Decide for each defendant whether punishment is deserved and, if so, how much. Record your answers on the scale provided in the text at the end of the case facts. Also record your answers on the attached scales, which you will hand in at class. A summary of the class' responses will be prepared and distributed to the class. (Responses by individual students are made in confidence and will not be recorded. Make up any name or number you like for the "student identifier" at the top of this page.)

In making your liability and punishment judgments, ignore what you know or think you know about criminal law. Also ignore any utilitarian considerations, such as the need or lack of need for deterrence of others or concern for future public safety from a dangerous person. Indicate simply what your own intuitive sense of justice tells you is the criminal liability and punishment deserved, if any, by each defendant. There are no right or wrong answers.

Do not work with others. (There will be plenty of time for that during the course.) Give your own personal judgment of what is deserved.

If you decide that some punishment is deserved, you are asked to give a sentence of imprisonment that reflects the appropriate amount of punishment. In some cases, you may think punishment would best be imposed through a sentence other than imprisonment, such as supervised probation, fine, or community service. For the purposes of this questionnaire, translate any such non-imprisonment sentence into a term of imprisonment of the same punishment "bite." (This makes it possible for us to compare and average the amount of punishment imposed by different persons and between different cases.)

You are given a scale like the following for each case. Mark only one choice.

N	0	1	2	3	4	5	6	7	8	9	10	11
☐	☐	☐	☐	☐	☐	☐	☐	☐	☐	☐	☐	☐
no liability	liability but no punishment	1 day	2 wks.	2 mo.	6 mo.	1 yr.	3 yrs.	7 yrs.	15 yrs.	30 yrs.	life imprisonment	death

1. Case of DeSean McCarty (Illinois, 1997)

Would you convict McCarty for the death of Officer Laura? If so, what amount of punishment would you impose?

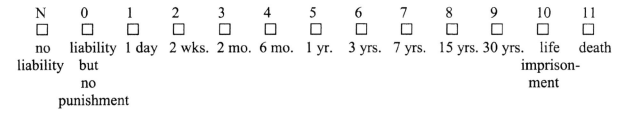

N	0	1	2	3	4	5	6	7	8	9	10	11
☐	☐	☐	☐	☐	☐	☐	☐	☐	☐	☐	☐	☐
no liability	liability but no punishment	1 day	2 wks.	2 mo.	6 mo.	1 yr.	3 yrs.	7 yrs.	15 yrs.	30 yrs.	life imprisonment	death

2. Case of John Landis (California, 1982)

Would you convict Landis for the deaths of Morrow, Le, and Chen? If so, what amount of punishment would you impose?

N	0	1	2	3	4	5	6	7	8	9	10	11
☐	☐	☐	☐	☐	☐	☐	☐	☐	☐	☐	☐	☐

no   liability 1 day 2 wks. 2 mo. 6 mo. 1 yr. 3 yrs. 7 yrs. 15 yrs. 30 yrs. life death
liability   but   imprison-
        no   ment
       punishment

3. Case of Bernice J. and Walter L. Williams (Washington, 1968)

Would you convict the Williamses for the death of their son? If so, what amount of punishment would you impose?

N	0	1	2	3	4	5	6	7	8	9	10	11
☐	☐	☐	☐	☐	☐	☐	☐	☐	☐	☐	☐	☐

no   liability 1 day 2 wks. 2 mo. 6 mo. 1 yr. 3 yrs. 7 yrs. 15 yrs. 30 yrs. life death
liability   but   imprison-
        no   ment
       punishment

4. Case of Thomas Dudley (England, 1884)

Would you convict Dudley for the death of Parker? If so, what amount of punishment would you impose?

N	0	1	2	3	4	5	6	7	8	9	10	11
☐	☐	☐	☐	☐	☐	☐	☐	☐	☐	☐	☐	☐

no   liability 1 day 2 wks. 2 mo. 6 mo. 1 yr. 3 yrs. 7 yrs. 15 yrs. 30 yrs. life death
liability   but   imprison-
        no   ment
       punishment

5. Case of William James Rummel (Texas, 1973)

What liability and punishment would you impose on Rummel for his air conditioner fraud?

N	0	1	2	3	4	5	6	7	8	9	10	11
☐	☐	☐	☐	☐	☐	☐	☐	☐	☐	☐	☐	☐

no   liability 1 day 2 wks. 2 mo. 6 mo. 1 yr. 3 yrs. 7 yrs. 15 yrs. 30 yrs. life death
liability   but   imprison-
        no   ment
       punishment

6. Case of Canna Baker (Arkansas, 1948)

Cannie can be held liable for the welfare fraud, but authorities are more upset about her treatment of Ed White's dead body. Would you impose criminal liability on Cannie Baker for her handling of White's body? If so, what amount of punishment would you impose for it?

N	0	1	2	3	4	5	6	7	8	9	10	11
□	□	□	□	□	□	□	□	□	□	□	□	□
no liability	liability but no punishment	1 day	2 wks.	2 mo.	6 mo.	1 yr.	3 yrs.	7 yrs.	15 yrs.	30 yrs.	life imprison-ment	death

7. Case of Julio Marrero (New York, 1977)

Would you convict Marrero? If so, what amount of punishment would you impose?

N	0	1	2	3	4	5	6	7	8	9	10	11
□	□	□	□	□	□	□	□	□	□	□	□	□
no liability	liability but no punishment	1 day	2 wks.	2 mo.	6 mo.	1 yr.	3 yrs.	7 yrs.	15 yrs.	30 yrs.	life imprison-ment	death

8. Case of Ray Edwin Billingslea (Texas, 1984)

What liability and punishment, if any, would you impose on Ray Billingslea for failing to care for his mother?

N	0	1	2	3	4	5	6	7	8	9	10	11
□	□	□	□	□	□	□	□	□	□	□	□	□
no liability	liability but no punishment	1 day	2 wks.	2 mo.	6 mo.	1 yr.	3 yrs.	7 yrs.	15 yrs.	30 yrs.	life imprison-ment	death

9. Case of Linda Ruschioni (Massachusetts, 1995)

Should Linda and Ricci Ruschioni be criminally liable for converting the lost ticket to their own use? If so, what amount of punishment would you impose?

N	0	1	2	3	4	5	6	7	8	9	10	11
□	□	□	□	□	□	□	□	□	□	□	□	□
no liability	liability but no punishment	1 day	2 wks.	2 mo.	6 mo.	1 yr.	3 yrs.	7 yrs.	15 yrs.	30 yrs.	life imprison-ment	death

10. Case of Joseph B. Wood (Vermont, 1879)

If Wood died from Luman's shot, would you convict Wood for the killing of Luman? If so, what amount of punishment would you impose?

N	0	1	2	3	4	5	6	7	8	9	10	11
☐	☐	☐	☐	☐	☐	☐	☐	☐	☐	☐	☐	☐

no   liability 1 day 2 wks. 2 mo. 6 mo. 1 yr. 3 yrs. 7 yrs. 15 yrs. 30 yrs. life death
liability but   imprison-
     no   ment
  punishment

Would you impose criminal liability on Wood? If so, how much punishment would you impose?

N	0	1	2	3	4	5	6	7	8	9	10	11
☐	☐	☐	☐	☐	☐	☐	☐	☐	☐	☐	☐	☐

no   liability 1 day 2 wks. 2 mo. 6 mo. 1 yr. 3 yrs. 7 yrs. 15 yrs. 30 yrs. life death
liability but   imprison-
     no   ment
  punishment

11. Case of Larry Eugene Phillips (California, 1993)

The two men are probably liable for at least some weapons offenses. (Their assault rifles are not at the time illegal in California, but there are registration requirements.) Should the two also be held criminally liable for attempted robbery? If so, what amount of punishment would you impose *for attempted robbery*?

N	0	1	2	3	4	5	6	7	8	9	10	11
☐	☐	☐	☐	☐	☐	☐	☐	☐	☐	☐	☐	☐

no   liability 1 day 2 wks. 2 mo. 6 mo. 1 yr. 3 yrs. 7 yrs. 15 yrs. 30 yrs. life death
liability but   imprison-
     no   ment
  punishment

12. Case of Roger Thomas (U.S. Military, 1961)

If the facts were as Thomas believed, would you convict him for rape? If so, what amount of punishment would you impose?

N	0	1	2	3	4	5	6	7	8	9	10	11
☐	☐	☐	☐	☐	☐	☐	☐	☐	☐	☐	☐	☐

no   liability 1 day 2 wks. 2 mo. 6 mo. 1 yr. 3 yrs. 7 yrs. 15 yrs. 30 yrs. life death
liability but   imprison-
     no   ment
  punishment

If the facts were as Abruzzese believed, would you convict him for attempted rape? If so, what amount of punishment would you impose?

N	0	1	2	3	4	5	6	7	8	9	10	11
□	□	□	□	□	□	□	□	□	□	□	□	□
no	liability	1 day	2 wks.	2 mo.	6 mo.	1 yr.	3 yrs.	7 yrs.	15 yrs.	30 yrs.	life	death
liability	but										imprison-	
	no										ment	
	punishment											

Knowing the complete facts, would you convict Thomas for his having intercourse with Alvis' body? If so, for what offense? What amount of punishment would you impose?

N	0	1	2	3	4	5	6	7	8	9	10	11
□	□	□	□	□	□	□	□	□	□	□	□	□
no	liability	1 day	2 wks.	2 mo.	6 mo.	1 yr.	3 yrs.	7 yrs.	15 yrs.	30 yrs.	life	death
liability	but										imprison-	
	no										ment	
	punishment											

Knowing the complete facts, would you convict Abruzzese for attempting but failing to have intercourse with Alvis' body? If so, what amount of punishment would you impose?

N	0	1	2	3	4	5	6	7	8	9	10	11
□	□	□	□	□	□	□	□	□	□	□	□	□
no	liability	1 day	2 wks.	2 mo.	6 mo.	1 yr.	3 yrs.	7 yrs.	15 yrs.	30 yrs.	life	death
liability	but										imprison-	
	no										ment	
	punishment											

13. Case of Joseph A. Bailey (Virginia, 1983)

Would you convict Bailey for the death of Murdock? If so, what amount of punishment would you impose?

N	0	1	2	3	4	5	6	7	8	9	10	11
□	□	□	□	□	□	□	□	□	□	□	□	□
no	liability	1 day	2 wks.	2 mo.	6 mo.	1 yr.	3 yrs.	7 yrs.	15 yrs.	30 yrs.	life	death
liability	but										imprison-	
	no										ment	
	punishment											

14.   Case of Keith Mondello (New York, 1989)

Would you convict Fama for the death of Hawkins? If so, what amount of punishment would you impose?

N	0	1	2	3	4	5	6	7	8	9	10	11
☐	☐	☐	☐	☐	☐	☐	☐	☐	☐	☐	☐	☐

no liability   liability but no punishment   1 day   2 wks.   2 mo.   6 mo.   1 yr.   3 yrs.   7 yrs.   15 yrs.   30 yrs.   life imprisonment   death

Would you convict Mondello for complicity in the death of Hawkins? If so, what amount of punishment would you impose?

N	0	1	2	3	4	5	6	7	8	9	10	11
☐	☐	☐	☐	☐	☐	☐	☐	☐	☐	☐	☐	☐

no liability   liability but no punishment   1 day   2 wks.   2 mo.   6 mo.   1 yr.   3 yrs.   7 yrs.   15 yrs.   30 yrs.   life imprisonment   death

15.   Case of Jordan Weaver (Indiana, 1991)

Would you convict Jordan Weaver for his attack of Wendy Waldman? If so, what amount of punishment would you impose?

N	0	1	2	3	4	5	6	7	8	9	10	11
☐	☐	☐	☐	☐	☐	☐	☐	☐	☐	☐	☐	☐

no liability   liability but no punishment   1 day   2 wks.   2 mo.   6 mo.   1 yr.   3 yrs.   7 yrs.   15 yrs.   30 yrs.   life imprisonment   death

Would you convict Weaver for the death of Jerome Sweeney? If so, what amount of punishment would you impose?

N	0	1	2	3	4	5	6	7	8	9	10	11
☐	☐	☐	☐	☐	☐	☐	☐	☐	☐	☐	☐	☐

no liability   liability but no punishment   1 day   2 wks.   2 mo.   6 mo.   1 yr.   3 yrs.   7 yrs.   15 yrs.   30 yrs.   life imprisonment   death

16. Case of John Charles Green (Missouri, 1967)

Green is charged with escape. Would you convict? If so, what amount of punishment would you impose?

N	0	1	2	3	4	5	6	7	8	9	10	11
☐	☐	☐	☐	☐	☐	☐	☐	☐	☐	☐	☐	☐

no liability 1 day 2 wks. 2 mo. 6 mo. 1 yr. 3 yrs. 7 yrs. 15 yrs. 30 yrs. life death
liability but   imprison-
   no   ment
punishment

17. Case of Johann Schlicht (Germany, 1919)

Would you convict Schlicht for his assault of the thief? If so, what amount of punishment would you impose?

N	0	1	2	3	4	5	6	7	8	9	10	11
☐	☐	☐	☐	☐	☐	☐	☐	☐	☐	☐	☐	☐

no liability 1 day 2 wks. 2 mo. 6 mo. 1 yr. 3 yrs. 7 yrs. 15 yrs. 30 yrs. life death
liability but   imprison-
   no   ment
punishment

18. Case of Wolfgang Daschner (Germany, 2002)

Would you convict Daschner for ordering his lieutenant to torture Gäfgen? If so, what amount of punishment would you impose?

N	0	1	2	3	4	5	6	7	8	9	10	11
☐	☐	☐	☐	☐	☐	☐	☐	☐	☐	☐	☐	☐

no liability 1 day 2 wks. 2 mo. 6 mo. 1 yr. 3 yrs. 7 yrs. 15 yrs. 30 yrs. life death
liability but   imprison-
   no   ment
punishment

19. Case of Motti Ashkenazi (Israel, 1997)

Would you convict Ashkenazi for his theft of the backpack? If so, what amount of punishment would you impose?

N	0	1	2	3	4	5	6	7	8	9	10	11
☐	☐	☐	☐	☐	☐	☐	☐	☐	☐	☐	☐	☐

no liability 1 day 2 wks. 2 mo. 6 mo. 1 yr. 3 yrs. 7 yrs. 15 yrs. 30 yrs. life death
liability but   imprison-
   no   ment
punishment

20. Case of Janice Leidholm (South Dakota, 1981)

Would you convict Janice Leidholm for killing her husband? If so, what amount of punishment would you impose?

N	0	1	2	3	4	5	6	7	8	9	10	11
☐	☐	☐	☐	☐	☐	☐	☐	☐	☐	☐	☐	☐

no liability — liability but no punishment — 1 day — 2 wks. — 2 mo. — 6 mo. — 1 yr. — 3 yrs. — 7 yrs. — 15 yrs. — 30 yrs. — life imprisonment — death

21. Case of Barry Kingston (England, 1991)

Should Kingston be held criminally liable for sexual assault of the boy? If so, what amount of punishment would you impose?

N	0	1	2	3	4	5	6	7	8	9	10	11
☐	☐	☐	☐	☐	☐	☐	☐	☐	☐	☐	☐	☐

no liability — liability but no punishment — 1 day — 2 wks. — 2 mo. — 6 mo. — 1 yr. — 3 yrs. — 7 yrs. — 15 yrs. — 30 yrs. — life imprisonment — death

22. Case of Andrea Yates (Texas, 2001)

Should Andrea Yates be held criminally liable for the deaths of her children? If so, what amount of punishment would you impose?

N	0	1	2	3	4	5	6	7	8	9	10	11
☐	☐	☐	☐	☐	☐	☐	☐	☐	☐	☐	☐	☐

no liability — liability but no punishment — 1 day — 2 wks. — 2 mo. — 6 mo. — 1 yr. — 3 yrs. — 7 yrs. — 15 yrs. — 30 yrs. — life imprisonment — no punishment but civil preventive detention for as long as she is dangerous

23. Case of David Kenney Hawkins (Nevada, 1986)

Would you convict Hawkins? If so, what amount of punishment would you impose?

N	0	1	2	3	4	5	6	7	8	9	10	11
☐	☐	☐	☐	☐	☐	☐	☐	☐	☐	☐	☐	☐

no liability — liability but no punishment — 1 day — 2 wks. — 2 mo. — 6 mo. — 1 yr. — 3 yrs. — 7 yrs. — 15 yrs. — 30 yrs. — life imprisonment — death

24. Case of Richard R. Tenneson (Federal, 1954)

Would you convict Tenneson? If so, what amount of punishment would you impose?

N	0	1	2	3	4	5	6	7	8	9	10	11
☐	☐	☐	☐	☐	☐	☐	☐	☐	☐	☐	☐	☐
no liability	liability but no punishment	1 day	2 wks.	2 mo.	6 mo.	1 yr.	3 yrs.	7 yrs.	15 yrs.	30 yrs.	life imprison- ment	death

25. Case of Alex Cabarga (California, 1982)

Should Alex Cabarga be held criminally liable? If so, what amount of punishment would you impose?

N	0	1	2	3	4	5	6	7	8	9	10	11
☐	☐	☐	☐	☐	☐	☐	☐	☐	☐	☐	☐	☐
no liability	liability but no punishment	1 day	2 wks.	2 mo.	6 mo.	1 yr.	3 yrs.	7 yrs.	15 yrs.	30 yrs.	life imprison- ment	no punishment but civil preventive detention for as long as he is dangerous

26. Case of Robert "Yummy" Sandifer (Illinois, 1994)

If Robert, now 11, is prosecuted as an adult, would you convict? If so, what amount of punishment would you impose on Robert?

N	0	1	2	3	4	5	6	7	8	9	10	11
☐	☐	☐	☐	☐	☐	☐	☐	☐	☐	☐	☐	☐
no liability	liability but no punishment	1 day	2 wks.	2 mo.	6 mo.	1 yr.	3 yrs.	7 yrs.	15 yrs.	30 yrs.	life imprison- ment	no punishment but civil preventive detention for as long as he is dangerous

†